# The Narcissist in You
# and Everyone Else

# The Narcissist in You and Everyone Else

## Recognizing the 27 Types of Narcissism

Sterlin L. Mosley

ROWMAN & LITTLEFIELD
Lanham • Boulder • New York • London

Published by Rowman & Littlefield
An imprint of The Rowman & Littlefield Publishing Group, Inc.
4501 Forbes Boulevard, Suite 200, Lanham, Maryland 20706
www.rowman.com

86-90 Paul Street, London EC2A 4NE

British Library Cataloguing in Publication Information Available

**Library of Congress Cataloging-in-Publication Data**

978-1-5381-6174-6 (cloth)
978-1-5381-6175-3 (electronic)

This book is dedicated to my mother, Faith, whom I love and miss dearly. I also dedicate this book to anyone who has endured the pain of narcissistic abuse and is trying to heal from their trauma.

Special thanks to my best friend, Aaron.
Thank you to Katherine Chernick Fauvre for her mentorship and the other teachers and mentors along the way who supported my journey.

# Contents

# Introduction

You're narcissistic. Yes, you read that correctly. You're narcissistic, but so am I, and so is your mother, father, brother, sister, partner, best friend, and neighbor. Before you put this book down in disgust, disbelief, and outrage, allow me to explain. When you hear the word "narcissism," I'd wager that you conjure images of smarmy, cutthroat business tycoons or arrogant, entitled movie stars. Maybe you're old enough to have been traumatized by Faye Dunaway's performance of Joan Crawford in *Mommy Dearest* or Christian Bale's chilling portrayal of Patrick Bateman in *American Psycho* (more on this in chapter 11).

Perhaps you hear the word narcissist and think of someone who believes they're pretty great and doesn't care what anyone else thinks. And while these are some manifestations of narcissism, the experience of narcissism in human beings is fascinatingly nuanced. Overall, the word has a pejorative implication and, thanks to pop psychology, has become a catch-all to describe anyone who possesses higher-than-average confidence and treats people carelessly. Unfortunately, these stereotypes fail to tell us what the heck narcissism is or what it does to us or others when it occurs in everyday life. So when I say you're narcissistic, I mean we all have a little bit of one of the twenty-seven subtypes of narcissism described in this book within us. The question is, how often does your inner Mommy Dearest or Patrick Bateman rear their head?

## A VERY QUICK AND INADEQUATE
## HISTORY OF NARCISSISM

Some of you may be able to pull from your cadre of ancient Greek mythology to recall the tale of Narcissus. He was an attractive, fit, virile hunter who rejected all potential love interests because he was so enamored with his beauty and thought he was too good for all of his adoring suitors. Think of Narcissus like the world's first Zoolander. Unfortunately, the poor guy became so enthralled with his dashing good looks that he stared for so long at his reflection in a pool of water, fell in, and drowned. He literally couldn't get enough of himself. The gods, to warn others, sprouted a flower in the pond in which he died that bore his name. The ancient Greeks had a way of personifying the human experience that was poetic, effective, and just a little bit macabre. So maybe you haven't drowned yourself in your bathroom sink staring at yourself, but who among us hasn't become so singularly focused on an aspect of ourselves or our experience that we've lost sight of the world around us?

You may think that narcissism is a clinical term reserved only for psychologists and psychiatrists. Still, while narcissism is a normal part of the discussion in these fields, its definition ranges from very broad to very specific. There was no clinical definition of narcissism or pathological self-absorption until 1898 when psychologist Havelock Ellis coined the term expounded upon by the bad boy of modern psychoanalysis himself, Sigmund Freud, in his 1914 essay *On Narcissism*.[1] The concept of narcissism as a disorder is a relatively new idea and one that arguably is exacerbated by life in the modern world. Many ancient societies were decisively collectivist. In many collectivist cultures, life focuses less on the individual's experience or psychological processes and more on community. The ancient Greeks are famous for birthing the concept of modern individualism. Because pathological narcissism as a concept of the human experience is only 220 years old, there is broad variance in what defines narcissistic behavior. Sigmund Freud was famously obsessed with human psychological development, particularly how human psychology relates to our libidinal relationship with our parents. Which is a nice way of saying Freud spent a lot of time thinking about whether or not people are attracted to their mothers and fathers and how that shapes and affects our personality and psychological development. Despite his proclivities toward sexualizing the psyche, Dr. Freud was a keen observer of human behavior. In "On Narcissism," which was his only paper on the subject, Freud theorized that *primary narcissism*, which he described as the instinct toward self-preservation and survival, was a normal part of human development. This notion helps to underscore my original presumption that we're all narcissistic. He also wrote that *"secondary narcissism,"* the creative fuel that ignites all good Lifetime movies about sneaky husbands with second families, is formed when there are problems in development that lend oneself toward overvaluation of one's importance to others.[2]

This book is concerned primarily with what Freud would call *secondary narcissism*. Most people beyond ages three to four have developed appropriate "primary narcissism," meaning they can survive in the world because they have a sense of themselves as individuated human beings. Many people also develop some degree of secondary or pathological narcissism. If secondary narcissism becomes too pronounced, we risk falling prey to the same fate as our friend Narcissus, as we become increasingly more enamored with ourselves. However, some of us become fixated, staring or clinging to an image of ourselves as somehow magnificently greater (or more grossly disadvantaged) than others, thus developing what modern psychologists would refer to as Narcissistic Personality Disorder.

The *Diagnostic Statistical Manual* (*DSM*) is the industry standard for diagnosing psychiatric and psychological disorders. The *DSM* outlines that, to be diagnosed with Narcissistic Personality Disorder (NPD), one must have problems regulating self-esteem without reference to others' perception of them, as well as an exaggerated inflated (or deflated) self-conception. The manual also defines those with NPD as having unreasonably high standards or goals based on gaining approval from others. People with NPD are said to have "problems with empathy" (both recognizing the feelings and needs of others or excessively attuned to the reactions of others, but only if relevant to themselves) and problems with superficiality and intimacy. On top of those characteristics, one must also exhibit these pathological traits throughout one's life, and the criteria can't be explained by other things, such as medical diagnoses or other psychiatric mood disorders.[3]

The vagueness of the DSM's diagnostic criteria regarding all the personality disorders has sparked much debate within psychological and academic communities precisely because they are ambiguous and nonspecific. Who hasn't at times had problems regarding the feelings of others, difficulty empathizing, trouble with intimacy, or sought approval or praise from others for their actions? So, effectively, we could all be considered clinically narcissistic at some point in our lives.

Now you see why I said everyone is narcissistic, and perhaps you'll forgive my introduction. We all exhibit these characteristics when stressed or overwhelmed to some degree. If you have an ego, which unless you are a Zen Buddhist monk dedicated to meditating your ego away, you do, which means you also have some degree (however tiny) of pathological or clinical narcissism.

Narcissism isn't in and of itself a problem but rather an occasional condition of modern life in an individualistic society. American cultural norms suggest that healthy, integrated people should follow their dreams, achieve their goals, make lots of money, be successful, and physically and emotionally take care of themselves. Yet these are singularly focused prescriptions for a healthy balanced life in the West. When we only focus on following our dreams, are relentless in achieving our goals, obsessed with making a lot of money, and need to be seen as successful at all costs, we risk dipping into the realm of malignant, destructive narcissism. However, defining and interpreting success varies depending on our personality type.

I've always struggled with the one-size-fits-all criteria for identifying narcissism. I remember sitting in my graduate school diagnosis classes thinking that extant definitions of narcissistic personality disorders only revealed three, maybe four different kinds of narcissism which were not indicative of every personality type. By that time, I was well versed in the Enneagram personality model, which outlines nine distinct personality types. Therefore, I knew that there had to be at least nine variations of narcissistic personality disorder. I also knew that any human being could devolve into narcissistic pathology temporarily and thus begin to display the narcissistic traits of our respective personality types.

## ENNEA-WHAT?

I like human typologies because you can easily recognize yourself in a well-developed, holistic system, and they can be a lot of fun. Unless you've been living under a technology-free rock, you have probably taken an online "What Harry Potter House Character Are You?" quiz or even a Myers-Briggs test. However, not all typologies are created equal. Modern psychological sciences prefer spectrum and trait-based models like The Big Five to explain human behavior because they are more easily quantifiable. The Big Five tests for traits like Neuroticism, Extraversion, Agreeableness, Openness, and Conscientiousness. The model's basic premise is that every person will display varying degrees of these traits. The Big Five traits have been identified in human DNA. However, traits alone don't give us a good personality composite. At best, they can point us in the direction of how a person may behave in a particular situation. For example, if you score high in neuroticism, you may become more anxious in unfamiliar situations. Or if you score high on agreeableness, you're likely to avoid confrontation. At worst, they can present a chaotic vision of the human psychological experience.

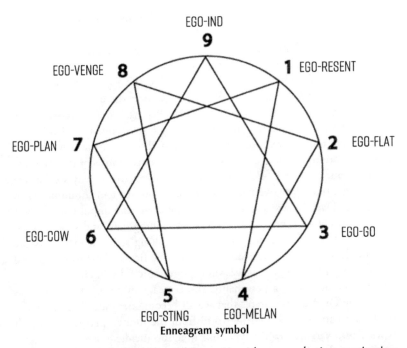

**Enneagram symbol**

They assume people are just swirling traits without a cohesive, motivating psychological goal which psychoanalytic and humanistic psychologists have refuted. I have always been more interested in the *why* behind people's behavior.

The Enneagram model gives us a framework for understanding the core motivations behind human behavior. The Enneagram of Personality has an interesting and somewhat dubious history of transmission that was primarily verbal and full of inconsistencies and power struggles (not unlike most fields of study). Much of what we know about the Enneagram of Personality's origins was disseminated through a murky and inconsistent verbal history (more on this in chapter 5).[4]

The Enneagram of Personality as we use it today comes from the work of Chilean psychiatrist Dr. Claudio Naranjo. Despite its relatively new presence in personality psychology, it has proven to be a highly effective means of identifying and working with ego and neuroses. The Enneagram types are nine distinct characterological archetypes, each type corresponding to one number. The Enneagram is a geometric symbol (Figure 0.1). The word Enneagram (pronounced any-a-gram) is Greek and translates to nine-sided drawing. Each type corresponds to a point on the symbol and has core motivations, fears, triggers, strengths, and blind spots. The Enneagram teaches us the *why* behind behavioral clusters and, as such, is an excellent shorthand for quickly under-standing ourselves and others.

There are variations and shades within the nine basic personality types based on three basic primal, instinctual drives of human beings, which pre-date the modern human ego: the *Social* drive, the *Self Preservation* drive, and the *Sexual* or Intimacy drive. We'll discuss these three drives more fully in chapter 4, but the idea is that our personality types are triggered in one of these three domains. For now, think of the three instinctual drives as evolutionary imperatives. All humans have within them the drive toward self-preservation (we eat, drink, sleep, seek shelter, and acquire resources to ensure our comfort). We all have a social drive (this is why we formed tribes in the first place; we need people, rules, norms, and communities to thrive). And we all have a sexual or intimate drive (the impulse to connect to one other person, procreate or create something new, and share our in-nermost selves with another). There is fascinating research to underscore the prevalence of these three domains from the fields of neuroscience and evolutionary psychology that we will explore more fully in chapter 4.

By virtue of having a personality, the Enneagram personality model, as posited by Dr. Naranjo, states that we all become neurotically fixated and stuck in a pattern of seeing the world from the limited perspective of our types. Also, Naranjo saw the types like nine specific diagnoses.

His work is certainly not for those who want warm, fuzzy feelings about their personality. As a Freudian analyst, he was interested in neurotic patterns and beliefs. These patterns become more fixated because we over-focus our attention on one of the three instinctual domains.

These defenses, patterns, and mechanisms are meant to keep us alive and are necessary for a healthy ego (remember Freud's *primary narcissism*). However, the ego doesn't know the difference between a real or a perceived threat—our egos become shadowboxers accustomed to fighting visible and invisible enemies. For example, the flippant dismissal of a temporarily self-involved parent forgetting to compliment our school project can become a source of long-standing emotional pain. We then begin to interpret dismissal everywhere in the world around us. So, we learn to compensate. We begin to exaggerate our strengths and conceal our weaknesses, hoping to divert, defend, or distract ourselves from potential criticism, pain, or abandonment. Secondary narcissism develops when our physical or emo-tional survival and individual focus trumps others'. This level of narcissism usually brings a lack of empathy and the inability to consider others' needs or desires.

This book is about the convergence between the Enneagram personality types, the three primary instinctual drives, and narcissism. Chapter 1 will unpack empathy: what is it, how do we use it, and why some people have more or less than others. Then we will break down the levels of the empathy spectrum in chapter 2 to begin to understand how the lower levels of empathy can result in the development of narcissism, sociopathy, and psychopathy in chapter 3. After unpacking all the underpinnings of what can go wrong in the personality's development of empathy, we will move to a quick and dirty synopsis of personality psychology and the basic structure of the Enneagram model in chapter 4. In chapter 5, you will learn about the three instinctual drives (Social, Self Preservation, and Sexual). Then, chapter 6 moves through a detailed description of the nine basic Enneagram personality types.

In part II, you'll be empowered with enough background knowledge to dive into the twenty-seven subtypes of pathological narcissism (9 personality types ✗ 3 instinctual types = 27 subtypes). By the end of the book, I hope you will understand yourself and how and to what degree narcissism shows up for you in your everyday life and for those around you. The purpose of this book isn't intended to tell you how wrong, terrible, or defective you or anyone else with narcissistic tendencies are (which, remember, is *all* of us). Instead, this book is meant to create greater compassion, understanding, and forgiveness for ourselves and others.

# I

# ON THE NATURE OF PERSONALITY AND NARCISSISM

# 1

## On the Nature of Empathy

If you ask five people to define empathy, you'll undoubtedly receive five different answers; trust me, I've done it. In fact, in a survey of over 300 people who were asked to define empathy, I rarely received similar definitions, yet most point to the same guiding idea. Is empathy an emotion, an action, a thought, an intuitive insight, or some combination of these? I like to think of empathy as a complex biocultural intrapsychic phenomenon, but that's a little wordy to spout off at a dinner party. Suppose you were to ask Siri to define empathy. In that case, she will generate a canned Wikipedia definition that defines empathy as the ability to understand another's emotions as they would their own. If you ask a psychologist their definition of empathy, you will likely hear them discuss the ability to identify, relate to, and respond to another person's feelings. When I've polled my students to define empathy, someone invariably says it is "being able to see the world through someone else's eyes." Another way of considering this is through the colloquialism of learning how to "walk a mile in someone else's shoes." These definitions, analogies, and reflections point to the same thing. Still, empathy is a complex and nuanced process that many conceptually understand but can't quite put their finger on. While a complete discussion of empathy's psychological, neurological, sociological, and communicative aspects is beyond this book's scope, we need to distill some of these basic concepts surrounding the phenomenon to understand the nature of narcissism. The two are invariably linked.

## Chapter 1

## A BIOLOGICAL PERSPECTIVE

If you listen to a geneticist discuss empathy, they will tell you that empathy exists in the human genome sequence along with our other measurable traits. And indeed, there is significant evidence to suggest that there are quantifiable components of empathy, or at least the ability to demonstrate empathy, that have a positive correlation to specific DNA strands. Simon Baron-Cohen and a team of other researchers at the University of Cambridge conducted a study using responses from an Empathy Quotient questionnaire in conjunction with respondents' 23andMe genomic data to determine whether higher levels of empathy could correlate to specific genetic markers.[1] The study reached a few interesting conclusions. First, researchers found that respondents' self-reported empathy levels have positive correlations to specific genomic sequences. Second, women tended to express more empathy than men (although this did not correlate with the empathy genome sequences, which suggested an environmental or developmental difference). And finally, genetic sequences that suggested lower empathy also indicated a higher risk of autism due to other genes that correlate to autism spectrum disorders.

Rather than one specific magic gene that indicates empathy, it is more likely that empathy is related to a series of genes that, if present in an individual, tend to increase the likelihood of the expression of empathy. Rarely is one gene responsible for any singular function in the human organism. The genes that point to empathy increase the development of oxytocin, dopamine, and other hormones and sympathetic nervous responses that help us relate and respond to others in a way that we would define as empathetic. From this, a more holistic biological perspective, empathy is a process that, if functioning, allows us to seemingly feel or relate to others' experiences and emotions as if they were our own.

In the early 2000s, I recall a great deal of excitement within the neurological community around the discovery of "mirror neurons." These neurons, located in the anterior cingulate cortex, help us relate on a cellular level to other human beings and resonate most strongly when we see others suffering or in pain. The neurons react to witnessing another's pain as though they are our own experiences. This part of our brain's processes responsible for sending pain signals to other systems in the body can be mysteriously stimulated by others' emotions, thoughts, and experiences that make their experience indistinguishable from ours. Researchers discovered that if these neurons are activated, we quite literally feel someone else's pain. The mirror neuron hypothesis certainly helps to explain why I always avoided TV shows like *Jackass* or *America's Funniest Home Videos*. There was always something sadistically excruciating about watching people slam onto the ground after falling off their roofs or smacking into a closed door. I felt like I was falling off a roof or smashing into doors rendering the entertainment value minimal. This doesn't mean that other stimuli wouldn't activate the mirror neurons of those unaffected by tumbling off a roof, but rather that kind of physical experience didn't excite their mirror neurons in the same way it did mine.

Interestingly, some people can watch others' pain with little to no cingulate cortex arousal; even more interestingly, others seem to experience pleasure from watching others experience pain. If we look at the history of human civilizations, we have no shortage of examples of humans enjoying others' pain or misfortune. The Germans call this peculiar emotional response schadenfreude. Predictably, those who self-reported lower degrees of empathetic response seemed to have less mirror neuron activation when observing others' physical or emotional pain. Some research suggests that these neurons can only be activated for some people if they have firsthand experience of the kind/type of the event or emotion. However, some people experience their natural empathy circuitry arousal without having equivalent experiences. This suggests a developmental or experiential component to empathetic responses that activate our ability to access the biological understanding of empathizing with another. Some research also suggests that mirror neuron deficits occur in people with autism spectrum disorders, which contribute to their difficulty in identifying the emotions and experiences of others.[2]

## AN ENVIRONMENTAL PERSPECTIVE

If genome science has taught us anything, our genetic code undoubtedly shapes so much of who we are. Our hair color, eye color, our preference for sweet or salty foods, even our muscle composition or tendency to patrol the kitchen at night for a late-night snack seem to express themselves in our genetic blueprint. However, gene science has also taught us that the presence of a particular DNA sequence does not guarantee its expression in our lives. Genes must be activated to express themselves. That activation could be the injection of a protein released in utero, which jump-starts our predisposition to having freckles, brown eyes, or asthma.

Some genomic activation may give us a leg up in reaping the benefits of developing innate intelligence if our caregivers properly nurture those innate aptitudes. In other words, our environment shapes the expression of our genetic potential. In a perfect world, every human being would be raised in safe, nurturing, and favorable environmental circumstances. We would all receive the optimal level of nutrients in utero, be reared by loving and intelligent caretakers, and never be deprived of physical security, food, money, creative stimulation, positive reinforcement, and the optimum level of discipline and challenges to become the ideal version of our genetic potentiality. This, of course, is not the case for most, if not all, human beings. We have varying experiences in utero, complications occur, caregivers are imperfect, and environments are, by their very nature, consistently inconsistent.

Our developmental environments' inconsistent and variable interpretation explains the divergence between siblings raised in the same home. Even identical twins, who may have had identical environments in utero, have different interpretations of their childhood environmental circumstances. Often, twins express different personality types despite the genetic predisposition to certain traits being the same, which pokes the perennial question, which came first the chicken (child) or the egg (personality type). I believe that, like all our other traits, we have a genetic predisposition to a particular personality structure. Our environment and developmental experiences shape, enhance, or diminish aspects of our personality types.

From studying children in abusive or neglectful homes, we know that they experience a greater incidence of health-related complications such as asthma, diabetes, depression, anxiety, and other behavioral or cognitive delays that are not present in peers raised in safer or healthier environments. Over the last decade, there was a boom of expectant parents playing classical music to their unborn children to foster the development of greater intelligence. This trend arose due to the popularization of studies that suggested that exposure to classical music and other creative stimuli may encourage higher intellect in children. However, it became clear that it wasn't necessarily the music that stimulated the children, but more likely the intimacy between mother and child that became a positive indicator of the development of higher intelligence. Nurturance and responding to the needs of young children have a prominent link to the development of healthy adults.

Like our other mammal friends, humans need touch, affection, and attention from active and engaged caregivers to have a chance at optimal development. Without these conditions in our lives, we have less chance of expressing some of the gifts that may already be latent in our genetic code. Suffice to say that our environments profoundly affect our brains, and the longer an environmental condition exists, the more likely it will affect our brains. For example, being in a jail cell for six hours may temporarily increase the body's production of stress hormones like cortisol, but being in prison for thirty-six years will have a more profound neurological effect and contribute to a higher incidence of permanent brain trauma.

Some research suggests that if we are raised by loving, attentive caretakers who administer to our emotional pain and teach us the value of understanding and tending to the pain and experiences of others, we have a greater chance of expressing our hard-wired empathetic intelligence. But of course, some people are reared in neglectful and sometimes extreme abusive environments and develop empathy anyway, and seemingly, because of it. Some people grow up in near-ideal environments and seem to express less empathy than environmental models of empathy would suggest. I have known people raised by severely narcissistic parents who developed highly tuned empathetic faculties despite their parent's inability to demonstrate compassionate responses. It could be that the absence of empathy activated their mirror neurons in a heightened way to be able to deal with the deficits of their parents. Perhaps it is simply that they just had more of a genetic predisposition toward greater empathy, and the genes in question skipped a generation, or, more likely, it is something in between these two hypotheses.

Undoubtedly some seem to be predisposed to expressing empathy due to certain genetic conditions. Still, without the outside world's influence, it may remain latent or perhaps become overexpressed due to the conditions in which one finds oneself. As a professor of Human Relations, I often tell others that I'm in the business of teaching my students how to develop greater empathy. My job is to create a learning environment that pushes students to see the world through another's eyes. Those students can project themselves into another's shoes more quickly because of prior experiences or a predisposition to increased empathy. Other students may come into the classroom with a diminished capacity to empathize with others but strengthen latent empathetic neural pathways during a semester. And still, there are those students who cannot develop greater empathetic skills for one reason or another. No amount of prodding, conditioning, reading, or interactions with other students can shift their lack of empathy. So while the environment is essential, it's certainly not the whole show.

## A DEVELOPMENTAL PERSPECTIVE

We've seen how our biological imprint and our environments could shape the development and expression of empathy in our lives. However, we are not simply physical beings that exist statically in our environments, but instead, we evolve within those environments. We begin in the womb and progress through childhood, adolescence, adulthood, and eventually old age. Within those stages of growth, we experience various shifts of consciousness, ability, and perception that are predictable across the average human life span. Many sociologists, psychologists, and other behavioral scientists have charted these developmental stages. Still, perhaps no insights are more widely regarded as the blueprint of human development than those of Swiss psychologist Jean Piaget. Piaget postulated that humans follow a predictable trajectory of four cognitive development stages: the sensorimotor stage (18–24 months), where humans begin to develop object permanence (i.e., mom's not gone; she's just hiding behind my blanket); the preoperational stage (2–7 years old), where humans develop symbolic thought (i.e., my backyard is a pirate ship and I'm the captain); the concrete operational stage (7–11 years old), where children develop the ability to perform complex operational procedures; and the formal operational stage (12–adulthood), where we develop abstract problem-solving skills (i.e., learning how to "adult," have adult relationships, navigate multiple responsibilities, and generally manage the various twists and turns of adult life).[3] While Piaget mapped the basic blueprint of cognitive development, he wasn't as interested in developing emotional/mental states as they relate to our sympathetic or empathetic responses to others and the world around us. Piaget might have believed that the average person should have developed complex emotional reasoning by adulthood, of which empathy factors into our operational decision-making.

Because Piaget's insights were primarily concerned with what we can do and perceive, rather than what we may be feeling, he left the door open for more interpretative models of human emotional development. Lawrence Kohlberg, for example, was interested in understanding the trajectory of moral and ethical development. In addition to cognitive development, Kohlberg believed that humans should ideally develop increasingly complex methods to process ethical or moral dilemmas.[4] He postulated that humans move through three distinct phases of ethical development. These phases helped explain why infants and children are more self-interested and seemingly less sympathetic or empathetic to others when their desires/wishes aren't cared for. Kohlberg expressed each phase by highlighting the dichotomy or dilemma at each stage. The stages are Pre-conventional stage, where we don't care about rules or guidelines; we take what we want. The Conventional stage is where we learn to ask permission for what we want for fear of punishment. And the Post-conventional stage is where we can ethically reason through the consequences both to ourselves and others for flouting rules or conventions.

Kohlberg believed that our ethical/moral reasoning should develop accordingly as we progress through these stages. From not caring about what is right or wrong, because we're simply trying to satiate our basic desire, to becoming increasingly more concerned with and adhering to the rules so that we don't get punished by an authority figure. And finally, to a higher level of ethical reasoning where we can see the impact of our decisions on the world around us.

In terms of empathy, we could say that empathy doesn't fully develop until the third, post-conventional stage of ethical reasoning for Kohlberg. Interestingly, Kohlberg believed that most never reach the post-conventional stage of empathy but instead live by what's "right and wrong" to avoid punishment rather than reasoning why and how one's actions and choices may or may not impact those around them. So, for Kohlberg, the post-conventional moral reasoning abilities would correlate to the potential to express or experience more empathy. This would assume that some people only express empathy when they believe someone may be judging, evaluating, or observing their compassion. This matches Kohlberg's assertion that the conventional level of ethical reasoning is the upper limit for many adults.

Carol Gilligan, a student of Kohlberg, developed a theory of moral development from a social interactionist perspective. Gilligan wanted to understand why women seemed to develop and demonstrate greater concern and care for the well-being of others. She was very conscious of how young girls were socialized to show more concern for the emotions of others because they are taught to preference others' feelings over their own. Like other feminist scholars of her era, Gilligan saw this as preparation for assumed future motherhood or other feminine caretaking roles it's presumed they'll inhabit later in life.[5] However, Gilligan's stages proved to be impactful for an alternative way of understanding the development of morality or ethics for all people and help us understand why men tend to express less emotional concern for others. Gilligan believed that people moved through conventional stages of morality and developed a greater awareness of the well-being of others. Gilligan thought that the post-conventional stage was related to the development of a need to protect the well-being of humanity as one has recognized themselves as part of an interconnected whole. Until recently, Gilligan's post-conventional stage was the closest developmental psychologists came to attempting to explain the differences in care and attention that people show toward their fellow humans.

Finally, in 2000 psychologist Martin Hoffman conceptualized his developmental theory of empathetic development. Hoffman's stages of empathy are compelling in that he believes that under "normal" circumstances (we can assume that to mean the relatively normal, safe biological and environmental conditions as we discussed earlier), humans should follow four stages of empathetic development:[6]

1. Global empathy (0–12 months old): The infant experiences sympathetic, albeit unconscious, responses to the pain or experiences of others.
2. Egocentric empathy (12–18 months): Children begin to understand themselves as separate entities from those around them and may have some understanding of the other's pain and offer support through the lens of their own experience.
3. Empathy for another's feelings (18 months–8 years old): At this stage, we begin to recognize others' emotions and distinguish those emotions in ourselves and another.
4. Empathy for another's life experience (adolescence–adulthood): At this stage, we begin to recognize the conditions or experiences that may have shaped an individual's emotions and can "feel" that person's experience in the context of our mental/emotional life.

In both Gilligan and Hoffman's models, as we develop through the life span, and certainly by adolescence, we should have developed the potential toward greater recognition, understanding, and empathetic resonance. So adulthood, from the developmental framework, should ideally include increasingly complex experiences and expressions of empathy. However, many factors can thwart "normal" development, such as trauma or other disruptions in the trajectory of what might be the theoretical empathetic or moral development that the theories we've discussed suggest.

## A SPIRITUAL PERSPECTIVE

While we've covered a few models to help explain empathetic development from the biological/genetic, developmental, and environmental domains, there is the equally essential but invariably less concrete domain of spirituality. Humans are more than just the mechanical firing of neurons in an environment (that is, if you're not a staunch materialist). Many human subjective experiences vigorously test, if not flat out defy, scientific explanation. The spiritual development of human beings has long been a subject of intense philosophical inquiry for religious scholars and mystics throughout the ages, partly because the development of the inner world lies squarely within the consciousness of the experiencer and doesn't easily conform to the instruments of scientific testing. There is something ephemeral about the idea of empathy, as it is both pointing to an affective state and interpersonal or collective way of interacting with the world around us.

Most of the world's revered religious texts, at their root, teach the principles of compassion and goodwill toward fellow humans. Numerous quotes in the Bible, the Koran, the Talmud, the Bhagavad Gita, the Mahayana, and the Tanakh point its adherents to the development and expression of loving consideration toward others. In most of these texts, the goal is for the devotee to strive for more profound and deeper states of communion with a divine source(s) which is often said to embody the principles of love, compassion, kindness, and goodwill. Ideally, the more devoutly one delves into the teachings of a particular spiritual tradition, the more one develops more profound empathy and understanding of the pain and plight of others.

These traditions point to the development and widening of one's consciousness or awareness of others and the world around them. As humans develop wider and broader perspectives of consciousness, they invariably develop more profound experiences of love, compassion, and empathy. Understanding one's impact on the world around them and the care and attention toward becoming a conscientious steward of their effect on themselves and the world or even the Universe is the deepest (or highest) level of human consciousness. There are as many different models of consciousness as there are philosophies themselves. Suffice to say that almost all of them denote a marked shift from focusing on the self and one's emotions, needs, and perspective to recognizing and considering those around them. These consciousness models differ from developmental and biological views of empathetic development because these states of consciousness do not typically follow a chronological or linear trajectory.

In some traditions of Hinduism (and other perspectives that espouse a worldview rooted in the principles of reincarnation), as one moves through each successive lifetime, they gain experience as different life-forms. This successive movement from lifetime to lifetime deepens one's level of understanding of the Universe and brings one closer to the wisdom and knowledge of God or the Universe itself. From this perspective, as one envolves (the consciousness equivalent to evolution), one also develops more empathy as one draws from a multitude of past-life experiences stored in their consciousness to access, however unconsciously. As many religious texts refer to it, this historical consciousness, or soul, houses the capacity to understand and empathize with other beings. The more experiences one has in various bodies, situations, and experiences, the more content the current personality can draw from intuitively understanding others. In this context, the term "old soul" refers to someone who has lived many lives and has the soulful wisdom to prove it. However, spiritual intelligence or understanding does not consistently create higher greater levels of empathy.

A client of mine who was in the middle of a divorce from a high-profile and highly respected New Age thought leader sought coaching to deal with the aftereffects of what had been years of both overt and subtle narcissistic abuse. They were hesitant to share their ex's name with me out of fear of backlash should word get back to their ex. My client was at once very relieved that I believed that their partner was indeed narcissistic because everyone else erroneously thought that because this person was spiritually gifted that they couldn't also be narcissistic. I assured my client that I understood that spiritual gifts, intellectual aptitudes, or the ability to inspire others don't necessarily comport with high empathy. I explained that, from my perspective, having a higher perspective of the human experience and providing a spiritual assessment of humanity requires a mental/emotional detachment that can accompany a type of spiritual narcissism whereby the person believes they're more elevated than others. My client let out a massive sigh of relief and began to recount obvious markers of narcissistic abuse that would otherwise be shocking to their ex-partner's followers.

## A HOLISTIC APPROACH

You may have gathered by now that I'm unconvinced that there's one over-arching model of empathy. A holistic approach to understanding how we develop and demonstrate compassion is needed to scratch the surface of this complex process entirely. One can have all the genetic and environmental advantages in the world and then hit a snag in the developmental process or have the highest values of empathetic relating modeled to them by their parents, yet lack the empathetic genetic components. As you'll see when we break down the elements of personality later in this book, I'm a big believer in looking at human beings as a holistic byproduct of their biology, environment, development, and life experiences to understand what makes someone tick. I would be remiss if I didn't acknowledge that empathy comes in degrees and waves and can be highly situational like our other emotional responses. Simon Baron-Cohen discusses the phenomenon of individuals "shutting down" their empathy to survive.[7]

A good example in history is the overwhelming participation of regular, everyday German citizens in the persecution of Jews and other scapegoated people during World War II. It is unlikely that a large swath of the German population was already predisposed to experiencing less empathy. Instead, during that time, survival conditions necessitated a need for some to shut down a portion of their empathetic resonance to survive. However, situations like those experienced during the Holocaust also awakened the compassion and empathy of some people who otherwise may not have given much thought to others' experiences. People can quickly shut down their empathy when stressed, angry, or otherwise hurt by another person. We can also suddenly open our hearts to a stranger's pain for no explicable reason. Research on the complexity of the human brain and genetic code is unfolding rapidly and will undoubtedly shed more light on the biological components of empathy. However, there is still much to learn about why, when, and under what circumstances empathy is diminished or eliminated. Next, we will shift our attention to what happens at the lower ends of the empathetic scale and at what point primary narcissism becomes secondary or pathological narcissism? In the next chapter, we will explore the various levels of the empathy spectrum.

# 2

## The Empathy Spectrum

The experience of empathy is not a zero-sum game. Most human traits are measured along a continuum, and empathy is no exception. Empathy exists on a continuum, and I believe (and the data supports this notion) that we function within a bandwidth of a couple of levels above or below our empathetic set point. Even the most empathetic of people can become exhausted and experience empathy fatigue and may, momentarily, seem to have lost their empathy. However, research has shown that people return to an average set point within these levels. I should add that learning how to relate better to others, or increasing communication skills, does not necessarily translate to higher levels of empathy.

Empathy is primarily an internal experience, and one can perform kind acts for various reasons and not necessarily experience empathy. In my 2021 study of empathy and personality, I found that people seem to fall within a range of seven levels of empathy. Similar empathy scales exist, but perhaps the most widely used is the empathy quotient scale conceptualized by Simon Baron-Cohen.[1] While Cohen does assert that some people have no empathy, he doesn't contend that someone can have too much empathy because part of having empathy, in his estimation, is the ability to know how to manage that empathy in the world.[2]

While I agree that effectively managing the occasionally difficult emotional fallout of having unusually high empathy is ideal, many who scored on the highest end of the empathy spectrum found it challenging to manage their empathy. This phenomenon likely exists because we live in a culture that doesn't understand that level of empathetic resonance. It's evident to me that one can experience undifferentiated empathy and struggle with how to translate their experiences into sympathy, or even how to best relate to others without feeling or becoming overwhelmed by the intensity of their empathy.

## LEVEL 0

At this level of empathy, there appears to be no recognition or understanding of empathy. People at Level 0 may seem normal to the onlooker. Many hold jobs, go to school, have children, maintain relationships, and engage in the world like everyone else. Some may have a reasonably developed sense of ethics in that they may understand the principles of right and wrong and adhere to laws and rules, so they are not punished or rejected. However, people with zero degrees of empathy tend not to feel much toward others. They often lack a certain degree of tact when dealing with people emotionally. They may be brutally honest in their opinions of others regardless of how their thoughts might affect another or can be relentless when teasing or admonishing someone for behavior they find to be objectionable. They may be completely clueless about why other people become upset at what they say and report not caring much about what others think about their commentary. If they find that they've hurt another's feelings, they may apologize in a dry and clinical way that feels devoid of remorse or emotion.

This level of empathy can show up with people who demonstrate some degree of autism; however, many people on the spectrum report wanting to cognitively understand how or why other people's feelings become hurt so that they can avoid transgressing others (which is a demonstration of empathy). Additionally, research suggests that people on the autism spectrum tend to express empathy in ways that aren't fully understood because they use different means of connecting with themselves and others. Hence the term "neurodivergent" destigmatizes those whose processing doesn't match conventional ways of relating in the world. However, some do not exhibit other qualities of those on the autism spectrum and may be functionally neurotypical in every other way. Some people with zero degrees of empathy can experience contempt, disdain, or anger at the expectation that they care what other people may be feeling or thinking. They tend to be self-involved and express exhaustion and avoidance when expected to engage in human interaction.

There can be significant difficulties in relationships at this level due to conflicts over their often-harsh communication style. They may be quick to anger and feel justified at expressing the brunt of their displeasure through insults, revenge, or even physical violence. They report no understanding of what other people may or may not be feeling and are unmotivated to shift their behavior to demonstrate more care toward others, even at the request of loved ones.

People at this level tend to experience no regret, guilt, or remorse when they have hurt someone. It's common for people at this level of empathy to feel a sense of justification or entitlement to treat others in whatever way they deem necessary. They often have limited emotional expression (unless it relates to someone hurting their feelings). When they express their emotions, they tend toward the "harder" end of the emotional spectrum (anger, irritation, frustration, outrage, etc.). There's often little to no compulsion to tend to others' experiences unless they are directly affected. It's not uncommon to find people at this level in the prison system (particularly if they have co-occurring antisocial or narcissistic personality disorders). Not because people with zero empathy are inherently criminally minded, but because they are often unaware and unconcerned with the needs or expectations of those around them. Their lack of awareness can sometimes land them in precarious situations when their need for self-gratification collides with others' interests or the law overall.

## LEVEL 1

At this level, there is some degree of empathy present, and as such, the person can often feel "twinges" of understanding their impact on others. People at this level also tend to have difficulty understanding where other people are coming from, particularly if others expect a particular emotional response. They may cognitively understand that their behavior or words harmed another after repeatedly hurting someone, and they can occasionally curb their natural reactions. They have difficulty attuning with others and prefer to keep to themselves as they find relationships draining. They may feel little attachment to the people in their lives (even children or spouses) but enjoy being around others because they are interesting, stimulating, attractive, or otherwise compelling. However, relationships become cumbersome at the point at which they are expected to tend to others' needs, and they may then distance themselves to be free from emotional expectations. Because they have some degree of empathy, they may navigate the emotional world well enough to recognize that they sometimes need other people to get their needs met. Many can even be well versed in reading and intuiting the emotions of others around them but are still typically unconcerned about whether others are in pain or need. If they're intellectually minded, they may lean on typologies or other systems of understanding the world so they can navigate relationships "normally" and maximize the likelihood of satiating their desires or immediate goals.

The emotional experience of someone at this level is relatively elementary. Many can recognize if they feel sad, angry, happy, or scared but tend to be uninterested in the emotional world because they're not feeling the same level of feeling they observe other people are experiencing. Unlike those at Level 0, where emotional regulation is even more difficult, those at Level 1 may be more adept at temporarily altering their behavior to affect the results in the environment or others to suit their needs. Learning to regulate their emotions enhances their ability to be in the world and with others without constantly being reprimanded, punished, or shamed for being selfish, unkind, or uncaring. People at this level have some inkling that they may lack empathy but often believe that it's other people's problem rather than their own. However, they can value rules and regulations to keep their own potentially destructive impulses in check. If they also have some degree of narcissism or antisocial tendencies, they may be more secretive and cunning about how to effectively hide or mask their exploitative, violent, or unscrupulous behavior.

People at Level 1 will try for a while to meet others' behavioral expectations. Still, most grow agitated and frustrated quickly, and eventually, the true breadth of their lack of concern reveals itself. The nonsubjective world feels more congruent for people at this Level of empathy, and they often feel more comfortable with hard facts, numbers, data, or the physical world.

Again, we must distinguish Level 1 and those on the autism spectrum who prefer the predictable world of data, figures, or calculations. While someone on the spectrum could indeed be at Level 1, many simply have trouble parsing the often-ambiguous world of emotional or interpersonal cues. There are many people with autism who have difficulty relating to other human beings yet are incredibly attuned to animals, trees, bugs, plants, or other nonhuman entities. Inventor and author Temple Grandin became a vocal advocate of autism awareness. Grandin, who was autistic, was famously uncomfortable and clueless in interpersonal relationships with people, yet she felt a deep and soulful connection to livestock. Thus she made it her life's work to devise a humane slaughterhouse so that the cows did not have to experience the fear she sensed from the animals. Again, this is a powerful demonstration of empathy toward an animal many people believe to be devoid of feelings.

## LEVEL 2

At this level of empathy, there is more recognition and understanding of one's own emotions and those around them. While there is still relatively little concern for other people's emotions, people at this level report experiencing slight feelings of guilt or remorse if their lack of empathy or concern for others is exposed. Typically, at this level, there is more ability to regulate emotional responses, especially anger, and a broader perspective on the consequences of their actions on those around them. People at this level are still primarily oriented toward self-gratification. There is often a greater propensity to conceal their self-interested actions because there is a stronger motivation to stay in positive rapport with others. It makes getting the things they want easier.

At Level 2, people tend to experience more emotional content, particularly their happiness or well-being issues. They are more emotionally sensitive than those at Level 1 or 0. They can become upset that people don't tend to their emotions and thus feel justified in treating others with callousness or lashing out when hurt. They feel guilty if they act in ways that cause others to reject or retreat from them. While their emotions are marginally more moderated than those at Level 1, they are still prone to outbursts of anger or callousness and may be unwilling to stop or curb those behaviors when called out at the moment. Tending to the emotional expectations of others is still exhausting to those at this level. Still, because they experience more emotions themselves, they are better able to mask their lack of caring with charm or, over time, learn how to give others the appropriate sympathetic responses (although their sympathies may lack emotional affect). There's a tendency for those at this level to feel misunderstood because of frequent experiences of others pointing out their lack of empathy.

> I've been accused of being unempathetic many times in my life, and I think people are just trying to make me feel guilty because I don't cater to other people's emotions or desires. I have no problem asking for things nicely, but if I don't get what I want, I'll find a way to make sure I get it, and sometimes I hurt people's feelings. I get fed up a lot because I do a lot for people, and I deserve to be selfish sometimes. I got tired of feeling like the bad guy all the time, so I just learned to keep my distance from other people. A few people get me, but I don't need people around me calling me selfish or making me feel guilty for doing what I want to do. If I don't look out for me, then no one will.
>
> ——Mary, 35, attorney, Type Two

## LEVEL 3

At this level, a person often becomes more adept at masking or demonstrating sympathy, and consequently, they feel a bit more comfortable around other people. They still experience empathy only sporadically and may have to directly experience something to develop an appreciation for how a particular situation may affect someone else. They may have healthy, functional relation-ships, yet they are more aware of the gaps between their empathy and others'. They may become adept at producing the correct responses to others' feelings but report feeling anxiety, irritation, or avoidance when expected to spontane-ously respond to someone's pain or experience (mainly if it's far outside of their own experience). They can often miss the mark and experience more shame or embarrassment when others point out their lack of empathy. They tend to do well in situations that don't require much emotional relating. While they may experience a fair amount of emotional content, they can become confused at others' emotions. They can sometimes be blunt and lack finesse in how they approach others, particularly if it's related to completing a task or meeting their immediate gratification needs.

Many at this level of empathy understand that there is a need to learn how to communicate effectively, and thus they may have a slightly professional or rehearsed interpersonal quality. At this stage, depending on the person's personality type, they may believe themselves to have empathy (or to have developed their empathy). Still, often the person has developed a practical, sympathetic communication circuit. They may avoid deep or intimate con-versations, not only because these kinds of conversations don't interest them for the most part, but also because it could reveal their deficits in emotional relating and potentially bring about rejection or abandonment.

Much like those at Level 2, at this level, depending on personality type, their emotional reactivity can be spontaneous and quick. Often, with practice, they gain greater control over how their emotions display to others. They want to be effective but may be exhausted by those who want to connect emotion-ally. They can often study the feelings, responses, and language of those who demonstrate the people-skills they wish to possess and master those behaviors. However, they report being aware of the distance between the appropriate responses they give others and the frustration, irritation, or exhaustion they're feeling internally. Few would classify those at Level 3 as "sensitive." They may be emotionally reactive, dismissive, or angry, particularly if they've grown tired of trying to match or cater to those around them. Many at this level recognize that they lack something when it comes to empathy but aren't sure how to find the emotions within themselves. Instead, they try to imitate empathy as best they can.

For people at this level, being told that they're unempathetic, unemotional, or cold can be distressing because they feel things for others in certain circum-stances. When empathy does arise, it can feel overwhelming, so they often prefer to shift back into a more objective perspective and not to be swayed by the emotions of those around them. Many at this level have a greater sense of experiential empathy and can be more inclined to be thoughtful or helpful if they have been through the same experience themselves.

# LEVEL 4

Level 4 is the beginning of the lower-average level of human empathy. People at this level still tend to experience a strong preference for preserving their self-interest but wish to appear and behave in ways that others will perceive as empathetic. Empathy at this level functions not as a constant state of being (as this is difficult for even the most compassionate to maintain) but can be called upon to help fix an immediate or developing problem. People at this level have greater experiential empathy than those at Level 3. They frequently report being guilted into empathizing by those close to them (much like those at Level 3). However, unlike those at Level 3, they may have learned both the appropriate sympathetic responses to others in addition to feeling more genuine guilt or remorse for hurting others' feelings or acting in selfish or uncaring ways.

They want to understand what they can do to improve a problem or fix someone's feelings. They employ empathy as a tool with which to return to relational equilibrium with others. They can become frustrated when their attempts toward sympathetic or empathetic relating go unnoticed or are ineffective. They see empathy as a means to an end. They may need others to specifically spell out why their behavior was bothersome or hurtful to feel motivated to change their behaviors. They may be very caring and loving toward those in their immediate spheres but can more easily dismiss the emotions or concerns of people outside their close circle.

Interestingly, as is expected at the higher levels of empathy, those at this level experience more significant distress at others' emotional pain because they want to solve the problem. This will be especially true of those close to them. People at this level feel even more shame for not feeling the same emotions that they believe other people feel. They may also compensate for their lack of empathy by caring and being attentive to others to show they care.

They do experience genuine care and love toward those they've attached to but report feeling a very conscious pull toward their self-interests, desires, and needs compared to those they care about. They may be quicker to develop empathy toward someone else if they have experienced the same situation but otherwise can still slip into callous or dismissive behavior. Many adopt a "fake it until you make it" approach to empathy and genuine compassion because they don't want other people to be upset with them.

At this level, some may feel that religious, spiritual, or philosophical ideologies help them to help foster their empathetic philosophies and guide their actions. Their focus on solutions can prevent them from understanding the need to process deeper emotional content. They will often have a strong preference for engaging in emotional sharing if it's a means to an end (i.e., improving their marriage or relationship, getting along with others, increasing productivity at work, increasing life satisfaction, etc.). Aside from seeking solutions, empathy can seem inconvenient to those at this level because when it does arise, they can feel overwhelmed with guilt or remorse if they've hurt someone due to their lack of empathy. Because they experience more shame for hurting others' feelings, people at this level want to conceal when a lack of empathy is present as much as possible. Research has shown that this tends to be the average level of empathy for men, likely due to socialization and expectations of masculine behavior.

I feel like if I didn't have my wife around, I would be a much less empathetic person. Before I met her, I was pretty clueless about why people got their feelings hurt so easily. I don't want to be an ass to anyone, but sometimes I find people's emotional baggage ridiculous. My wife helps me see things from someone else's perspective, especially when I've hurt her feelings. When it clicks, I totally get it. I just need someone to put me in their shoes. It's not something I do naturally, but when I get there, I will try my hardest not to repeat the offense. I learned that sometimes talking about feelings has a positive outcome in marriage counseling. I'm all about positive outcomes, and if empathy helps me get there, awesome!

—Daniel, 36, media manager, Enneagram Type Seven

## LEVEL 5

At Level 5, people begin to experience what could be considered average empathy. People at this level may feel more at ease interacting with others and their emotions because they can recognize a range of emotions within themselves. The tendency to avoid deeper relationships or sharing at the lower levels diminishes significantly as the person may feel more significant connections to other people and their experiences. However, the person at this level may still struggle with balancing their agendas, needs, and emotions with others around them. They do what is emotionally expected, and if their communication skills are well developed, they are more adept at responding to others' emotions with compassion. Those at Level 5 still prefer talking about themselves and their activities, interests, and desires but experience more guilt and shame if selfishness or self-interest is exposed. Although more comfortable with emotional expression, most people at this level tend to prefer activity-based interactions because they prefer to keep their relationships free from the painful or negative emotions that others could communicate in more intimate settings. They want some level of intimacy but ultimately become frustrated and agitated if interactions do not stay within their emotional comfort zone.

Some people can be quite empathetic to the negative emotions of others because they have experienced more pain or heartache but may feel disdainful or intolerant of others' positive emotions. Conversely, if the person has a more positively focused personality type, they may be intolerant of negative emotions in the other. Either way, there is a tendency to stay within one's emotional "wheelhouse" accompanied by some lingering struggles with empathizing with the experiences of those who are very different from them or in some way violate their morality or sensibilities.

There can be greater cognitive or conceptual empathy at this stage as many people tend to increase their empathy with more familiarity or knowledge of the people and situations they encounter. For example, someone who may have never experienced famine and hunger may be able to watch a news story about starving children and become emotional as they imbibe more information about the experience of starving. Those at Level 5 are still more adept at cutting off or shutting down their empathy for others, especially if the situation or person is removed from their immediate awareness or violates their morality or values. Empathy at this level relates to their direct experiences, friends, family, and loved ones. If helping someone else requires too much mental, emotional, or tangible effort, they may avoid helping to avoid being inconvenienced and resort instead to sympathetic responses.

It's common at this level for people to be more conscious of the impact of their words and actions on others and, as a result, be more averse to conflict or discord in their environments. People at Level 5 typically demonstrate greater emotional control because of their increased awareness of how others receive their emotional energy. However, they may become stubborn, dismissive, incorrigible, argumentative, or inflexible if they disagree with someone's perspectives, experiences, or opinions.

# LEVEL 6

At this level, empathy begins to become more finely tuned. People at this level report having had some awareness of their high empathy early in their lives and may feel like they have always been able to tell what others are thinking or feeling without being told. Many at this level report feeling a certain level of sensitivity, particularly to others' negative emotions or pain and a desire to help or assist those in need. Those at Level 6 are often aware of their emotional impact and take more care in how they speak and interact with others, and can adjust their communication style to match the situation at hand. People at this level are more emotionally resonant and seek relationships to foster an emotional bond with the other. They tend to enjoy sharing confidences and emotional experiences with others as a means of connecting. When connected to someone, they will offer support and compassion in the way that will most benefit the other person.

People at this level can at times overestimate their empathy. Thus they may find themselves in situations where they are the primary means of assisting or support and become overwhelmed or resentful. At this level, people are more forgiving because they can intuitively understand the choices, emotions, and decisions others make even if they don't agree or fully cognitively understand the other's actions. They make time for other people, particularly if people are suffering or in need, and often feel a strong sense of responsibility to be available to others who need their empathy or compassion. At times, people at this level can develop arrogance about their empathy. Recognizing that they have more empathy than other people, they may feel a sense of judgment, indignance, or outrage when others aren't as sensitive as they are. They may separate their disagreement from their care or concern for others and are often more adept at maintaining relationships over time because they value the feelings, emotions, and quality of the relationship over being right or getting their immediate needs met.

Many at this level can feel inundated with the emotional demands of others, not because they can't understand them (as we saw with those at Levels 1–3), but because they feel an overwhelming need to offer their emotional support or assistance. There can often be patterns of empathizing to exhaustion. Many people at this level report some emotional, psychological, or financial strain on their lives due to their tendency to fret or worry about others' being in emotional pain.

## LEVEL 7

This is the highest level of empathy and at the farthest end of the empathy scale. Consequently, it's rare to find this level of empathy in the general public. They experience the same pull toward intimacy, emotional relating, and the desire to bear witness and offer support to those in emotional pain as those at Level 6. However, at this level, there is an additional metaphysical or spiritual element to the experience of their empathy. People at Level 7 appear to possess a level of understanding or wisdom about the impact of their actions, words, and experiences on the world around them that can transcend their personal experiences and age.

They tend to experience their empathy as almost entirely energetic, spiritual, or otherwise less tangible—many report spontaneous empathy with humans, animals, plants, and even inanimate objects. There's a universality in their empathetic experience that transcends space and time that can make them appear enigmatic or strange to others.

> I remember when I was a little girl, I would have funerals for flies my mother would kill in our house because I felt like their life was snuffed out too early simply because we didn't want them around. I felt bad for them. I don't particularly love being bothered by flies either, and I understand why my mom did it (she hated filth and bugs), so I understood her as well. Now, as an adult, I can feel what anyone or anything is feeling if I plug into it, and sometimes it's lovely. At other times, it can be excruciating. I became a therapist because I felt it was the best way for me to use my empathy to help others. I now work with convicted child sex offenders to help them heal. It's excruciating sometimes hearing about their crimes, but I also feel deeply for them, and everyone deserves to have someone listen and try to understand them.
>
> —Carol, 54, psychotherapist, Enneagram Type Four

Interestingly those at this level report feeling less distress about their empathy as they age as many learned coping mechanisms that allowed them to develop healthy detachment from the experiences of others so they could be of greater service. Many at this level possessed a kind of sixth sense about what others were thinking, feeling, or the actions they may take and can empathize with those that others may find reprehensible, dangerous, or taboo. What distinguishes this level from Level 6 is the level of ego identification with being empathetic and the spontaneous, unconscious experience of empathizing with or understanding the world around them. They are very sensitive to tone and easily track others' emotional nuances and mood changes. At times they can be too sensitive and absorb others' moods, emotions, and needs and need to be alone to differentiate their emotional needs from people around them.

People at this stage want to give meaning and significance to others and feel a need to find ways to translate suffering into something transcendent or transformational. As a result, many find themselves drawn to work as therapists, psychologists, social workers, or other healing professions. Even those not in those fields of study have an aptitude for quickly understanding others' needs and motivations and will try to respond to others in a way that best matches their intuitive understanding of the person's situation at the moment.

* * *

As you consider where you may fall on the empathy scale, I will remind you that it's rare for someone to live at one level all the time. Most people run the gamut between the level above and below their set point, and there can be a variety of experiences that can elevate or decrease our level of empathetic resonance at any moment. For example, when we experience intense emotional trauma, stress chemicals in our brain can reduce our ability to experience empathy or compassion for others as our bodies go into fight or flight. Extended periods of trauma can erode our ability to empathize with others as we spend most of our mental/emotional energy trying to find neurological equilibrium.

Some studies have demonstrated that certain kinds of trauma can catapult our empathetic capabilities to higher levels than we might typically experience. For example, during natural disasters or widespread catastrophic events, people may feel a swelling of compassion and thus feel compelled to perform acts of service for those they may otherwise not have helped. However, you didn't likely decide to read this book to understand those in the higher ranges of empathetic resonance but wanted to understand what happens when empathy is lacking. In the next chapter, we will explore some of the common diagnoses of those at the lower empathy levels, namely, narcissism, sociopathy, and psychopathy, and the difference between these often uttered but rarely discerned terms.

# 3

## Narcissism, Sociopathy, and Psychopathy

Now that we have covered the conditions that contribute to narcissism, we will explore some variations of narcissism in the human psyche. Narcissism, like empathy, exists along a continuum. We all have some measure of narcissism present in our egos as the ability to focus on our personal needs, desires, and wants to the exclusion of those around us, which is, at times, a necessary defense mechanism to ensure we meet our needs. When we're feeling hurt because someone forgot our birthday, desirous of attention for our contributions at work, or when we feel the compulsion to cut in front of a long line because we have an appointment in fifteen minutes, we're demonstrating "everyday narcissism." Moments of selfishness, disregard for the feelings or needs of others, and a desire to be important are features of a "normal" and healthy ego. Our egos need a certain degree of narcissism to survive because having our self-image mirrored back to us is how the ego knows it exists.

You may have heard the term "mirroring," which points to the action of having our identity projected back to us by people in our lives. An example of mirroring is when you take a personality test and can't wait to read your results to see if it's pinned you. Mirroring can feel good, like when our third grade teacher tells us the book report we worked hard on is excellent. Or mirroring can be incongruent, like when we find out our first crush thinks we're ugly or not cool enough.

Each personality type deals with and needs differing amounts of mirroring, and the effects of mirroring deviate from type to type. However, we're all seeking accurate, honest, and constructive mirroring from the world around us in one way or another. If we receive consistent feedback that we're attractive and charismatic, we begin to see ourselves accordingly. Positive mirroring gives us the confidence to move through the world in a way that allows us to meet our goals and feel deserving of positive attention. But what happens when positive mirroring is given in abundance or given without equal honest and critical feedback for our deficits? Moreover, what happens when our sense of self is built purely on the positive feedback of others to the extent that we cannot handle any negative or critical commentary, even when we may be in desperate need of a reality check? Some believe this is one condition for the development of narcissism.

As we saw in chapter 1, narcissism develops for various reasons. And frankly, we don't yet fully understand all the facets that contribute to developing an abundance of narcissistic traits. We don't know why some people become more narcissistic than others. Some think it's a trait variance created due to a particular sequence of inherited genetic codes or brain chemical imbalances that shape the personality's defense strategies. Others believe that difficulties or traumas experienced in the psychological development of some people create a greater propensity for narcissistic tendencies. While still others believe that narcissism is simply a lack or disregard of one's behavior on the world around them. I think any (or all) of those things contribute to developing narcissistic spectrum disorders such as Narcissistic Personality Disorder (NPD), sociopathy, and psychopathy. So, rather than rehash prevailing theories of how narcissism develops, let's spend our time building an understanding of the various expressions of narcissism in the human psyche.

## NARCISSISM

Narcissism and Narcissistic Personality Disorder are not mutually exclusive. When we colloquially label people narcissistic, we're usually talking about those with a greater propensity of narcissistic traits and not the personality disorder itself. In recent years narcissism has become a buzzword that sweeps everyone from the cocky guy at work who likes to brag about his achievements to Harvey Weinstein or Ted Bundy into the same bucket. These generalizations miss the importance of the degrees to which narcissism exists in the average human personality (which we'll explore further in part II) instead of those whose narcissism has manifested significant impairment in their personal or professional lives. Usually, the higher the degree of narcissism, the lower the presence of empathy. It would be a misnomer to say someone is an "empathetic narcissist." However, a subset of narcissism called the Dark Empath does report higher levels of both affective and cognitive empathy (more on this in chapter 8).

Some people with narcissistic traits can seem very nice. The term "nice narcissist" refers to those who appear pleasant and amicable, but their narcissistic traits are less evident on the surface. However, by definition, narcissism focuses on oneself to the exclusion of others. While someone may have learned behaviors that others may deem polite or even kind, if they are a true narcissist, empathy is less accessible or consistent.

Narcissism and identifying people as narcissists have become pop psychology trends. Examples of narcissistic behavior flood our media as prominent, rich, and famous exemplars have become the gold standard for recognizing the harmful effects of malignant narcissism. However, I work with clients daily who refer to their mothers, ex-spouses, fathers, brothers, and former bosses as "narcissists," and they may very well be narcissists. Still, very few of those examples would qualify for a clinical diagnosis of narcissism, in my opinion. Indeed, many likely have low empathy or a combination of low empathy and a personality style that tends toward self-aggrandizement or an abundance of confidence.

What is the line between arrogance, cockiness, and narcissistic bravado? Are all braggarts narcissists, or does narcissism foster self-aggrandizement? Are all selfish and callous people narcissists? The answer is yes and no. Indeed, narcissists tend to prioritize their concerns, emotions, and needs over those of others. Still, they may not necessarily think highly of themselves, at least not in the "I'm so amazing" way people tend to think of narcissism. Some exhibit "negative narcissism" and see themselves as fundamentally flawed, hopelessly broken, or desperately less fortunate than others and thus deserving of special treatment (such as the narcissistic subtypes of Enneagram Types Four, Five, and Six). In its extremes, negative narcissism is evident in those who suffer from Borderline Personality Disorder (BPD). In those with BPD, there may be such a lack of a sense of self that they require levels of attention and psychological mirroring that can't be satiated. While BPD is beyond the scope of this book, and there are immense complexities at work with those who suffer from BPD, it's worth noting that if BPD is present, narcissism is often one manifestation of the disorder. Additionally, addiction can foster narcissistic traits due to the nature of the addict's preoccupation with their immediate needs.

Some personalities are more prone to having greater innate confidence and bravado than others, but this does not necessarily make someone narcissistic. These behaviors are often ego defense strategies intended to keep someone from feeling deflated, weak, or looking bad in front of others. Still, these defenses aren't codified in a person with average psychological health, and the person can reveal more vulnerable emotions and motivations. Narcissists utilize a set of defense mechanisms that makes themselves more significant than others in some way.

It's when we start habitually doing so at the expense of others (or ourselves), we have entered Narcissistic Personality Disorder territory. Those with higher degrees of it tend to believe that what they want, need, think, and feel is more important than it is for others. Even after transgressing another, they will be unable to acknowledge how they've hurt someone else, let alone engage in interpersonal repair strategies.

Another essential feature of narcissism is the apparent lack of ability to self-reflect on one's deeper motivations or impact on those around them. Most people with narcissism are not intent on harming others (this is more the orientation of the psychopath). Narcissists have difficulty caring much about others unless the issue is directly related to their wants, needs, or desires.

Research suggests a greater incidence of those with higher-than-average narcissistic traits in the general population than previously theorized.[1] We have popular media to thank for identifying these traits more easily. However, clinical narcissism or Narcissistic Personality Disorder (NPD) is less common and requires more than an inflated sense of self and lack of empathy for diagnosis. If I remember anything from my clinical diagnosis classes in graduate school, unless someone is experiencing personal or professional impairment, a diagnosis shouldn't be assigned. However, the necessity of diagnosis to appease insurance providers and the cost-prohibitive nature of mental health care paired with an overreliance on the medical model of disease has created a culture in which diagnosis is a necessary component of treatment. Most narcissists we encounter in everyday life aren't particularly dangerous to society. They maintain friendships, have jobs, kids, romantic relationships, contribute meaningfully to the world and live rather happy and healthy lives.

Those with higher narcissistic traits may, however, experience more interpersonal conflict or professional difficulties due to lower empathy and a tendency toward prioritizing their needs over others. Many have learned effective strategies for mitigating the impact of personal or professional damage from their behaviors. Most people with high narcissistic traits do not seek treatment, therapy, or help of their own volition. Many enter treatment to deal with secondary issues related to the effects of their narcissism, such as marital or relationship difficulties, losing a job, depression, anxiety, addiction, or other life problems. Some extreme cases may enter therapy due to a court order, particularly if their narcissism accompanies violent behavior or antisocial personality traits.

Depending on the person's specific subset of narcissism, their harmful behaviors may be more self-directed or other-directed and come from a different core wound. Thus, understanding each of the twenty-seven narcissistic subtypes is integral in effectively managing the adverse effects of narcissistic behavior. Only with the presence of psychopathy, and to a lesser degree, sociopathy, does one's behavior become habitually and predictably opportunistic, exploitative, or more calculated.

## THE SOCIOPATH

There is no diagnosis in the DSM-V for sociopathy. Most theorists consider sociopathy a subset of Narcissistic Personality Disorder that includes a high degree of narcissistic traits and a low degree of empathy. Sociopaths display most of the characteristics of a clinical narcissist paired with a low degree of concern or understanding of other people's feelings, needs, wishes, or desires. Sociopaths can appear emotionless, measured, cold, or quite expressive, explosive, and emotionally volatile. Many understand right and wrong, and some have a greater developed sense of ethics or conscience. However, even those with some degrees of empathy may be unable to adjust their behavior or presentation to consider others' emotions or needs meaningfully. In part II, as you're reading each of the twenty-seven subtypes, you can think of the unhealthier range of each narcissistic subtype as the "sociopathic zone." Many of the exemplars in part II will be demonstrative of the sociopath. When narcissism enters the sociopathic zone, someone's psychological health becomes compromised to the extent that they can no longer regulate or mask their lack of concern or care for others (at least not for long).

There are various reasons a narcissist may dip into sociopathic territory. I believe sociopathy is a condition of untreated narcissism, low empathy, poor behavioral modeling, and, typically, childhood trauma or neglect. Sociopathy is a degree of narcissism, and I would submit that those with sociopathy could almost always be diagnosed with Narcissistic Personality Disorder. Sociopathy is the affective and actively manipulative or exploitative branch of narcissistic behavior. Sociopaths are doing *something* to ensure their needs are met, whereas narcissists may be self-absorbed and unempathetic but not quite as consciously plotting as a sociopath.

A high-functioning sociopath may do quite well in the world. They can be successful in business or other endeavors focusing on production, efficiency, and profit but may struggle when dealing with people (unless their personality style is naturally interpersonal and warm, like Enneagram Type Two). Their primary concern will first and foremost be tending to their needs and desires. Still, some experts believe that sociopaths can develop a conscience or learn to consider others when positively reflecting on them.

However, research overwhelmingly asserts that narcissism is notoriously challenging to treat because those with NPD are inherently unconvinced that they have any problems. It is unlikely they would develop empathy, compassion, care, or concern for others even with treatment. I think that some forms of sociopathy, if well channeled, can be beneficial in specific professional contexts. For example, sociopathic politicians may ensure that they manipulate, calculate, and coerce their way to the top of the political food chain. Low empathy and high sociopathy are assets in other professions where results are hard-won if too much empathy is present.

For many sociopaths, empathy and compassion are hindrances to success. However, most sociopaths do not identify themselves as seeking or enjoying violence or cruelty. They believe life is survival of the fittest, and they're determined to survive. They can delay gratification for a short time and may employ various strategies (flattering, manipulation, lying, cajoling, appeasing, etc.) before resorting to overt aggression because even sociopaths do not want to be shamed or punished for their actions, thoughts, or behaviors. Their fear of punishment is why they often work so hard to conceal their transgressions (gaslighting is a favorite strategy).

The primary difference between a narcissist and a sociopath is the degree to which they calculate their behavior. Sociopaths think a few steps ahead of others to ensure their needs or desires are satiated. Narcissists are typically not as highly calculated but are still grandiose, entitled, self-absorbed, and egotistical. If a sociopath can get their needs met in a socially acceptable way, which creates less interpersonal drama, they will opt for the route of least resistance. However, they often believe they must orchestrate or manipulate all or most situations to ensure they come out on top. Sociopaths tend to have more emotional affect and response to shame or punishment (at least temporarily) than psychopaths.

Some research suggests that sociopaths suffered some degree of trauma that forced them to resort to exploitative, abusive, or manipulative engagement strategies.[2] From a developmental perspective, we can view the sociopath's behavior like that of a toddler attempting to meet their needs and avoid shame, punishment, or obstruction. However, unlike most toddlers, they lack concern for how their behavior affects those around them. When narcissism, low empathy, and a tendency toward violent or premeditated aggression toward others collide, the result is the most malignant variation of the narcissistic spectrum: the psychopath.

# THE PSYCHOPATH

The term "psychopath" derives from the Greek word "psyche," which means soul or essence, and "pathos," which means suffering. This is a profound way to view the condition of psychopathy in humans as it's easy to forget that the psychopath, or those with psychopathic traits, are not only creating suffering for others but also are likely experiencing a degree of unconscious suffering themselves. What characterizes psychopathy varies from theorist to theorist. At a basic level, it is the existence of heightened aggression, a lack of inhibition, and a bold or grandiose sense of one's dominance, strength, or superiority over those viewed as threatening, weaker, or somehow deserving of their aggression. Psychiatrist Alexander Lowen, known for conceptualizing somatic character structures, saw the psychopathic character as seeking power over pleasure and characteristically charismatic, multi-talented, intelligent, or otherwise very well equipped to utilize their considerable energetic reserves to inspire others.[3,4] Lowen describes the psychopath as dazzling, persuasive, and influential but possessing an underlying and pervasive rage that compels them to find enjoyment in overpowering or controlling others. I appreciate Lowen's psychopathic character composite because he acknowledges that psychopathy can be a beneficial quality in some contexts.

Consider the charismatic leader who appears strong, fearless, and persuasive and can be an effective agent for change. Lowen also recognized that when we need to demonstrate our anger and power, we can become psychopathic, making ourselves bigger, more formidable, and intimidating to scare away potential attackers. For some, however, psychopathy becomes their dominant stance in the world. When paired with low empathy and other biological, environmental, or developmental disturbances, this can create the infamous "psychopath."

For psychopaths, the primary aim is to channel their rage and appetite for dominance onto others for their pleasure or satisfaction. The Psychopathic Personality Inventory assesses a few common traits of psychopathy, such as meanness (a lack of empathy or concern toward others) and disinhibition (the inability to delay gratification, urge control problems, or problems with planning or foresight). Psychopaths also exhibit boldness, a lack of fear, and a feeling of self-confidence or grandiosity.[5]

In popular culture, the psychopath plays an influential role in our collective nightmares. Many fictional and real-world boogey-monsters are psychopathic. Popular archetypes of the psychopath include serial killers, serial rapists, blood-thirsty crime bosses, and evil rulers focused on inflicting pain and suffering on unsuspecting or otherwise innocent people. Indeed, many psychopaths are calculated, cold, and cunning predators who approach interactions with others as a power struggle between predator and prey.

Harrowing stories of some of the world's most infamous serial killers like Jeffrey Dahmer, John Wayne Gacy, the Zodiac Killer, or serial rapists like Harvey Weinstein or Jeffrey Epstein are reminders of the unimaginable pain psychopaths can inflict on their victims. Psychopathy paired with other mental illnesses such as Antisocial Personality Disorder, mood disorders like depression or bipolar, or even neurological conditions can exacerbate or, in some instances, even trigger psychopathic behavior. Most psychopaths do not commit murder and are never caught committing a crime. Many psychopaths do exceptionally well in business, politics, or the entertainment or sports industry. Their cutthroat and ruthless aggression and propensity toward exerting power and influence are rewarded in high-performance fields. Psychopathic behavior is particularly highly regarded in the finance industry, where a predatory sensibility is often necessary for success and advancement.

The political stage is a perfect opportunity to pursue power and influence. Manipulation, ruthlessness, and intimidation are expected tactics for career success. Many corporate and political psychopaths enjoy seeing the fear they can elicit in others because it reminds them of their power. Of course, the way the person exerts their need for domination and submission will vary depending upon their personality type. Some may employ less overt tactics to prey on those they've identified as weak or vulnerable such as flattery or seductive coercion. In contrast, others may prefer more overtly aggressive intimidation and force, but most fall somewhere between those two poles. What remains consistent with those who display psychopathic traits is that there is conscious malice underlying their behavior, which differs from the partially innocent behavior of the sociopath who struggles to consider the needs of others.

Part II provides you with a cross-section of interview excerpts of more typical presentations of the subtypes interspersed with extreme examples from various media (film, literature, and real-life psychopaths or sociopaths). However, it's helpful to delineate between the degrees and severity of narcissistic behaviors from their more benign forms to the most malignant forms so that we recognize that the condition of narcissism in the human condition, like everything else, exists on a continuum and can be influenced by a multitude of other factors from biology, culture, environment, mental illness, and even intelligence. In the following few chapters, we will delve more into the Enneagram personality system, which we will use as the scaffolding to understand the twenty-seven narcissistic subtypes that we'll unpack in part II.

# 4

# Understanding the Enneagram Personality System

We're working backward a bit, but now that we have a firm foundation in how healthy egos can become compromised by narcissism, we can add a little more texture to the concept of the ego and, more specifically, the personality. Throughout the remainder of this book, I will utilize the terms personality and ego interchangeably. Most personality psychologists submit that all human beings have an ego and that in many ways, without it, most of us would not know how to function in the world. The ego's function is to keep us safe from perceived threats. However, the ego's idea of what constitutes "safe" and "threatening" may be quite different from what may be innocuous or frightening objectively. Before the development of the ego, safety and security were very literal. For example, if a saber-toothed tiger runs toward us our primary defenses include fighting, fleeing, or freezing to prevent being killed. The modern ego can interpret anything from a sideways comment from a friend to someone startling us like a proverbial saber-toothed tiger. Fear and danger are highly subjective depending on our personalities, culture, personal history, and genetics.

## MOTIVATION-BASED SYSTEMS

The most enduring psychological systems delve beyond behavior and look to our motivations to help us understand why we do what we do. These systems can also enable us to change behaviors that may be limiting or self-defeating.

Applied psychology is interested in the behaviors themselves and the motor or fuel that powers them. The Enneagram model of personality is one such personality system that is both elegant and complex enough to paint a satisfying composite of the human ego.

## EARLY HISTORY OF THE ENNEAGRAM OF PERSONALITY

### Ichazo's Enneagram Fixations

The Enneagram, at its root, is a system of nine basic ego or personality fixations. It was brought into popular awareness in the early 1960s by Bolivian mystic Oscar Ichazo, who first outlined what he termed the nine points of the "Enneagons." These nine fixations were intended to illustrate the psychological and spiritual limitations of the human ego, and were seen as obstacles to psychological and spiritual freedom. Ichazo termed the methodology he used for ascertaining one's primary fixation(s) *protoanalysis*. For Ichazo, nine points of the Enneagram corresponded to psychospiritual "stuck points" that limited a person's psychological development and awareness and ability to be free from egoic limitations.

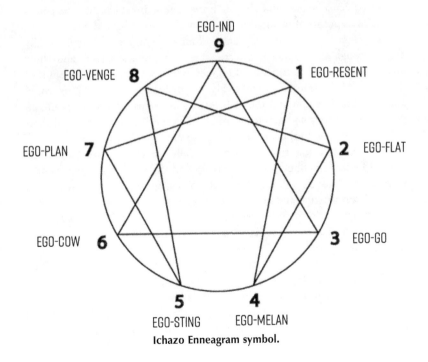

Ichazo Enneagram symbol.

Protoanalysis analyzed the person's physicality, energy, and mental fixations. Ichazo believed, much like his predecessor G. I. Gurdjieff, that Enneagram work was a somatic and spiritual undertaking. Gurdjieff (born in or around 1877) utilized the Enneagram symbol like a koan, which was intentionally difficult to understand and meant to serve as a meditative figure for his students. Gurdjieff had people "dance" the symbol in ritualistic and meditative bodywork and breathwork practices meant to unlock stuck energies from the body to help his students reach greater psychological, emotional, and spiritual freedom.

No one is entirely sure where Gurdjieff first encountered the Enneagram symbol, but he is credited for introducing the symbol to the world as a tool for personal growth. Gurdjieff's teachings of the Enneagram bear little if any resemblance to what would later become the Enneagram of personality. Ichazo, like Gurdjieff, was first and foremost a spiritual teacher, and identification of the ego using the Enneagram was only one tool in his transformational work. But he recognized the power of naming the nine facets of the ego utilizing the geometric symbol of the Enneagram as a visual guide to the evolution and development of the various aspects of the human experience. Ichazo taught hundreds of "Enneagrams" in which the nine points were used as points of meditation for his students. For him, the Enneagram was a system to be "worked." Ideally, human beings would symbolically move through the symbol with ease, able to access the virtues and "holy ideas" to mimic the holistic, fluid human experience free from the binds of the distorted ego. However, Ichazo also taught that few, if any of us, could maintain this freedom and thus fall into egoic "traps" at various points in the human journey and develop a fixation at a specific point of one of these virtues, giving rise to the idea of an Enneagram type.

The passion, virtue, trap, fixation, and holy ideas all became part of the original Enneagram of personality typology and are part of the tapestry of the system. The Arica school still guards Ichazo's teachings because he wanted to avoid misconstruction and misinterpretation by those who hadn't experienced his teachings firsthand. However, the Enneagram points could not be contained, and his teachings on the Enneagram were disseminated by his student Claudio Naranjo.

Naranjo, a Chilean psychiatrist, and protégé of Gestalt psychiatrist Fritz Perls, began to develop a theory of the "Enneatypes" after attending Oscar Ichazo's training at the Arica school.[1] While initially skeptical of the Enneagram's applicability toward understanding the human ego, he nonetheless translated the Enneagram into psychoanalytic terms that could be useful for those working with patients in a clinical setting and those who wished to delve into the intricacies of their psyches.

Naranjo, a post-Freudian psychoanalyst, viewed the nine Enneagram types as neurotic fixations and aspects of psychological disease that needed to be identified and cured. Naranjo's conceptualization of the Enneagram drew upon his work with patients. He is best known for mapping and extrapolating Ichazo's basic Enneagram type archetypes with other psychoanalytic theories of his generation (including Karen Horney, Alexander Lowen, and Carl Jung) to create the Enneagram of Personality. Naranjo's Enneagram differed from Ichazo's in that it was decisively psychological and, while Naranjo himself was quite spiritual, his Enneagram system was placed decisively within the medical disease model. He built upon Ichazo's esoteric/spiritual explanations of the nine types to create a brutally honest but incisive composite of each "Enneatype." Naranjo compiled his clinical reflections, interactions, and observations of Arica participants and began his study group to further his theory and research of the Enneagram.

In 1971 Naranjo started his Seekers After Truth (SAT) groups in Chilé and began teaching the Enneagram in small workshops in South America and eventually the U.S. (specifically in and around Berkeley, California). Early American study group participants such as Father Robert Ochs, Richard Rohr, and Naranjo's (then) girlfriend, Kathy Speeth, were primarily responsible for the widespread dissemination of the Enneagram. In the mid-to-late 1970s and early 1980s, these early students disseminated the system to Jesuit scholars who helped to popularize the Enneagram in Catholic and Christian self-help groups. The spread of the Enneagram in the United States sparked worldwide interest. When various "schools" of Enneagram theory cropped up around the U.S., Naranjo stopped teaching in the United States in 1973 because he felt his work was mistaught and improperly disseminated.

Since Naranjo disseminated Ichazo's Arica material, the Enneagram and its nine types and three instinctual subtypes have become global phenomena. In the 1990s and 2000s, prolific Enneagram teachers such as David Daniels, Helen Palmer, Deborah Ooten, Don Riso, Russ Hudson, Eli Jaxon Bear, Tom Condon, Katherine Chernick Fauvre, and others developed their approaches to, postulations of, and theories about various aspects of Ichazo and Naranjo's original dissemination to varying degrees of similarity to the seminal teachings.

## THE ENNEAGRAM: AN OVERVIEW

The word Enneagram itself is Greek. It roughly translates to "nine-sided drawing" (Ennea=9, gram=drawing). The Enneagram is a psychospiritual

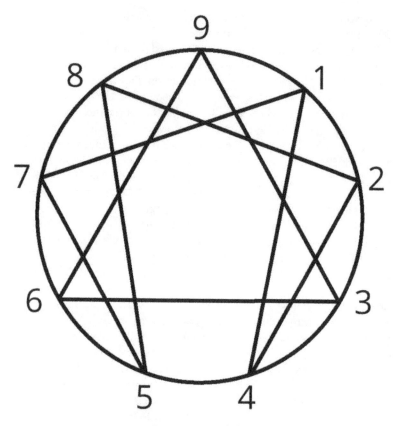

**Enneagram symbol.**

system that espouses nine basic personality types. There is a fascinating and compelling mathematical history of the symbol beyond the scope of this work (and quite frankly beyond my expertise). However, the system functions based on what Gurdjieff referred to as "The Law of Three" and "The Law of Seven," which he contended were universal laws of symmetry, evolution, and involution that map growth and change in the universe.

As a trialectic system, everything within the Enneagram is divisible by threes. Within the system, there are three *centers of intelligence* related to the processes by which each type interprets information about themselves and the world at large: The gut types (Eight, Nine, One), the heart types (types Two, Three, Four), and the head types (types Five, Six, Seven).

There are three *instinctual types* related to the primitive survival mechanisms that, when activated, trigger the defenses of the Enneagram types; these include the Social instinct, the Self-Preservation instinct, and the Sexual/Intimate instinct. The Enneagram is not a static system because it maps movement in the universe and the human psyche. Instead, it is a dynamic system where various points on the Enneagram intersect and interact with other points on the Enneagram, adding color, flavor, and complexity to each type.

Each center of intelligence has a particular flavor, focus, or habit of attention and energetic and psychological imprint that is consistent throughout each type in the center. Ichazo heavily emphasized the importance of the centers to understand the human beings' movement through the world.

## CENTERS OF INTELLIGENCE

The Enneagram maps the human psyche and recognizes that we have various ways of filtering information about the world. Some often-cited colloquialisms refer to multiple mechanisms of decision-making that are shorthand to refer to the centers of intelligence. In English, phrases such as "Don't lose your head," "Follow your heart," and "What does your gut tell you?" all point to these intelligence centers. Each center is like a filtering mechanism through which we absorb information and interpret our worlds. Everyone uses all three centers of intelligence. We act instinctively, going off our visceral, somatic reaction to something. We recoil when we see something we don't like, we push away that which is too close, or we may suddenly feel convicted about something which springs us into action. We all use our rational minds to sort through information, know whom to believe, what to think, and find information to help us make more informed and safer decisions.

Finally, everyone uses their heart; emotions arise, and we react to them; we follow our passions toward that which may not be entirely rational but ultimately feel good. Or we feel elated and valued when we're seen or met by another human being who understands us. Alternately, we feel despondent and rejected when someone doesn't see us accurately.

These intelligence filters do not work independently but rather work in tandem to comprise the complex machinery of the mind. We prefer one intelligence center over the others. Some people are more prone to intellectualizing and rationalizing, while others are keen to trust their instinctive responses to the world with little analysis.

Ichazo believed that humans, unbound from their human psychological process, can utilize all three intelligence centers with equal vigor and grace. Ideally, we could easily shift between the head, heart, and gut, depending on the situation. However, defenses arise because we do not live in an ideal world. We become fixated or stuck in a defense strategy in each of these centers of intelligence.

### The Gut Center: Types Eight, Nine, One (also referred to as the Instinctive Types)

The three types in this intelligence center navigate the world primarily through their visceral, reflexive reactions. They make decisions based on instinctive memories of where to go to meet their needs, and their convictions guide their behavior. This center of intelligence governs the visceral experience of empathy in its most rudimentary form. By using our gut, which some research has shown acts much like a second brain, we process stimuli about the world and make decisions based on our gut impressions. This intelligence center helped us know where to get water, food, or how far to travel to find shelter.

The types in the gut center are inherently rooted, self-possessed, and self-protective. They're focused on identifying what will be satisfactory for their survival and respond instinctively to threats to their autonomy or independence (in slightly different ways depending on the type in question). As such, Types Eight, Nine, and One can have issues with being too open, empathic, and resonant (a feature of their well-developed somatic intelligence) or be too closed, callous, and dismissive.

The gut center is also the seat of power, so all three types in this center "own" their authority and need little direction or prescriptions from others, preferring to follow their instinctual guidance. Each of these types can struggle with rage because threats to one's autonomy or right to exist are experienced viscerally and feel like a fundamental violation.

Eights, Nines, and Ones can have difficulty adjusting to the demands and needs of others. Instead, they repress or deny themselves what they need or want rather than risk changing themselves and losing a sense of control over their destinies. Their tendency to deny their impulses and their need to exert their power gives rise to the dichotomy of power vs. resignation.

**The Heart Types: Two, Three, Four (also referred to as the Image Types)**

The three types in this center of intelligence navigate the world primarily through their emotions and are most comfortable following their "heart," or what their emotions tell them about the world around them. These types constantly assess their level of closeness with others and judge their safety by whether they are appealing in some way to others. Unlike the gut types, Twos, Threes, and Fours are adept at adjusting their presentation to match their own or others' ideas of who they should be. They are also naturally sympathetic and adaptable. Attunement to one's impact on others is an asset and a curse. They can easily make a favorable impression and become lost or discouraged when others do not like or approve of their presenting image. Relating to others and playing a role can become habitual, and problems with authenticity, spontaneity, and shame about one's self-worth can arise.

This intelligence center developed out of the human need to connect and relate to others emotionally. It allowed us to adapt to life with close intimates and the community by assessing whether our presentation creates our desired impact in the world. We use this center to quickly shift into and out of our various roles to meet our needs.

Twos, Threes, and Fours are the most likely to confuse their role for their authentic selves and risk becoming inauthentic, insincere, or overly adjusting to what others expect or want. These types specialize in image manipulation and emotional intuition. Twos, Threes, and Fours naturally understand the necessity for emotional attunement in relationships. The result of their shifting emotional relationships to themselves and the way others see them creates the dichotomy of authenticity vs. image.

**The Head Types: Five, Six, Seven (also referred to as the Mental Types)**

The three types in this center focus on gaining the "know-how" or knowledge to survive in the world. The head center is where we as human beings attempt to make sense of our environments and relationships through our postulations, projections, ideas, formulas, and theories. We use this center to help us recognize who and what is safe and how to properly fit in (or stand out) from others to make ourselves feel secure. These types understand the necessity for mental constructions, theories, information, and calculations to sort and make sense of the world. Types Five, Six, and Seven look for who and what information they can trust to quell anxieties about the uncertainty of human life.

After the instinctive and emotional/heart centers, humans developed the head center, primarily residing in the human brain's neocortex, which neuroscientists believe is the "newest" portion of the human brain to evolve. This center functions more independently from the heart and instinctive center. Those who lead with this center of intelligence access their emotions or visceral instincts through the intellect and thus may unconsciously bypass their visceral responses or raw emotional data.

The mental types rely on their theories and ideas about the world to dictate their opinions. All three types in this center rely on their interpretation of objective data. The mental types are affiliative by nature. Through this center, humans utilize rational processes to identify a friend or enemy. This process allows us to discern what ideologies, philosophies, and theories are safe to help us find people and communities that match our ideas. With these types, the necessity to test the limits of one's understanding or interpretation of the world against what they observe or identify in others helps alleviate fear.

Anxiety arises when discrepancies appear between what they think and feel they have learned and what others say, think, or feel. Fives, Sixes, and Sevens are most likely to abdicate their authority and intuition in favor of externalized authorities or data. Because they tend to feel uncertain, they struggle more acutely to find certainty and guidance for who or what information is worthwhile to devote their considerable attention. Their oscillating anxiety results in the dichotomy of trust vs. mistrust.

## DOMINANT ENNEAGRAM TYPE

Research shows that we utilize one type's defenses, strengths, and blind spots in each intelligence center (head, heart, gut). Our dominant Enneagram type is the defense strategy that we use most frequently and with the most ease. I often refer to this as the "primary operating system." Much like your cell phone runs an OS depending on its brand and model, the OS is responsible for executing and running other programs; the dominant Enneagram type plays a similar role. Finding and understanding our dominant Enneagram type is a journey that, for some, can be complicated. Because our primary defense mechanisms are vested in staying out of our conscious awareness, this phenomenon occurs because if we learn to deprogram these patterns, our egos believe we will be rendered defenseless. Remember, like all entities, the ego wants to stay alive at all costs.

Our personality defense strategies are employed to protect us from perceived threats, and we have a variety of sophisticated (and elementary) tricks up our sleeve to this end. I've seen dozens of people spend years vacillating on their dominant Enneagram type as a way of unconsciously preventing themselves from settling and beginning the work of unraveling their defense mechanisms and egoic distortions.

# FINER DETAILS OF THE ENNEAGRAM SYSTEM

## Wings

At the beginning of this chapter, we discussed the Enneagram as a trialectic system whereby patterns of three create symmetry and reinforce the system's dynamic nature. Each type on the Enneagram has two types on either side; these types are called "wings." Each type's relationship to its wings influences the behaviors and presentation of each type depending on which wing type is more dominant in someone's expression. For example, Type One is flanked by Types Nine and Two; Type Two is flanked by Types One and Three; Type Three is flanked by Types Two and Four, and so on. I think of each type as the tension between the types surrounding it. For example, Type Two is created by trying to resolve the tension between trying to be good, correct, and above reproach like a One and striving to be seen as successful, admirable, and attractive like a Three.

No matter how you chalk it up, this tertiary pattern exists throughout the system overall. Some Twos may be slightly more Oneish, whereas some may present slightly more Threeish. Depending on the Two, we may refer to them as a 2w1 (shorthand for Two with a One wing) or a 2w3. In either case, the dominant type itself doesn't change. Some people identify more with one wing over another, but both wing types influence the dominant type because this completes the trialectic pattern.

## Lines of Connection

Gurdjieff and Ichazo (along with countless philosophers, scientists, mystics, mathematicians, and physicists) recognized that nothing in the universe is static. To illustrate the elasticity of the human psyche, movement within the Enneagram symbol is shown by the way each type connects to two other types on the system (these two types are not its wings). In a Seekers After Truth workshop in the 1970s, Claudio Naranjo postulated these "connecting lines" could be pointing to the path of integration (or growth) of one type toward greater freedom from its limiting and neurotic patterns, and the path of disintegration (decline) when the type moved into unhealthy territory.

For example, Naranjo identified as a Type Five. He considered that when he was becoming healthier and liberated from his typical Fiveish defenses, he acted more like a Type Eight and became more embodied, confident, and "lustful." He then thought that if he moved to Type Eight in health, he must move toward Type Seven when he became more neurotic and fixated and was more scattered, prone to exaggeration, and untethered from practicalities.

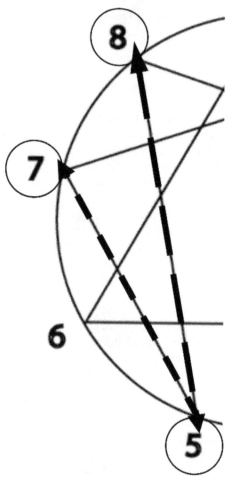

**Lines of Connection**

Naranjo quickly revised his understanding of these connections and stated he could also see some of the neurotic defenses of Type Eight and the healthier traits of Type Seven[2]. In the same workshop, Naranjo revised the theory that we "integrated" in one direction when healthy and "disintegrated" in the other when unhealthy.

### Trifix, Tritype, or Enneagram Trifecta

While we will have one dominant type and feel most comfortable in one center of intelligence, we still must access and utilize the other centers of intelligence. After the initial dissemination of the Enneagram, Oscar Ichazo observed that people preferred an ego "fixation" in each center of intelligence which he called the Trifix. Independently from Ichazo, in 1994, Enneagram researcher Katherine Chernick Fauvre observed a pattern where participants utilized the talk style, defense strategies, core fears, passions, fixations, convictions, strengths, and weaknesses of three different types (one in each center of intelligence).[3] Sometimes, this could be explained by a wing-type or line of connection, but there were many times in which a person would have the core fears and patterns of a type they had no "access" to naturally within the flow of the Enneagram system. Chernick Fauvre originally called this phenomenon

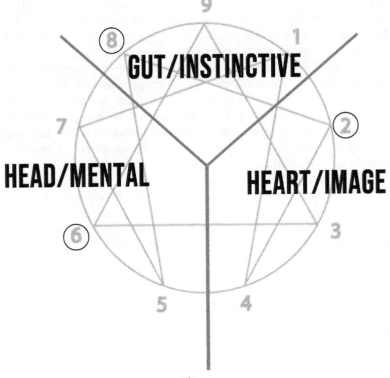

**Tritype.**

"3 Types" and later trademarked "Tritype" to differentiate her work from Ichazo's. Chernick Fauvre later learned of Ichazo's Trifix in December of 1996, which further validated her findings that, without exception, people use all three centers of intelligence in a preferred order.[4]

The idea of Tritype gives greater dimension, nuance, and complexity to the Enneagram system overall. It completes the notion that the system should follow the patterns of three that are evident throughout the system. Trifix explains the puzzle that some types have no access to all three intelligence centers, which flies in the face of the system's mathematic elegance.

For example, Type Two has access to the gut center via its potential wing of One on one side and its line to Eight. However, Type Two has no natural access to the head center, either through a wing or a connection line. Does this mean that Twos are unable to utilize the head center? No, they have access to the head center through the mental type in their Trifix. Alternately, Type Seven has no access to the heart center via its connection lines to Type One and Type Five or its potential wings of Type Eight and Type Six. Does this mean that Sevens have no access to their emotional intelligence center? Again, the answer is no because Sevens access the heart center through their Trifix.

Without Trifix or Tritype, the lack of trialectic symmetry present throughout the rest of the system poses a mathematical dilemma because it breaks from the trialectic pattern that underlies the system overall. Ichazo explained this pattern interruption using his idea of Trifix. I corroborated the findings of Chernick Fauvre and Ichazo's Trifix concept in that people utilize the defense strategies, defenses, and blind spots of a type in each intelligence center in a "stacking" order in my 2021 study on the Enneagram and Lexicon.

I observed that the Tritype types converge to create an archetype that adds refinement and specificity of behavioral strategies and defense mechanisms beyond the dominant type theory. However, this book will focus on the intersection of the dominant type and the dominant instinct and how those combinations create the twenty-seven narcissistic subtypes for simplicity.

## PUTTING IT ALL TOGETHER

The Enneagram is a nuanced system that can be as detailed or as simple as you'd like. To understand the narcissistic subtypes, you will need to remember that there are three instinctual drives and the nine basic Enneagram personality types. There are a variety of resources that discuss and explain the Enneagram system (refer to the suggested reading at the end of the book). In the next chapter, we will expand on the concept of the instinctual drives as these seem to be the fuel that ignites the flames of our Enneagram types, so understanding the role of the instinctual types is key to understanding what triggers us to behave narcissistically.

# 5

## The Three Instinctual Drives and Narcissism

In chapter 4, I briefly introduced the concept of the three instinctual types (or instinctual drives). However, we need to unpack this critical idea fully before we delve into the twenty-seven narcissistic subtypes. It will also be helpful to understand the instincts before we delve into the nine Enneagram types in chapter 6.

Dr. Claudio Naranjo was the first to conceptualize the twenty-seven instinctual subtypes as we know them today. While Naranjo didn't publish anything about the instincts in English until the 1990s,[1] prior to writing about the subtypes, he taught the instincts in his workshops and psychotherapist training intensives beginning in the 1970s. Katherine Chernick Fauvre expanded upon Naranjo's teachings and first published her research findings in 1995.[2] Much of what is currently available about the instinctual types and subtypes can be credited to Naranjo and Fauvre's contributions. Other notable Enneagram pioneers like Russ Hudson and Don Riso, Tom Condon, and Helen Palmer are responsible for disseminating other teachings and perspectives on the three instinctual types. The following descriptions are a synthesis of my own research and the insights of those who came before me.

### WHAT ARE THE INSTINCTUAL TYPES?

The instincts are the primal, evolutionary hardwiring of the human psyche. We can even think of the instincts as rudimentary, basic personality types that aided our early ancestors' survival before developing complex thought patterns and emotional responses. Sigmund Freud posited the "Id," which he theorized is a relentless, satisfaction-oriented, immature impulse within the human psyche that seeks to satisfy its immediate gratification needs without care for social concerns or self-image.[3] The raw impulses of the Id to hunt, kill, fornicate, and seek self-gratification lurk in the unconscious of the human psyche but is mitigated by the more socially acceptable behaviors of the ego. The ego, according to Freud, has greater awareness of how to gratify its impulses through more socially acceptable or appropriate means. The Id functions stealthily underneath the surface no matter how sophisticated the ego's defenses are. Like the Id, the instinctual drives operate in the background as the foundational operating system through which the Enneagram type functions.

There are three primary instinctual drives; Social, Sexual, and Self-Preservation. These drives function in everyone because we evolved to utilize all three instincts to survive. Additionally, because the Enneagram is a trialectic system, all three instincts must be present according to the theory to maintain its symmetry. However, most Enneagram researchers agree that one instinct dominates. At the same time, the other two play a secondary or tertiary role in our awareness (much like the concept of Trifix outlined in the previous chapter). For some people, their primary instinctual drive is more consciously accessible than their dominant Enneagram type due to its apparent influence on their conscious thoughts. For others, a couple of instinctual drives seem to compete equally for attention. And still, for some, particularly those who have engaged in a significant amount of psychological or spiritual work, their instinctual drives have become more balanced.

Balancing the three instinctual drives is quite tricky as it requires mastery over one's visceral impulses. For most of us, one instinctual type dominates our unconscious decision-making. When that instinct is "triggered," the dominant Enneagram type and Trifix are deployed to satiate the instinct's perceived deficiencies or threats. The instinctual drives function on the premise of fear of lack.

As we move into the descriptions of the three instinctual drives, it might be helpful to notice which instinctual description intuitively or instinctively resonates with you to help you ascertain its importance in your awareness. Tracking which instinctual type is dominant in you shouldn't be confused with which instinct you like more, as we can often idealize an instinct that's secondary or tertiary to our primary instinctual drive.

# THE SELF-PRESERVATION INSTINCT

The Self-Preservation instinct ("Self Pres" for short) was likely the first instinctual drive to develop in the human species because it directly connected to the essential maintenance of physical survival. The Self-Preservation instinct governs the domains of safety, comfort, hunger, wellness, and sufficient attention to one's physical environment and body. The Self Pres instinct was the primary instinct our distant ancestors used to ensure we had enough food to eat, protection against the elements, a suitable dwelling, and protection from intruders or invaders who could threaten our food reserves or physical safety. The Self-Preservation instinct propelled the discovery of natural remedies to cure ailments and illnesses and inspired the development of the various creature comforts that make life on earth more bearable and comfortable. Issues of mortality are inherent within the Self-Preservation instinct. So Self Pres–dominant people tend to be acutely aware of themselves as independent beings responsible for their survival (regardless of how independent they may be in reality).

Many Self-Preservation people firmly believe, "I came into this world alone, and I'll leave alone." This solitary worldview doesn't mean that Self-Preservation people don't have close relationships, families, friendships, and communities but that there is a solitary and independent orientation to the way people with this dominant instinctual drive approach life. Being Self-Preservation dominant shouldn't be confused with being introverted, shy, or preferring one's own company. However, Self Pres people of all temperaments tend to enjoy more time alone than the other two instincts.

Self-Preservation concerns include money, health, wellness, food, diet, exercise, sleep and sleep quality, sensuality/physical pleasure, insurance, décor, ambiance, vitality, comfort, routines, conservation, grounding/stability, emotional and physical safety, and resource acquisition (or hoarding).

When any of us are ill, we must tend to bodies or die (or at least remain uncomfortable). When we are worried about our money, our homes, our health, or the health and financial security of intimates, family, and friends we utilize our Self-Preservation instinct to solve these fundamental survival concerns. For those who are Self-Preservation first (as with all the dominant instinctual drives), the awareness of these domains happens at such a subconscious level they may not immediately recognize themselves as leading with this instinctual drive. We don't often appreciate the extent to which we monitor these unconscious instinctual needs until there is an obvious and direct threat to those needs.

The Self-Preservation instinct functions on a visceral, gut-centered response to ensuring our physical safety and the physical safety and comfort of our loved ones. For Self Pres dominant people, there is a conscious and constant tracking of their energy to ensure that whatever resources they deem necessary to their overall survival are plentiful. If they aren't abundant, they will focus attention on worrying, fretting, or strategizing to adequately meet the Self-Preservation concerns. In relationships, the Self-Preservation instinct seeks grounding, security, and comfort to ensure survival.

It's important to note that some Self-Preservation types ensure their basic needs are met through the financial, emotional, or physical support of a mate, family, friend, or institution. In these cases, Self Pres support systems help attain, retain, and ensure vital survival resources are consistent.

## SOCIAL INSTINCT

Once we, as a species, understood how to ensure that our basic survival needs were met, prehistoric humans began to look to establish affiliations and alliances with others as a means to ensure survival. Like most mammals, humans are inherently social. We need other people to survive the various threats, trials, and tribulations of human existence. We could have the most secure and secluded cave in the world, but if a saber-toothed tiger wandered into our cave, we would be hard-pressed to fight the beast alone. However, if there were at least a few other people to have our back, we might make it out alive. The Social instinct was born out of our instinctual knowledge that there's "strength in numbers." However, the Social instinct is more than just the desire to band together to survive, although this is the biological precursor to the more complex concerns of the Social instinct overall.

Once we formed into small tribes, we quickly began to communicate, and this communication inevitably developed into a series of negotiations of how best to live. Social negotiations included the assignment of various community roles necessary for survival. For example, deciding who would keep watch at night for predators, hunt, nurture children, gather plants for medicinal purposes, or surveil surrounding tribes for potential allies or foes were all vital to the propagation of the tribe. Humans quickly understood that their quality of life improved with the cooperation of others with a common goal of survival. As tribal cultures evolved, so did the various group roles and rules of engagement, which led to the development of what we now refer to as a culture.

The social instinct is most concerned with maintaining, preserving, and proliferating culture and connections as a means of safety. Because the Social instinct involves three or more people, assigning, managing, and monitoring power, influence, and communication can be complex, thus creating political factions, in-groups/out-groups, norms, mores, customs, and protocols. In tribal systems, it was a matter of survival to ascertain which of the other tribes were safe or unsafe. The ability to quickly assess who is one of "us" and who is one of "them," of course, has become less vital with globalization and modernization. However, diplomatic interactions are still necessary to navigate the potential fraught waters of national or international relations.

The Social instinct should not be confused for extroversion or enjoying being around groups of people. Trait-based personality features drive these preferences. Instead, the Social drive is about monitoring the group(s) as a whole. A group is any combination of three or more people and includes but isn't limited to: political parties, work/school groups, church or religious groups, sports teams, cultural groups, countries, nations, or racial or ethnic groups. Some people have an avoidant or mistrustful association with the Social instinct and thus mistrust and avoid groups or affiliative activities, but still monitor and track the social world to stay safe. This mistrust stems from fears the Social person harbors that being shunned or rejected by the group will result in danger. There is some evolutionary truth to this assumption. Once tribal alliances form, rejection by the tribe could reasonably result in annexation, punishment, or death.

From the Social instinct, we develop a desire to be recognized, noticed, and honored for our contributions to the whole. Conversely, if we step outside the bounds of what the group finds acceptable, we risk being ignored, singled out, shunned, or punished. These sometimes formalized, but often informal, rules of engagement characterize human and other complex animal civilizations.

Other Social concerns include gossip, fame, notoriety, lawmaking, manners, hierarchies, philanthropy, trends, cultural narratives, history, government, religious and cultural customs and rituals, team building/making, bullying/anti-bullying, honor, shame, and the creation and maintenance of ideological paradigms.

Being part of a group can have advantages and contribute to the rich and exciting development of camaraderie, culture, and a sense of belonging and community. For many Social types, while tracking, joining, or opposing the group feels like a necessity for survival (and at times exhilarating), it is also a significant source of anxiety, uncertainty, and tension. Social dominant people understand that if annexed from the group, we risk bearing the hardships of life alone.

## THE SEXUAL INSTINCT

Of course, there's more to human existence than self-preservation concerns and social engagement. Human beings crave intimacy, connection, and profound emotional experiences with themselves, the Divine, and other living beings. The Sexual instinct pushed human beings to explore the deeper aspects of human relationships to ultimately know ourselves and others more intimately. At a basic level, the Sexual instinct focuses on the creation and procreation of the species. All animals exhibit this instinctual drive as it ensures the species' survival.

Once ancient civilizations developed more advanced levels of cognitive sophistication, the Sexual instinct consequently became more refined (along with the other instinctual drives). Mate selection became less about who was easily accessible for mating and instead focused on individual preferences, whims, and desires. We began to select mates based on what we found attractive, desirable, and alluring and began to present ourselves to potential mates in ways that gave us a sense of power and signaled fertility, virility, or dominance over the competition (a trait seen in most mammals). While the physical or sexual pleasure of sexual activity remains in the domain of the Self-Preservation instinct, the desire for sexual interaction to communicate deeper or intimate bonds with another lies within the realm of the Sexual instinct. Research suggests this focus on intimacy appears to be unique to human beings.

Most animals evolved biological rituals designed to attract potential mates. Anthropologists believe differentiating oneself from others has helped animals ensure that the most desirable traits passed into successive generations. Some elusive but beautiful bird of paradise species, found primarily in Indonesia, Australia, and Papua New Guinea, demonstrate animal mating rituals' near universality. The male creates an elaborate display of masculinity and superiority by showcasing his nest-building capabilities. He cleans the rainforest floor of debris and any unsightly twigs or leaves before dancing for potential mates. His elaborate dance, fanning of tail feathers, and the display of hidden beautiful plumes on his head aim to win over the female so that he can ensure the proliferation of his genes. The female bird of prey, who may watch dozens of these dances from potential partners, selects her mate based on which dazzled her the most. Researchers are still unsure what causes females to choose one suitor over another. However, as with all matters of sex and romance, there seem to be chemistry, personal preference, and correct timing involved in the final selection.

Competition is an essential theme of the Sexual instinct as most species have grooming, courting, or adornment practices designed to set themselves apart from others to gain a mate(s). Aside from attraction, intimacy, and desirability, the Sexual instinct also rules over the domains of secrets, mysteries, personal adornment, relational power dynamics, depth of connection, fascination, intensity, eye contact, obsession, and repulsion.[4]

For Sexual types, being unattractive, unalluring, and unable to compete for the attention of the desired mate, partner, or best friend increases anxiety (much like the Social who is annexed from the group or a Self Pres person who doesn't have enough money, food, or security). It is not unusual when people first learn about the instinctual drives to believe they're Sexual because almost everyone wants to be desirable on some level to someone. When we actively search for a mate or seek intimacy with another, we employ the energy of the Sexual instinct. However, for those Sexual types, the need to maintain one's desirability, relational intensity, and allure does not subside or lessen once the mate is secured. The Sexual instinctual operating system believes that if one's desirability or the deep connection between themselves and the desired intimate isn't maintained, they are as good as dead.

A discussion of the Sexual instinct isn't complete without discussing the role of the Sexual instinct in human spirituality. The creative impulse of the universe, as many mystics, sages, religious scholars, and even quantum physicists have espoused, mimics the creative urge present in the human Sexual instinct. The Sexual instinct fuels the creative impulse in human beings as it reigns over the desire to bring something new into existence. It is, in essence, a manifestation of the "procreative" impulse of the human organism. We typically think of procreation as the physical propagation of a species. It also indicates the desire to express oneself through creating something new (art, music, poetry, myths, ideas, etc.). In my research, those who reported higher scores in the Sexual instinct drive conveyed an increased need to express themselves through some creative medium. Many religious traditions discuss the longing of the spiritual seeker to commune or merge with the Divine. The desire for connecting with another human mirrors the yearning for spiritual merging with something immortal, eternal, or vastly more remarkable than the temporal nature of human existence.

However, this does not suggest that the other instincts don't or can't express spirituality. The Self-Preservation instinct leads us to connect with our spiritual selves through the physical body with practices such as yoga, fasting, and other body-centric or naturalistic approaches to transcend human temperance or limitation. Alternately, the Social Instinct expresses this impulse by creating communal ritual practices, the spirit of philanthropy and charity, and through efforts to create utopian communities based on shared spiritual, philosophical, or religious ideals.

## WHEN THE INSTINCTS FALTER

The instinctual drives, when properly functioning, are invaluable evolutionary necessities that have kept human beings alive for millennia. However, instinctual drives do not always function optimally (like all human biological, psychological, and emotional processes). As previously mentioned, human beings evolved and developed more complex methods of protecting us from danger. As a result, many of the immediate threats to our survival are mitigated by advances designed to improve our quality of life (the move from the cave to huts, and from huts to brick-and-mortar dwellings, food storage systems, medicine, scientific advancements, governments, the internet, etc.). In the modern world, threats to our survival have become increasingly subtle. Thus, the ego perceives danger less through the lens of imminent physical death (although this, of course, is still hardwired into our brains) and instead through a symbolic, metaphoric, or psychological lens.

For example, a human with a dominant Self-Preservation instinct in 3000 B.C.E. had reason to believe that without hunting or gathering enough food to last the long winter, they would die. However, in the twenty-first century (for most people in both industrialized and most developing nations), food scarcity, although still a global problem, is significantly less likely to result in death as the invention of grocery stores, markets, food banks, farming, and other sources of sustenance have made food generally more accessible. Nonetheless, a Self Pres type in the United States with plentiful financial resources and reliable access to food sources may still fear that they might starve if they don't stockpile enough food for the winter.

The remnants of the biological imperative of the primitive instinctual drives are like a ghost of our more basic anthropological beginnings. The Self-Preservation instinct in modern humans cannot distinguish between not having access to food for a midnight snack any more accurately than a Neolithic person could distinguish between how much meat would last through the coming winter. They both seem vital and urgent needs worthy of immediate attention.

As mentioned earlier, the instinctual drives trigger the Enneagram types to deploy their defense strategies. Reiterating this concept is crucial in understanding the profiles of the twenty-seven narcissistic subtypes presented in part II. As a set of personality traits, narcissism acts as a general blanket over the entirety of the Enneagram personality typology.

Those familiar with Enneagram theory likely know the twenty-seven subtypes within the Enneagram system based on the nine types interacting with the instinctual drives. Dr. Claudio Naranjo made this assertion in the 1980s and finally wrote about it in 1995.[5] What's not yet fully explored is what happens when narcissism, a curiously more prominent feature in the modern personality structure, overlaps the existing twenty-seven instinctual subtypes as postulated by Dr. Naranjo. Research suggests we can identify three distinct variations on each of the nine types that illustrate a predictable and consistent pattern in how one's narcissism is activated and demonstrated in everyday life.

Much more can be said about the instinctual drives, as they are a fascinating and complex system in and of themselves. I would need many more pages to unpack the instinctual type system's intricacies fully, and fortunately, other Enneagram scholars have done much to advance this area of research.[6] You may be asking yourself at this point, but what about the Enneagram types themselves? And in the next chapter, we will delve into the nine basic Enneagram types so that in part II, we will have an adequate foothold to understand the underlying psychic structure of the twenty-seven narcissistic subtypes.

# 6

# The Nine Enneagram Types

Chapter 5 introduced the concept of the Instinctual types or drives as the operating system and the Enneagram types themselves as applications or programs that the OS governs. The Instinctual drive always activates the type and will direct the energy of the Enneagram type's defense mechanisms depending on the focus of the Enneagram type. The Enneagram types are referred to by number. However, the numbers themselves are merely signposts and do not denote any kind of hierarchy. For example, Type One is no better than Type Three.

## WHAT IS AN ENNEAGRAM TYPE?

The Enneagram type is a cluster of defense mechanisms designed to meet our instinctual needs. Unlike the instinctual type, the Enneagram type is ego based rather than "Id" based and thus tends to have more sophisticated methods of getting what it wants and needs. Harkening back to our computer imagery from chapter 5, our Enneagram type is like an application launched in service of our instinctual drives' needs at any given time. It contains our deepest fears and inherent psychological strengths. Our Enneagram types are personas intended to keep us safe from perceived inner and outer threats. Our types function primarily to uphold our self-image and its defenses deploy in service of maintaining a cohesive and coherent sense of identity continuity.

*Chapter 6*

My research has demonstrated that everyone operates from at least one of these defense structures. The primary Enneagram type combines two other types (one in each center of intelligence), which form the Trifix.[1] The oral history of the Enneagram states that Oscar Ichazo and his predecessor G. I. Gurdjieff postulate that we must have access to all nine types of the Enneagram to be a holistic system. Indeed, we have easier access to some types over others depending on the lines of connections and adjacent types next to the primary type on the symbol. Mathematically, however, if we allowed for all calculations of type, wings, Trifix, and lines of connection eventually, we find that no matter what someone's dominant type, they would have access to all nine types. Such is the beauty of the mathematical symmetry of the Enneagram symbol.

While it is unclear how we settle on which defense strategies we utilize throughout our life span, it is likely a combination of genetics, upbringing, environment, culture, and experiences. Whatever factors merge to create our personalities, our Enneagram type, Trifix, wings, and instinctual type remain stable throughout the life span.

I've coached clients and students who report being more like one type in their youth and as they age, they believe that they've become another type with increased wisdom and temperance. While I understand this interpretation of personal evolution, it does not comport with the data nor match the basic assumption of identity coherence. As we develop, we may become less defensive and thus have better access to the strengths and gifts of our type, hard-fought through years of psychological or emotional self-work. So while it may look like another type altogether (typically one of the types in the lines of connection), this is merely an expression of the healthy strategies of a type becoming more accessible. The fundamental core fears, defenses, and identity remain the same.

## THE ENNEAGRAM LEXICAL ANALYSIS RESEARCH STUDY

Katherine Chernick Fauvre's "Enneastyle" research was the first of its kind to gather data from participants about how people conceptualize and describe their self-image within the Enneagram framework.[2] Chernick Fauvre utilized her Enneastyle questionnaire, born out of her work as an image consultant, to gather data about how people conceptualized their self-image. By asking respondents to write five adjectives, describe their greatest strength, weakness, how they want to be seen by others, and other qualitative free-response questions, she identified patterns among people of the same type.

To confirm that a respondent's self-typing, test result, and self-description matched, Fauvre developed the "deep inquiry" interviewing method to quickly ascertain the deep-seated core fears behind a respondent's self-description. Her postulation underlies psychoanalytic theories of personality and asserts that people nurture traits, characteristics, strengths, and personas based on deep egoic insecurities and fears.

Utilizing Fauvre's premise, my 2020 Lexical Analysis Research study aimed to replicate, validate, and expand upon Fauvre's original research. I was able to confirm that the Enneagram type, Trifix, and instinctual type are predictable by analyzing a respondent's self-description, Enneagram test results, and depth interviews designed to tag the conscious and subconscious fears behind people's self-description.[3]

Upon analyzing the Lexical Analysis data, I could confirm Fauvre's findings that each of the nine Enneagram types, and three instinctual types, utilize self-reflexive language that matches the core fears, strengths, and weaknesses of the type as described by existing descriptions of the types. More than individual adjectives or phrases, it is the combination of words, phrases, and self-descriptive statements that were more predictive of type. On the Enneagram Lexical Analysis test, the instrument I designed to gather data about respondents' self-image, striking patterns emerged that reinforced the existent descriptions of the nine Enneagram types and twenty-seven instinctual subtypes first posed by Claudio Naranjo and Oscar Ichazo. However, because Oscar Ichazo did not conduct formal research, his assertions about the nine egoic fixations were based primarily on his intuition, observation, and postulations.

## ANALYSIS OF THE DATA

I analyzed the data leaning on my training as a qualitative researcher and decided the best method to ascertain whether people's self-description matched their Enneagram type was to triple-check their written self-description, Enneagram test results, and verbal explanation of their self-image matched. Depth interviews revealed predictable patterns in how people use language to describe their psyche. The deeper meanings behind their self-reflexive vocabulary proved more compelling than the word choice itself.

A typical case analysis would look like this. If I selected a study participant named "Amy," who scored highest on Type Two and wanted to confirm that Amy was indeed a Two, I would begin to analyze her Lexical Analysis Questionnaire. Imagine Amy wrote adjectives like "caring," "loving," "strong," "generous," and "people pleaser" to describe herself on her self-reflexive questionnaire. This collection of adjectives typically points toward a potential Type Two (or at least someone with Two in the Trifix). However, I need to know what Amy intends to communicate by her questionnaire responses. Specifically, I want to determine what Enneagram type(s) her deeper fears, anxieties, and strengths indicate to ascertain the core motivation(s) behind her self-description. I would then contact Amy for an interview. Upon interviewing "Amy," she reveals that these adjectives help assuage deep fears of being inconsequential, forgotten, or unlovable. I could then code Amy as a Type Two with a high degree of certainty.

For over 300 respondents, the triple validation method was effective for mapping words, phrases, and other type-specific markers. The adjectives and test results are massive clues toward pinpointing someone's type, but unless we understand the meaning behind someone's self-description, they are only theoretically relevant. Hence why the interviews proved more valuable than the questionnaire responses or the test results

The following Enneagram type descriptions are a very simplified distillation of the most common words and phrases to the Enneagram Lexical Analysis questionnaire by type obtained from study participants. For more complete and narrative Enneagram descriptions visit www.empathyarchitects.com/enneagram.

# TYPE ONE

### The Ethical Perfectionist

*Ones are ethical, measured, rational, detailed, and judgmental. Ones are motivated by their need to live by their sense of morality, ethics, and what they believe is right. They are responsible and feel it's up to them to maintain a sense of decorum, standards, and appropriateness. Ones have a robust ethical code and must adhere to their convictions of correctness to avoid feeling bad or wrong.*

> *Motivation*: To live by their sense of morality, ethics, and what they believe is right
>
> *Common Adjectives*: Fair, considerate, conscientious, wise, idealistic, responsible, resolute, idealistic, ethical, judgmental, strong-minded
>
> *Other People Describe Me As*: Judgmental, fair, balanced, polite, uptight, responsible
>
> *Strengths*: Reliability, can be counted on to do the right thing, fair-minded, organized, rational, reasonable
>
> *Weaknesses*: Anger, criticality, uptight/rigid/tense, fretting, judgmental, angry
>
> *Personal Image Style*: Clean, simple, practical, put-together, neat, classic, plain, elegant
>
> *I Avoid People Who Are*: Chaotic, selfish, reckless, irresponsible, crass, irrational
>
> *Biggest Fears*: Making a mistake/error, being reprimanded/reproached, being wrong, carelessness, missing an important detail, being bad
>
> *It Upsets Me When Other People*: Are inconsiderate, rude, selfish, unkind, unprincipled, unmannered, or reckless
>
> *I Avoid Feeling*: Complacent, wrong, corrected, bad, chaotic, irritated
>
> *I Need*: Order, time, rest, kindness, autonomy, relaxation

# TYPE TWO

### The Charming Supporter

*Twos are effusive, emotionally expressive, people-oriented, willful, and manipulative. Twos are motivated to be seen as helpful and want to be the "special person" in the lives of others. Attuned to others' needs, Twos know how to present a pleasing image that can make them desirable, generally likable, and well-received to compensate for feelings of being inconsequential.*

> *Motivation*: To be seen as helpful, supportive, and special to important people
>
> *Common Adjectives*: Kind, supportive, fun, ambitious, loving, nice, charismatic, generous, too nice, friendly, strong, willful

*Other People Describe Me As*: Caring, helpful, loving, sympathetic, kind, nice, bossy, flirtatious

*Strengths*: Loving, "able to see the best in others," helpful, encouraging, positive, giving others what they want/need, positive

*Weaknesses*: Too helpful, selfish, meddling, too nice, pushy, angry, resentful, people-pleasing

*Personal Image Style*: Cool, appealing, attractive, friendly, approachable, cute, sexy, warm

*I Avoid People Who Are*: Selfish, too anxious ("because it makes me anxious"), sad, angry, negative, unkind

*Biggest Fears*: Loneliness, being unlovable, being forgotten, depression, insignificance, rejection, valueless

*It Upsets Me When Other People*: Are negative and unhappy, don't have confidence, are rude, selfish, take me for granted

*I Avoid Feeling*: Sad, unhappy, negative, angry, depressed

*I Need*: People, love, attention, positivity, to be cared for, appreciation

## TYPE THREE

### The Successful Achiever

*Threes are motivated to be viewed as successful, attractive, accomplished, and competent. They derive their sense of self by being seen favorably by others. They seek value through accolades, success, and efficiency. Threes strive to be the best at everything they do and focus on developing the perfect image to compensate for feelings of worthlessness and valuelessness.*

*Motivation*: To be viewed as successful, attractive, accomplished, and competent

*Common Adjectives*: Ambitious, energetic, perfectionistic, overachiever, image-conscious, goal-oriented, popular, attractive, driven, expedient

*Other People Describe Me As*: Successful, attractive, alpha/dominant, smart, charismatic, capable

*Strengths*: Leading, winning, adjusting to the situation, being a good example, motivating others, efficiency

*Weaknesses*: Impatient, workaholism, perfectionism, image-conscious, approval-seeking

*Personal Image Style*: Professional, cool, stylish, effortless, trendy, smooth, polished

*I Avoid People Who Are*: Unmotivated, negative, lazy, people who make me look bad, slow

*Biggest Fears*: Losing, looking bad, incompetence, rejection, being exposed/unmasked

*It Upsets Me When Other People*: Are lazy, unmotivated, negative, slow, depressed

*I Avoid Feeling*: Like a loser, negative, lazy, too emotional, unmotivated, sad

*I Need*: To win, to succeed, to look good, approval, awards/accolades, positive attention, praise

# TYPE FOUR

## The Intuitive Romantic

*Fours are insightful, melancholy, creative, and analytical. Fours are motivated to be seen as authentic, deep, intuitive, and original. They have a deep need to express their emotional experiences and share their innermost feelings in the hopes of being seen and mirrored. Fours seek emotional intensity to compensate for feelings of inadequacy, lack, and meaninglessness.*

*Motivation*: To be seen as authentic, deep, intuitive, original, beautifully flawed

*Common Adjectives*: Intuitive, empathetic, creative, sad, intellectual, tasteful, elegant, beautiful, monster, hateful, envious

*Other People Describe Me As*: Aloof, sensitive, intuitive, intellectual, moody, snobby, remote

*Strengths*: Creating beauty, analyzing self and others, creating meaning, insightful, truth-telling, sensitivity

*Weaknesses*: Rumination, depression, lack of confidence, envy/jealousy, feeling lost, easily discouraged

*Personal Image Style*: Elegant, tasteful, creative, interesting, one of a kind, unique, beautiful, striking, rare, original, irresistible, natural, bohemian

*I Avoid People Who Are*: Shallow, unintelligent, boring, superficial, too happy, "basic"

*Biggest Fears*: Lack of meaning, being forgotten, ordinariness, inadequate, consumed by grief, not reaching potential, feeling lost or abandoned

*It Upsets Me When Other People*: Are harsh or unkind, mistreat others, are controlling, too positive, invalidating, unrefined, or insensitive

*I Avoid Feeling*: Ordinary, flat, too depressed, uninspired, too happy, content, lost, inadequate

*I Need*: Time to develop my potential, intensity, creativity, freedom, hope, more confidence

# TYPE FIVE

## The Remote Investigator

*Fives are remote, logical, sensitive, and intelligent. Fives are motivated to seek knowledge, avoid being overwhelmed and depleted, and conserve their time and energy to pursue their intellectual interests. They are sensitive, idiosyncratic, perceptive, and observant of their world. Anxiety and fear are quelled by seeking and hoarding information as a defense against the unknown.*

*Motivation*: To seek knowledge, avoid being overwhelmed and depleted, and conserve time and energy to pursue intellectual interests

*Common Adjectives*: Intelligent, aloof, shy, avoidant, studious, perceptive, odd, weird, private, sensitive

*Other People Describe Me As*: Aloof, removed, smart, odd, complicated, stingy, remote

*Strengths*: Synthesizing complex data, researching, understanding ideas, idiosyncrasy, being invisible

*Weaknesses*: Bad with emotions, anxiety, socializing, shyness, afraid of people

*Personal Image Style*: Smart, unassuming, clean, nerdy/dorky, nondescript, eccentric, quirky

*I Avoid People Who Are*: Loud, ignorant, manipulative, have nothing to say, clingy, shallow

*Biggest Fears*: Invasion, being incompetent/stupid, other people, emotional expression, being depleted/drained, nothingness, ignorance

*It Upsets Me When Other People*: Manipulate, are too emotional, irrational, nosy, illogical, stupid

*I Avoid Feeling*: Overwhelmed, invaded, emotional, incompetent, pressured, obligated

*I Need*: Safety, time, books/the internet/more information, space, privacy, solitude

# TYPE SIX

## The Loyal Skeptic

*Sixes are loyal, relatable, skeptical, anxious, and provocative. They are motivated to avoid anxiety, uncertainty, being blamed, or being caught off guard. Sixes are the alarm systems of the Enneagram and are frequently misunderstood by themselves and others because they are a mass of contradictory mental positions, emotions, and behaviors. They seek certainty in themselves and others to feel secure.*

*Motivation*: To avoid feeling fearful, anxious, uncertain, unsafe, or caught off guard

*Common Adjectives*: Loyal, sensitive, complicated, anxious, defensive, determined, emotional, responsible, complex, clever, over-thinking, friendly, angry, smart, reactive

*Other People Describe Me As*: Loyal, confusing, smart, anxious, funny, warm, friendly, reactive

*Strengths*: Creative problem-solving, seeing potential problems, loyalty, encouraging, analytical, skeptical

*Weaknesses*: Anxiety, reactive, cowardly, uncertainty, lack of confidence, poor boundaries, impulsive, too loyal, people-pleasing

*Personal Image Style*: Casual, athletic, cool, quirky, tough/unassuming, edgy, "normal"

*I Avoid People Who Are*: Judgmental, mean, bossy, brash, disloyal, insensitive, fake, snobby

*Biggest Fears*: Anxiety, uncertainty, being alone, dying, losing support, abandonment

*It Upsets Me When Other People*: Are mean, controlling, inconsistent, blaming, lie, fake or insincere

*I Avoid Feeling*: Anxious, uncertain, caught off guard, alone, targeted, blamed

*I Need*: Support, confidence, patience, courage, to know what's expected of me, consistency

# TYPE SEVEN

## The Excited Enthusiast

*Sevens are upbeat, fun-loving, curious, creative, and distractible. Sevens are motivated to avoid pain and to seek novel experiences to prevent feelings of boredom or emotional distress. Sevens need exciting plans and ideas and constantly think of ways to satiate their need for the new, exciting, or unexpected. They need variety to circumvent feelings of emptiness and fears of being trapped or limited.*

*Motivation*: To avoid pain, and seek novel experiences to prevent boredom and feeling trapped

*Common Adjectives*: Free-spirit, upbeat, loving, creative, interesting, clever, witty, cool, fascinating, fascinated, cheerful, funny, innovative

*Other People Describe Me As*: Interesting, fun, innovative, confident, high-energy, talkative

*Strengths*: Having fun, visionary, creative, influencing others, synthesizing, loving

*Weaknesses*: Lack of discipline, anxiety, imposter syndrome, scattered, impatience, commitment-phobic

*Personal Image Style*: Colorful, cutting edge, cool, clean, showstopping, flamboyant, avant-garde, interesting, stylish

*I Avoid People Who Are*: Boring, unfunny, uninteresting, negative, bland, complaining, unmotivated

*Biggest Fears*: Boredom, sadness, pain, being trapped, being stuck, feeling inferior, no options

*It Upsets Me When Other People*: Are limiting, negative, bitter, routinized, unmotivated, controlling

*I Avoid Feeling*: Depressed, emotional, pain, bored, inferior, trapped, or controlled

*I Need*: Freedom, fun, plans, excitement, variety, positivity, laughter

# TYPE EIGHT

## The Powerful Protector

*Eights are motivated to avoid weakness, vulnerability, and feeling disempowered. They seek power, influence, and strength to prevent others from controlling or taking advantage of them. Eights employ denial to disown their vulnerabilities and weaknesses, allowing them to plow through obstacles, intimidate, and overpower those who underestimate them.*

*Motivation*: To avoid weakness, vulnerability, and being disempowered or at the mercy of injustice

*Common Adjectives*: Direct, bold, creative, intense, confident, sensitive, honest, powerful, strong, authoritative, reactive

*Other People Describe Me As*: No-nonsense, intimidating, big-hearted, protective, angry, domineering, "too much," callous, insensitive, scary

*Strengths*: Strategizing, truth-telling, leading, directness, creativity, no-nonsense, intimidating, effective

*Weaknesses*: Too much, emotional/reactive, directness, rage, cynicism

*Personal Image Style*: Bold, confident, interesting, tough, comfortable, striking

*I Avoid People Who Are*: Fake, too sensitive, manipulative, too emotional, whiny, bullies, negative

*Biggest Fears*: Betrayal, weakness, disempowerment, being harmed, overpowered

*It Upsets Me When Other People*: Try to control [them], lie, betray [them], bully others, are unfair, are too sensitive, inconsiderate

*I Avoid Feeling*: Weak, naïve, used, sensitive, powerless, disempowered, sad, or controlled

*I Need*: Autonomy, control, power, loyalty, acceptance

# TYPE NINE

## The Peaceful Mediator

*Nines are easygoing, pleasant, conflict-avoidant, agreeable, and passive-aggressive. Nines are motivated to maintain their inner peace and want peace in the world around them. Nines want to feel even-keeled and seek moderation and evenness internally and externally. They avoid complication, conflict, and disconnection by suppressing their preferences, feelings, and desires.*

*Motivation*: To maintain inner and outer peace and avoid complication and conflict

*Common Adjectives*: Easygoing, calm, laid back, pleasant, balanced, stubborn, quiet, observant, conflict-avoidant, strong, open, receptive, good listener, kind, gentle

*Other People Describe Me As*: Easygoing, calm, chill, laid back, peacemaker, dependable, stable, a pushover, dismissive, stubborn

*Strengths*: Staying calm, keeping the peace, accepting, determined, nonjudgmental, empathetic, open-minded

*Weaknesses*: Pushover, anger, avoiding conflict, laziness, weak boundaries, stubbornness, anger, resistant, anxiety, naïve, skeptical

*Personal Image Style*: Comfortable, easy, clean, effortless, relaxed, classic, approachable

*I Avoid People Who Are*: Mean, angry, dramatic, uptight, judgmental, anxious

*Biggest Fears*: Conflict, anger, disconnection, separation, misunderstandings, no love

*It Upsets Me When Other People*: Are angry, dramatic, fighting, mean, pushy, bossy, pretentious

*I Avoid Feeling*: Too many feelings, intense, rushed, angry, overwhelmed, imbalanced

*I Need*: Love, autonomy, acceptance, patience, comfort, peace, time

# 7

## When Narcissism and the Enneagram Collide

As discussed in chapter 6, the nine Enneagram types will be the starting point for understanding the twenty-seven narcissistic subtypes. The core type intersects one of the three instinctual types (Social, Self Preservation, and Sexual), creating an instinctual subtype. These subtype labels combine the dominant instinct and the core Enneagram type (e.g., Self-Preservation Four, Sexual Two, Social Seven, etc.). Just as the twenty-seven instinctual subtypes create a unique archetype of the core type and the instinct intermingling, the twenty-seven narcissistic subtypes create an archetypal character structure. The twenty-seven subtypes in the following chapter are the product of the instinctual type, the Enneagram type, and narcissistic traits combined. However, we first need to understand the difference between narcissistic traits and Narcissistic Personality Disorder (NPD).

## NARCISSISTIC TRAITS VS. NARCISSISTIC PERSONALITY DISORDER

All of us, without exception, have some degree of narcissism present in our psyche. We touched on this concept in chapter 3; however, it bears repeating before we delve into the twenty-seven subtypes. Having an ego necessitates some degree (however small) of narcissism. The ego is primarily concerned with meeting its immediate needs (as dictated by one or more instinctual drives). Once we recognize a survival need, whether it's food, companionship, sex, shelter, money, or any other host of needs, our ego kicks in to help us ensure that our need is satiated. Depending on our psychological and emotional development, we employ a host of different strategies depending on our Enneagram type, instinctual type, and other developmental and environmental factors. Those strategies may be healthy, well-adapted, and largely effective. Our Enneagram type provides us with specialized skills in a particular arena.

For example, Twos are specialists in the realm of interpersonal relations. Their skills of persuasion, manipulation (both positive and negative), emotional support, and sympathizing with others ensure that they're valued, influential, and seen as indispensable in others' lives. At times they may be more transparent and clearer about their expectations and their desire for reciprocation or acknowledgment for their efforts. They recognize their tendency toward meddling, unsolicited advice-giving, and martyrdom and modulate their behavior to ensure they don't develop resentment or hostility. In this instance, the narcissistic goals of the Two's ego become mitigated by healthy self-awareness and effective behavioral and emotional strategies to reality check their expectations of themselves and others. However, in times of stress, trauma, or an increased propensity toward narcissistic traits, some Twos rely heavily on manipulative, maladaptive, or malignant strategies to get their needs met.

Under the right circumstances, any of us can be selfish, arrogant, or experience lapses in empathy or compassion. Most of us wouldn't label ourselves as narcissistic in those moments because we recognize that such behaviors are fleeting or temporary and aren't our normal state of being.

Adolescence, for most people, is a time of increased narcissism. Beginning around the age of eleven until approximately twenty-five, we experience a developmental stage where we focus primarily on what we need and want. Teenagers are notoriously concerned with image, social success, and house brains calibrated to focus on immediate gratification. Interestingly, this is also the period of development where empathy (however prevalent) amplifies strong emotions.[1] This fact of human development is why personality disorders aren't generally diagnosable in children or adolescents. For most of us, these developmental narcissistic traits are fleeting and are not pervasive as we mature. However, those maladaptive, selfish, or predatory methods of interacting with the world and others are chronic, pervasive, and lifelong patterns for some people. We have a variety of colloquial terms for people like this: "jerk," "selfish," "self-centered," "egotistical," and "megalomaniac," to name a few. Indeed, some people can be jerks, selfish, or self-centered, and some of those people aren't narcissists. However, some of them are.

Many researchers and clinicians note that narcissists are far more prevalent in the Western world than the data suggests.[2] The term denotes someone who exhibits enough observable traits and a pattern of behavior that fits within the narcissistic spectrum, as mentioned in chapter 3. Narcissistic Personality Disorder is a clinical diagnosis and is rare because NPD cases rarely present in clinical settings.

## NARCISSISM IN PLAIN SIGHT

My aunt persuaded me to watch a popular (and equally befuddling) reality show, *Married at First Sight*, which pairs two single people who have decided to trust a panel of experts (and producers) to pair them with a stranger whom they will marry sight-unseen. In this season, it was clear that one of the cast members was narcissistic (The Flattering Networker subtype). The audience is given a bird's eye view into how someone with the Social Climber narcissistic subtype and their corresponding abuse patterns operates in a relationship. It made for great television and received high ratings. Unfortunately, it was gut-wrenching to watch his estranged bride struggle to make sense of his behavior, gaslighting, and dramatic, selfish displays. The couple separated by the show's end due to his antics' interpersonal stress and drama. In the last few episodes, the couples sit with the show's experts and discuss their experience of becoming "married at first sight." The four experts (a psychologist, sociologist, pastor, and intimacy coach) went to great lengths to apologize for, rationalize, and at times, admonish the groom's behavior. But they avoided the word "narcissistic" like the plague.

On the one hand, it may not be necessary to call out narcissism by name because it appears everyone understood on some level something was "off."

Everyone on the show agreed that his behavior was unacceptable, problematic, and emotionally reckless. However, as I watched his confused bride struggle to make sense of what she experienced, I couldn't help but think that it would have been an excellent service to her (and the audience) to name her experience as narcissistic abuse. I am continually baffled at the verbal gymnastics some people use to avoid using the term "narcissist" when it's often the most straightforward and most concise explanation of some people's problematic behavior. Nonetheless, I understand the trepidation. The word seems too strong, a nasty label that conjures images of a Bernie Madoff or Harvey Weinstein. Indeed, those two "gentlemen" are observably narcissistic, but they are also on the sociopathic/psychopathic extreme of the narcissistic spectrum. For others, the word is not in their everyday lexicon, and it doesn't occur to them to use it. Also, I recognize the potential for reducing people's complex experiences and identities to one word, as there's typically an abundance of potential issues that interplay with narcissistic traits.

Narcissists like the groom in *Married at First Sight* are rampant in media. We love to watch them because they're often dazzling, entertaining, sometimes talented, and outrageous, and frankly, they make great television. Narcissism can produce entertaining, titillating, or compelling media figures, and it's no wonder that the reality TV, film, and music industries have hundreds of exemplars of observable narcissism hiding in plain sight. As American culture has grown more obsessed with image, power, money, and wealth, narcissists benefit from their efforts to gain attention, notoriety, fame, and money. There's nothing wrong with wanting fame, money, or power; however, the methods, tactics, and strategies narcissists use to reach their goals often leave a trail of pain in ascension to the top.

## THE NARCISSISTIC SUBTYPES:
## DISCERNING TRAITS FROM PATHOLOGY

My job as a researcher was not to discern whether participants in the following chapter fit the diagnostic criteria of NPD. However, there are instances of personal friends, family members, colleagues, or clients who exhibit narcissistic traits, which I share for illustrative purposes where appropriate. More commonly, I will point you to public figures and fictional characters to illuminate the archetypal behavior of a particular narcissistic subtype. And in these cases, I have not met or even interacted with the person in question. Much to my chagrin, I don't have access to some of the most famous narcissistic figures in human history. Still, there is ample data in historical accounts, interviews, documentaries, and biographies to make reasonable assessments of the presence of narcissistic traits and place them within one of the twenty-seven subtypes. A lack of personal interaction with these people does not preclude anyone who observes their behavior (with a moderate understanding of narcissistic personality traits) from identifying their narcissism. I also want to remind you to take the fictional examples as a signpost toward identifying the subtype in question. Most characters are not perfectly drawn, so they don't match the complete narcissistic profile, although, at times, they do.

We can leave NPD diagnoses to clinicians trained in those diagnoses. Dr. Ramani Durvasula,[3] for example, writes prolifically as someone who works with individuals with NPD disorder and their abuse survivors. As a personality scholar and researcher, I'm primarily interested in how traits of narcissism (including sociopathy and psychopathy) manifest in the twenty-seven Enneagram instinctual subtypes, as opposed to diagnosing individuals with NPD.

In my estimation, a move toward discussing narcissism as a set of observable personality characteristics is long overdue. We can discern narcissism in the same way we recognize introversion, sociability, emotional liability, a quick temper, or kindness. Moving the traits of narcissism out of their taboo associations and positioning them more prevalently in our everyday lexicon will hopefully help those dealing with some of the difficulties of having narcissistic traits and, more importantly, support those suffering from narcissistic abuse to heal.

It's crucial to remember as you read through the twenty-seven subtypes that you and everyone you know will demonstrate some degree of narcissism because you and everyone you know has an ego. As you're reading, consider whether the narcissistic patterns you're learning about are pervasive or, as will be the case for most people, whether those behaviors or thoughts flare and subside. In cases where you or someone else exemplifies the complete profile, you should also look for increased interpersonal conflict, a marked and pervasive lack of empathy or compassion for others, and some emotionally, physically, spiritually, or financially abusive patterns. If this is the case, a personality disorder could be present, and a personality disorder specialist can discern the severity and potential intervention strategies.

Finally, a word of caution: Running around to your friends, family, coworkers, and neighbors and telling them which narcissistic subtype they may be will likely go over like a lead balloon. First and foremost, try to identify which narcissistic subtype archetypes you identify with, which should be relatively easy if you've taken the Narcissistic Subtype Inventory (empathyenneagramtest.com /narcissism). That way, you can point out where you fall in these subcategories and maybe have a productive conversation with another.

# II

# THE 27
# NARCISSISTIC SUBTYPES

# 8

# Variants on the Narcissistic Spectrum

## PLACING THE TWENTY-SEVEN SUBTYPES IN CONTEXT

Each of the twenty-seven narcissistic subtypes described in the following chapters fits within a broader narcissistic personality spectrum dialogue within personality psychology research. It's essential to position the subtypes revealed in my study among established narcissistic spectrum delineations. I'm not attempting to reinvent the wheel entirely. I'm only adding spokes to an already well-constructed wheel. Narcissistic personality theorists have identified variants of narcissism and, for the most part, agree on the broad stroke character traits of these variants. I want to include these variants before delving into the twenty-seven subtypes, as each corresponds to one or more of these overarching variants. Many of these you've likely encountered, while a few I've added (primarily the intellectual and "nice/pleasant" narcissistic variants). The narcissistic spectrum variants are the grandiose, vulnerable, communal, nice/pleasant/benign, self-righteous, neglectful, dark empathic/spiritual narcissist, intellectual/cerebral, and malignant narcissists. These are not complete psychological profiles like you'll read in chapter 9 but rather subcategories under the larger narcissistic umbrella. I should also note the considerable overlap between the variants mentioned above. Like the Enneagram and instinctual types, one variant rarely captures the whole picture. For example, the malignant narcissist can also be grandiose, or the vulnerable narcissist can also be intellectual.

# GRANDIOSE NARCISSIST

Many people visualize this narcissistic profile when they hear the term "narcissist." They are confident, entitled, egotistical, arrogant, and boastful. They believe themselves to be larger-than-life and behave in cocky, arrogant, and at times off-putting ways that others may find objectionable (much to their surprise). They have a low threshold for the emotions of others (particularly vulnerable feelings). They enjoy attention, admiration, power, money, and praise and are unaware or uncaring of others' needs. They can be dismissive, harsh, rageful, and cutting when angry.

Grandiose narcissists can be formidable and dangerous when upset, particularly if they have a fair amount of psychopathic or sadistic tendencies present in their psyche. They are highly competitive and will go to great lengths to win. Those who fall within this variant, who tend toward psychopathy and sociopathy, may derive great pleasure in seeking revenge or humiliating those who've crossed them.

The Grandiose Narcissist is most comfortable tending to their immediate goals, often exceeding their actual abilities. Most grandiose narcissists are overt with their behaviors, meaning we can readily observe their inflated egocentricity. However, most grandiose narcissists also harbor vulnerable covert feelings and motivations (that will vary depending on their Enneagram narcissistic subtype) that belie their grandiose behavior.[1] Most will alternate between their inflated sense of themselves and a deflated lamentation of being misunderstood claiming nobody understands their genius or believing people don't appreciate their contributions. This variant of narcissism is prevalent in the corporate and entertainment industries, where high achievement yields big rewards.

# VULNERABLE NARCISSIST

At first, the vulnerable narcissist appears to be more self-contained, sensitive, or aggrieved than the Grandiose narcissist. They see themselves as getting the short end of the stick in life and are angry that they're not valued as much as they believe they should be. They may complain endlessly about situations and invariably blame others for their unrealized dreams and goals. They often have a more superficial understanding of their emotional landscape. They are internally convinced of their specialness and exemption from the rules but are resentful, mournful, or angry that people don't validate their elevated sense of self. Vulnerable narcissists are easily hurt and are quick to see insults and slights in others' benign behaviors or comments.

Vulnerable Narcissists primarily focus on themselves and their internal processes, thoughts, emotions, and desires. They may talk for hours about their problems to a friend who just revealed a death in the family or be unaware and uncaring of others' emotional needs. They have as many empathy deficits as the Grandiose Narcissist but often believe they are empathetic because they are aware of their own vulnerable emotions. They can become hateful or dismissive if they sense that others aren't listening to, validating, or honoring their emotional experience. This subcategory of narcissists is prone to sulking and can struggle with more depressive, anxious, or sad emotions than the other narcissistic subtypes.

## COMMUNAL NARCISSIST

This subcategory of narcissists focuses on appearing benevolent, generous, and well-liked. They are less overt with their arrogance and typically have more social charm and grace than the Grandiose or Vulnerable narcissists. They are image-conscious and believe that their worth and value directly relate to their standing in their chosen communities as gracious. They want to be recognized for their contributions and enjoy philanthropic endeavors to receive accolades for their social consciousness. They are less concerned with the causes they adopt and far more concerned with how their social standing will improve through their associations.

The Communal Narcissist is socially aspirational, and they want to know and be around the "right" people. They are very competitive and enjoy calculating how to achieve their goals. They need others to see them engaging in benevolent acts. Unbeknownst to the Communal Narcissist, other people sense the incongruency between their verbal sympathizing, apparent empathy or generosity, and their simultaneous preoccupation with status, power, and money. Some communal narcissists gravitate to spiritual, philanthropic, or religious communities and seek power and position through the appearance of selfless service. Others enjoy the power of contributing money to prestigious charities, sitting on boards and committees, and having buildings, plaques, and other accolades to commemorate their generosity or contributions. They can become angry, vicious, and competitive if someone seeks the attention and praise they're seeking and may resort to undermining or sabotaging behaviors to regain their status or position.

## SELF-RIGHTEOUS NARCISSIST

This variant is the most rigid and judgmental type on the narcissistic spectrum. They are moralistic, exacting, critical, and emotionally cold. The Self-Righteous narcissist focuses on ensuring they and those around them adhere to their strict standards. They can be sanctimonious, condescending, and highly disapproving of anyone or anything that doesn't match their ideals. Many have strong religious, ideological, or political opinions and values and readily share those opinions (and why they're the best opinions) with others. They fixate on order, efficiency, rules (as they've defined them), and control. Unable to admit they're wrong in any way, they go to great lengths (gaslighting, lying, sabotaging, manipulating, concealing, or intimidating) to ensure they maintain their moral, ethical, or ideological power.

The Self-Righteous narcissist may be more reticent and reserved than the other variants, while some can be very vocal and expressive about their ideologies and opinions. They are punitive and quick to anger and excessively need control over every aspect of their environment. This subtype is quite common in institutional settings such as military, law enforcement, government, or religious vocations.

## BENIGN OR NICE NARCISSIST

The Benign or Nice Narcissist is sometimes called the "narcissist light," as Dr. Ramani Durvasula coined this variant.[2] They typically have low (but rarely nonexistent) empathy and may have less interpersonal trouble than some other variants. They are more adept at navigating relationships and conflict. They are usually agreeable and conflict-avoidant. However, unlike non-narcissistic people who are conflict avoidant, they do not avoid conflict because they deeply value their relationships and connections. Instead, the benign narcissist avoids conflict to maintain emotional peace and be free of limitations or obstructions to their pleasure or fun. They value their peace of mind, positivity, happiness, and ease of living more than others. They seek validation and approval from others and are often well-liked and well-received by others.

The Nice/Benign Narcissist focuses on appearing friendly, kind, and agreeable, yet they harbor grandiosity, entitlement, and egocentricity under the pleasant exterior. They are frequently less contentious than the grandiose, vulnerable, or self-righteous variants. They believe that they deserve special treatment and care because of their niceness. They think they are entitled to others' attention, praise, and admiration because they are agreeable and pleasant. They often espouse a life philosophy of positivity, fun, or pleasure. Others may find their positive, sometimes overemotional, or Pollyanna-like orientation "toxically positive." They can also be legitimately entertaining to be around for short periods.

This variant's emotions are shallow and even child-like. They may throw temper tantrums when they don't get their way. Their displeasure comes through pouting or passive aggression. Due to their general likability, they are masterful at gaslighting or manipulating others to get what they want. Their selfishness will be evident in how they push and insist (however nicely) on what they want and need. They have difficulty maintaining intimacy and connection with others and may use others to get their immediate gratification needs met and move on quickly once they've satisfied the need. They have difficulty being helpful or generous without something in return for their efforts. When very frustrated, they may show quick and uncharacteristic fits of rage and then return to their normal pleasant set-point.

The Nice/Benign Narcissist's arrogance exercises their entitlement to pursue pleasure, enjoyment, or peace over other more pressing responsibilities. They want others to see them as some combination of easygoing, fun, attractive, likable, and positive. However, many people find them exhausting or tiresome due to their focus on staying light and airy. They cannot access their emotional depth and find connecting with others emotionally challenging. Once they sense that a relationship has soured or that the others' admiration has waned, they may become irritable, sulking, dismissive, or subtly antagonistic. This variant may be less recognizable as narcissistic by many because they are less malignant and challenging than the other variants. Nonetheless, their self-centeredness, superficiality, and hedonistic attitude can be draining when others want more depth from them.

## NEGLECTFUL NARCISSIST

This variant is less overtly aggressive but no less damaging. The Neglectful Narcissist harbors similar rage, entitlement, egocentricity, and grandiosity as the other variants. However, they channel their aggressive emotions through a lack of concern or attention to others. This variant often exudes a sense of cool, unbothered calm and refuses to be bothered by other people's problems, emotions, or concerns. They believe that their power comes from their unflappability and exemption from emotional or tangible responsibilities.

The Neglectful Narcissist is arrogant and dismissive when others request or need their attention. Some are overtly irresponsible and flippant, while others tend to their own immediate needs and concerns while ignoring responsibilities to friends, coworkers, family, or loved ones. They believe their time, energy, peace, resource, and relaxed image are paramount to their survival and cannot be bothered caring about others. They are very often emotionally flat and disdainful and dismissive of emotionality, displays of generosity, or expressions of care.

Some people of this variant are neglectful of their safety and security and make poor life decisions to satisfy their immediate gratification needs. They expect others to "sweat the small stuff" while they continue chasing their dreams, desires, or whims. Others are lazy and ineffectual and stubbornly refuse to contribute to a relationship, work project, or conflict resolution. For example, they are content to watch their spouse or partner clean the house without lifting a finger as they binge their favorite television series.

Their neglect is palpable and can be incredibly erosive to relationships and even cause problems in their professional lives. They evade responsibilities and fail to contribute meaningfully to projects. They are more passive-aggressive than overtly challenging but can have eruptions of rage or extreme contempt if others press them to take responsibility in their lives. It's common for this variant to use legitimate medical conditions (e.g., ADHD, chronic illness, trauma, depression) to evade responsibilities. Whether or not these conditions are present is highly variable, nonetheless the tendency to employ excuses for their behavior.

## DARK EMPATH/SPIRITUAL NARCISSIST

This variant is a relatively new variant of narcissism yet deserves explication. The Dark Empath or Spiritual Narcissist is the most emotionally and interpersonally conscious of all the narcissistic variants and has a higher degree of cognitive empathy than almost all the other narcissists mentioned in this chapter. They're adept at reading others' emotional cues and have a talent for reading people's motivations and vulnerabilities. Research shows that they demonstrate more affective and cognitive empathy and have lower levels of physical aggression.[3] They appear intuitive, wise, emotionally mature, and inspiring. They intuitively understand others' psychological, spiritual, and emotional experiences and utilize their understanding of the human psyche to manipulate, coerce, control, or abuse people.

Their intuitive and empathic faculties are better calibrated to feel or experience others' pain. They tend to be more adept at mirroring, pacing, and sympathizing with others to get closer to them and build trust. This subtype's grandiosity is displayed through their spiritually transcendent, intense, and psychologically sophisticated superiority. They are often very charming and adept at gaslighting, love-bombing, and trauma bonding.[4] The dark empath often engenders sympathy and support from people in their spheres of influence by sharing their traumatic experiences as well as the miraculous, transcendent, or impressive manner they overcame their tribulations. They are careful not to reveal information that could hurt, expose, or shame them, so their emotional revealing is often highly curated to paint a favorable image, with just enough vulnerability and emotional insight to be enticing. They target vulnerable, lost, or empathic people and hope to help these pathetic souls grow and flourish. They enjoy the power of guiding, mentoring, and teaching others and take pleasure in psychological molding and manipulating people.

This variant is one of the more emotionally dangerous narcissistic variants as there's typically a considerable amount of sociopathy present in their psychic structure. Because they're better able to get into the minds of those around them, their control of others can be profound and go undetected by their victims for years. They, like other narcissists, seek attention, admiration, money, and power. Yet, because of their aptitudes in understanding human motivations and emotions, they are better able to conceal their ultimate goals (sometimes even from themselves). Many fly under the radar until those closest to them feel safe to reveal their darker, more sinister manipulation tactics. Unfortunately, this variant populates helping professions (psychiatry, psychology, mental health or grief counseling, spiritual advisors, self-help, yoga, or religious gurus).

## INTELLECTUAL NARCISSIST

This variant typically appears less extroverted and bombastic than the Grandiose Narcissist. However, they are equally egotistical, inflated, and entitled. Nevertheless, they lack the extroverted, peacocking prowess of the Grandiose variant and are often remote, introverted, or hidden from public view. They're confident of their intellectual superiority and lord their knowledge, intellect, and expertise over others. They gain power and influence through their mental prowess. Some may be legitimately intelligent and mentally adept. Still, the arrogance and disdain they display toward others who don't understand their "brilliant" minds differentiate them from other knowledgeable yet empathic people.

The Intellectual Narcissist believes they are the most extraordinary intellect in the world. Still, they typically lack the interpersonal or emotional skills to communicate their ideas to others without being insulting or condescending.

They may neglect or avoid other responsibilities (parenting, work, housework, paying bills, etc.) because they believe that less intellectually capable others should care for their basic needs. Their lack of emotional intelligence or depth isn't due to other neurological or mental deviations (such as autism), but rather a pattern of disdain and dismissal of those they've deemed beneath them.[5] The Intellectual Narcissist is often less concerned about their appearance or other status symbols outside their intellectual or mental achievements; however, this can vary by Enneagram type. They typically harbor a fair amount of schizoid or schizotypal tendencies.

The Intellectual Narcissist may or may not have higher than average intelligence. Those with moderate or below-average intellects may avoid IQ tests or other measures that could expose or reveal their intellectual prowess. If they are indeed intelligent, they will often overestimate or overvalue their intellectual contributions. They are typically highly specialized in their field of knowledge and can be ruthless with others and compete for accolades or attention. Some may fabricate or invent stories about their intellectual achievements to appear more impressive. This variant abounds in academia, tech and research industries, STEM careers, or other scholarly circles.

## MALIGNANT NARCISSIST

The Malignant Narcissist is the most overtly aggressive, angry, and cantankerous of the variants. Typically combined with a generous dose of psychopathy or sociopathy, these people have a robust sadistic orientation toward interpersonal relationships. Psychological literature often refers to the malignant narcissist as the psychopath; however, there are fine distinctions between the two, as discussed in chapter 3. The psychopath often exhibits low inhibition, an increased propensity toward antisocial or violent behavior, and a lack of remorse or shame. While the Malignant Narcissist does often have low to zero degrees of empathy, their sadism is often subtle and less evident than the more unbridled sadism of the psychopath. Some argue that malignant narcissists are "sociopaths" because they're focused on meeting their immediate needs but can often modulate their presentation or behavioral strategies long enough to avoid violating social norms. However, unlike the textbook sociopath, their sociopathic or malignant behaviors are not triggered until someone betrays or abandons them. They then see their behavior as justified and may unleash various nuanced or overt attacks on the people, institutions, or organizations that dared to leave, rebuke, or deny them.

This Malignant Narcissist focuses on revenge, punishment, or retribution for perceived slights or insults. They may enjoy abusing others emotionally, psychologically, or physically because of the sense of power or dominance it affords them. Malignant Narcissists may like conning or swindling people and can be highly successful as they can often fly under the radar of legal repercussions. Like other narcissistic variants, they covertly struggle with feelings of emptiness and shame but often channel their emotional pain into the abuse or neglect of others. They feel their pain is somehow relieved through harming, controlling, or manipulating others. Due to higher psychopathy, they enjoy conflict, fighting, and violence more than some other variants. They may find ways to channel that energy in socially acceptable mediums (i.e., boxing, MMA fighting, litigation, violent video games, etc.). We can contrast their violent sublimation with the psychopath, whose social inhibition and impulse control problems often land them in legal trouble because of their propensity toward breaking the law or explosive violence.

Like the other narcissistic variants, they typically harbor a grandiose self-image, low empathy, a high degree of egocentrism and selfishness, and a lack of concern for others. They can be reckless (particularly if angry). If they experience a string of upsets, disappointments, or setbacks, they may devolve into full-blown psychopathy or sociopathy to manage their shame.

## PUTTING IT ALL TOGETHER

Now that we understand the basic variants of narcissism as a set of personality traits, we can (finally) dive into the specific twenty-seven subtypes. For each subtype, you'll see a radar graph visualizing which of the variants mentioned in this chapter are associated with the subtype. Where appropriate, I will indicate which variants are most common with each subtype.

The personality archetypes in the following chapters provide a snapshot of an Enneagram instinctual subtype when affected by the typical narcissistic traits (lack of empathy, lack of inhibition, difficulty accepting criticism, arrogant or self-centered behavior or thinking, and an excessive need for validation). Upon completing the Enneagram Lexical Analysis Test—ELAT (available at www .empathyenneagram.com) and the Narcissistic Subtype Inventory (www .empathyenneagram.com/narcissism), you should have a clear idea of which Enneagram type, instinctual type, Trifix, and the narcissistic subtypes that you most closely resemble.

I encourage you to pay special attention to the Trifix your ELAT suggests. Reading the narcissistic subtypes for all three types in the Trifix gives more nuance and complexity to how narcissism shows up for you or someone you know. Each description begins with an overall snapshot of the Enneagram instinctual subtype in normal to healthy psychological functioning. Then each description will evolve to reveal how narcissism affects and shifts the "psycho-typical" behavior and focus on increasingly more maladaptive behavior.

# 9

## Type One

### The Ethical Perfectionist

Narcissistic Subtypes:
*Self-Preservation One: The Puritanical Fussbudget*
*Social One: The Moralistic Inquisitor*
*Sexual One: The Zealous Crusader*

### SELF-PRESERVATION ONE

The Self-Preservation One is the most pragmatic, sensible, and anxiety prone of the One subtypes. Self Pres Ones are very conscious of "doing the right thing" related to their responsibilities. They are hardworking, diligent, and prudent in their personal and professional lives. Many are incredibly conscientious, careful, and mindful to avoid avoidable mistakes. They value and enjoy cautious attention to detail. Self-Preservation Ones are aware of making mistakes resulting in catastrophe or disaster. And rarely do they find themselves out of control of a situation. They also consciously modulate and monitor their behavior, actions, and thoughts to avoid being insulting, inconsiderate, or inappropriate:

> I am thoughtful, empathetic, and appropriate because it's the right thing to do. I never want to think that I might have offended someone around me, so I try to make sure that I'm demonstrating to others my character. Character is the most

important thing to me. If you are a selfish, unkind, and inconsiderate person, you're a leach to society, and that is unacceptable.

—Leila, 29, graduate assistant

Self-Preservation types focus on ensuring that their basic survival and comfort needs are met. Self-Preservation Ones frequently channel their self-preservation fears by concentrating on conservation and appropriate management of resources, time, and money. They strive for moderation and are not typically excessive in spending (or any other aspect of their lives). Many Self-Preservation Ones are incredibly conscious of their diets, health, budgets, exercise, and the tidiness and efficiency of their homes and workspaces. For the Self Pres One, cleanliness is next to godliness, and maintaining purity in their bodies, minds, and environments is of the utmost importance.

I try to avoid excess in most areas of my life. I splurge now and again, but it's my nature to be pretty moderate overall. I don't eat a lot of sugar, carbs, meat, or drink much alcohol. Mostly because I know that I don't feel good when I put those things into my body. I don't care what other people do, but for me, it's important to maintain a clean lifestyle.

—John, 36, tax accountant

Self-Preservation Ones believe that through proper preparation, attention to detail, and careful consideration, they will avoid errors, mistakes, or chaos through rational and reasonable decision making. In this way, they can mimic Type Six. However, unlike Sixes, Self-Preservation Ones do not struggle with decision making or anxiety in the same way. Instead, they are decisive and self-assured that their convictions lead them toward the correct course of action. They are frequently rigid and are often judgmental of frivolous, excessive, inappropriate, or inconsiderate people. Naturally puritanical, Self-Preservation Ones have self-control and prefer to indulge their whims (if they even arise) privately and without fanfare. Many feel burdened and slightly resentful of their innate sense of responsibility and often struggle with muscle tension, headaches, or chronic stress.

Within the average range of empathy, Self-Preservation Ones are compassionate, much to the surprise of others due to their characteristic stoicism. Their focus on avoiding being wrong or bad creates a self-critical internal dialogue that they believe pushes them to be compassionate and empathetic toward others. They can be stern and correcting when necessary. Self-Preservation Ones understand the value of empathetic and nonjudgmental communication because they know how negative judgment and callousness hurt their souls.

> I try to listen to people's struggles even when they're discussing something that morally or ethically, I might find wrong or inappropriate. We all make mistakes, and while I may judge myself harshly, I try to avoid doing that to others whenever possible. Of course, sometimes, my judgment creeps in. My sister bought a really expensive car when she had some debts that needed to be paid, and I didn't think it was the most prudent choice.
>
> —Rita, 44, elementary school teacher

## THE PURITANICAL FUSSBUDGET

When narcissism is present in the Self-Preservation One's psyche, their focus on pragmatics, practicality, and purity becomes heightened. They become obsessed with ensuring that their internal and external standards are upheld at all costs. Relationships begin to suffer because they have difficulty softening their expectations and becoming increasingly critical of others. They are stoic, unemotional, and seem hardened to any sensitivity. Their lack of emotionality makes it difficult for others to reach the sensitivity ordinarily present in the non-narcissistic Self Pres One. They are more outwardly tense, rigid, and inflexible when excessively stressed. Self-Preservation Ones are generally reticent about expressing too much direct anger or frustration. However, the Puritanical Fussbudget believes others will not learn their lessons without their displays of firmness, punitiveness, or anger. This subtype is nitpicking and irritable. They think it is their job to ensure that people in their orbit correctly adhere to their order protocols. Of course, this supports their ideas of what people *should be* doing according to their prescriptions of living life.

> I have exact standards, and yes, I will tell you if you've underwhelmed me because how else will you know how to improve. If I'm always improving, then other people should be doing the same.
>
> —Yani, 42, quality control manager

Because their narcissistic tendencies flare in the Self-Preservation domain, the narcissistic traits are most evident in matters relating to food, the home, money, comfort, and security. They can be immensely frugal and believe that their frugality is the only right or appropriate way to live. Excessive spending (or spending on anything they haven't deemed worthy) is degraded and avoided at

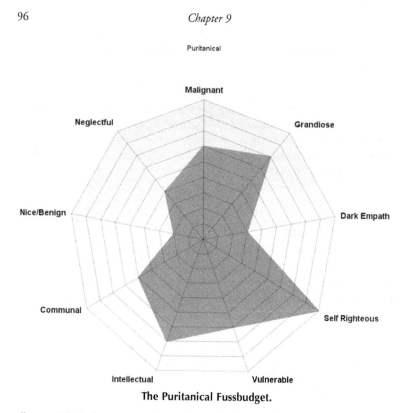

**The Puritanical Fussbudget.**

all costs. Their focus on money and resources can become hypocritical as they may secretly splurge on luxuries or indulgences for themselves while denying others comforts or even the smallest extravagances.

> I make good money, but I don't spoil my children. I only buy them clothes once a year before school begins, and I decide what they buy. No single clothing item should cost more than $50. This will teach them the value of hard work and that their friends' exorbitant prices on clothing are ridiculous and unnecessary. I, however, must have nice, high-quality clothing (because of my career), so I will occasionally spend good money on my suits and shoes. My kids say it's hypocritical, but their opinion doesn't matter much to me on this issue. Children should be seen and not heard.
>
> —Carolyn, 45, tax attorney

The Puritanical Fussbudget is rigid, insensitive, and uncompromising. They relentlessly manage their diets, exercise regimes, health, daily routines, religious or spiritual observances, and finances and often want others to follow their stringent protocols. Their practical affairs are meticulously supervised to avoid errors or surprises. They can be incredibly arrogant and convinced that the way they manage their diet, exercise routines, households, money, and daily affairs is superior. Many Puritanical Fussbudgets struggle with restrictive eating disorders, exercise, bulimia, or obsessive-compulsive tendencies to manage their anxieties.

> Our house was like an internment camp for kids rather than a home. We were only allowed to have a few toys. She would spot clean our room once a week with an actual white glove, and if she found dust, we weren't allowed to call or socialize with our friends. We lived in fear of her punishments which were never physical but were emotionally abusive. I never saw her cry or express any emotion but judgment, irritation, and anger. She softened a bit before she died, but she stayed that way most of her life.
>
> —Mary, 64, retired

They are inflexible and rarely smile or engage in leisure activities, giving them a reputation for being dour or dull. This subtype does not particularly enjoy having fun and often believes that too much fun will capsize their tightly run ship. If children, spouses, or other members reside in their household, they typically have unrealistic standards for the cleanliness and orderliness of the home. They dole out punishment or admonishment readily if disappointed.

Some people of this subtype may be less patrician but demonstrate their exacting standards in pursuing personal, moral, or professional excellence. However, they still secretly value money, status, and power (which they may publicly deny).

In the film *There Will Be Blood*, Paul Dano plays Eli Sunday, the severe, puritanical, and pious iteration of the Puritanical Fussbudget. Eli exemplifies the moral hypocrisy and characteristic callousness of this subtype. Sunday is the self-righteous variant who tries to extort Miserly Hoarder, Daniel Plainview (played by Daniel Day-Lewis). Plainview seeks to set up an oil well on Eli's family's land, potentially a proverbial gold mine for greedy, aspiring oil tycoon Plainview.

I discuss this film and Daniel Plainview in more detail in chapter 13. However, it's worth mentioning Dano's character here. Eli is devoutly religious, and his family and the surrounding town recognize him as a "powerful healer." Sunday aspires to start a church from the money Plainview's expected to pay the family from the oil he extracts from the land. Eli is suspicious of Plainview's motives and trustworthiness, and rightly so. However, Eli is far more concerned with amassing wealth, status, and power than his pious image suggests. Eli controls his family, having taken the role as head of the household, believing his father to be "stupid" because he doesn't press Plainview for more money. The scenes with Plainview and Eli are tense. Both men are narcissists vying for power and control over the other. Plainview is a cold, deceptive, and money-hungry expansionist, and Eli is moralistic, patrician, severe, and self-righteous. By the end of the film, Plainview and Eli finally face off. Eli became a successful radio televangelist but is in dire financial straits and approaches Plainview with a proposition to purchase a ranch so he can make money. Plainview agrees so long as Sunday renounces his faith, to which he agrees—revealing the superficiality of his religious convictions and satisfying his self-preservation needs was far more critical.

If this subtype is successful, they maintain an appropriate, neat, and pristine image for public consumption, as all narcissists are aware of public perception to some extent. Still, unlike other narcissistic subtypes (primarily those in the Heart Triad), the Puritanical Fussbudget is less concerned with appearances overall. The standards by which they maintain their worlds dictate their behavior, and narcissistic fits and rages illustrate when others inevitably fail to meet their expectations. They are often disappointed in others and will frequently undermine or undercut others' attempts to live up to their standards by taking over projects, work, or other endeavors because they believe nobody can do anything as accurately as they can.

> I hardly ever delegate anything anymore because everyone is sloppy and has poor standards. I've always said if you want it done right, do it yourself. I'm always doing things myself because I can't trust anyone to understand how important it is for everything to be perfect. It's the only reason I've had such a long and successful career.
>
> —Felindo, 56, chef

There's a fine line between striving for excellence and an unrealistic pursuit of perfection. This subtype often falls on the latter end of the pole, searching, uncompromisingly, for the ideal.

Severe narcissists of this subtype are cruel and punitive toward those they believe lack moral fortitude, competency, or match their preference for perfection. The puritanical streak at this stage often manifests as a stark ascetic orientation to life. They may believe that others who engage in activities they deem immoral, inappropriate, or imprudent deserve their judgment, wrath, and ire. They are openly disdainful and dismissive of anyone who doesn't meet their impossible standards while secretly envying others' freedom.

The typical attention to considerateness and appropriateness falls by the wayside as narcissism decreases self-awareness and self-modulation. This subtype can be blunt, brusque, opaque, and even cruel in communication with others.

They may make glib or even inappropriate comments to others about their conduct or behavior and will not recognize (or care about) the impact of their directness and disapproval. All the while, they maintain a self-image of being appropriate and considerate and yet are wholly unable to integrate or even listen to criticisms of their delivery or approach when dealing with others.

As is the case with all Ones, this subtype may indulge in "trapdoor" tendencies, particularly in the realm of sensual pleasure (binge eating, excessive sex or promiscuity, secret drug or alcohol abuse, or other activities they would typically find objectionable). They denounce others for their inappropriateness and frivolity while hypocritically demonstrating the very behaviors they find reprehensible or disgusting. Without empathy, they feel little to no remorse for their admonishment of others' perceived foibles and find it impossible to admit if they've made an error, mistake, or misstep in judgment (which at this stage may be quite frequent).

### When Dealing with a Puritanical Fussbudget:

1. Avoid criticism or correction. This is sure to trigger this subtype into fits of rage, and it's better to keep complaints to yourself.
2. Calling out a narcissist generally is not well received. With this subtype, they may be entirely unaware of their narcissistic tendencies. However, using words like "selfish" or "unreasonable" to describe their behavior may resonate in a way that will allow some slight adjustments in their toxic behaviors.
3. Be clear about your boundaries. If they become overly critical or nitpicking in a manner that you find objectionable, tell them calmly that you will not tolerate disrespect or rudeness.
4. If they become irate, verbally, or physically abusive, physically remove yourself from the situation and seek assistance from a trusted therapist, friend, or loved one.

## SOCIAL ONE

Social Ones channel their perfectionism and motivation into being good, ethical, and proper in the social arena. They are the most focused on social appropriateness, rules, and adhering to a set of ethical and moral standards that they believe align with their internal convictions and beliefs. This instinctual subtype focuses on the group, and attention goes to what is right and wrong related to behavior and conduct in the world. They are conscientious, well mannered, and believe that their role in the world is to help guide others toward what they feel is the ideal way to be in the world. They are hypercritical and judgmental. At times, they may openly correct or admonish others if they believe people behave objectionably in their spheres of influence.

Social Ones often gravitate to social roles where they exercise their aptitude for guiding or mentoring others. They enjoy teaching others to be reasonable, balanced, and socially conscious by cultivating correct thoughts and actions. Social Ones channel their frustration about the world's imperfections into the social arena to make meaningful contributions to society.

> I'm a tough grader because I want my students to work for their grades, but in the end, I think they respect me because I'm honest with them about their gifts and their shortcomings, when necessary.
>
> —Rita, 43, high school political science teacher

Morality is of the utmost importance to the Social One, and they can be relentless in their desire to ensure that their actions in the world and ideologies are congruent. This is the most orderly and socially conscious of the One instinctual subtypes, and they will work tirelessly to ensure that their ideals are in some way bettering themselves or others.

With average to high empathy, this subtype is often immensely generous with their time and energy toward causes, people, and projects they believe are worthwhile. They can be excellent mentors and patient teachers and help communicate the need for moral integrity with an awareness and appreciation for the emotional experience of those around them. They fight for what is right and put their necks on the line for people or causes they find meaningful. When appropriate, they can loosen their buttoned-up presentation and let loose with people in their chosen group without their typical self-criticality and fear of being judged as irresponsible by others.

## THE MORALISTIC INQUISITOR

This narcissistic subtype is the most "teachy, preachy" of all twenty-seven subtypes, and they believe that it is their job to show other people the correct way to behave and how others should think. When the Social Instinct, One, and narcissistic traits collide, it creates a character structure intensely focused on moral upstandingness and fortitude. This subtype is openly judgmental and typically has no problem expressing their judgment openly due to the decreased inhibition accompanying narcissism. However, because they still harbor the

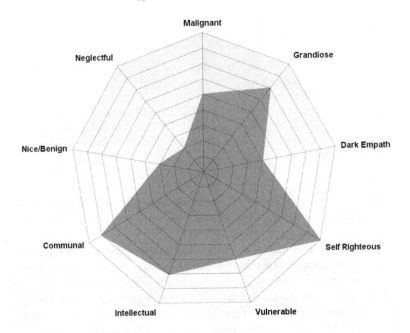

**The Moralistic Inquisitor.**

typical Type One rigidity, their delivery is often still appropriate, albeit pointed. Unlike the Puritanical Fussbudget, where their bluntness is more evident and attention to the social image decreases, this subtype channels their fear of being cast out from the group into maintaining a public persona in line with their moral and ethical standards. It is ubiquitous for this subtype to exhibit religious, philosophical, or ethical rigidity that is firmly nonadaptable.

> I believe that God put me on this planet to ensure that sin is eradicated from the human spirit. So, I don't have any problem shaming or publicly rebuking one of my congregants if I think this will help them see the error in their ways. People learn through shame, but I'm always there to help them see and grant them forgiveness.
>
> —Ted, 64, pastor

Even if this subtype isn't religious, they adopt standards of behavior and conduct that align with some ideological viewpoint and will be staunchly adherent to their chosen principles. Craig, a rather cold and admittedly tightly wound former student, identifies as an atheist, and expresses open and derisive disdain for religious zealots and believers while simultaneously extolling the correctness of a rational and scientific approach to life.

> I think religious people are ridiculous. There is no logical reason to believe any mystical force behind the universe. Science has taught us that reason and logic is the only way out of the terrible and doomed situation we find the world in. So, I enjoy demonstrating the silliness of frivolous thought through rationally and calmly poking holes in religious people's ideas. They often leave feeling frustrated and angry with me, but I don't care. At least they'll think about their beliefs more after they encounter me.
>
> —Craig, 26, student

This subtype believes emphatically in their decency, and the self-assuredness that accompanies narcissism helps solidify their moral convictions. The Moralistic Inquisitor may think that they are the only people who live "correctly," and some refuse to associate with people whom they've labeled as wrong. Or, which is more common, they see it as their mission to convert, convince, or prove to others that they have in some way fallen short of an ideal.

Some people with this narcissistic style may enjoy correcting others. If they have significant impairments in empathy, they relish proving others wrong, humiliating, or exposing other people's errors or wrongdoings. They insist others atone and apologize for transgressions and can extend their cold or cruel treatment for weeks, months, or years if they've been transgressed. They can crusade against perceived fallibility and go on proverbial witch hunts to expose anyone who is not on the up and up. They fail to see the effect of their relentlessness on those around them.

*Doubt*, John Patrick Shanley's play about a righteous and relentless nun convinced of a priest's inappropriate conduct toward a child in the Catholic elementary where they both work, is an excellent snapshot of this narcissistic subtype. In the 2008 film adaptation, Meryl Streep plays Sister Aloysius masterfully. Sister Aloysius' lack of doubt about Father Flynn's (played by Phillip Seymour Hoffman) accused indiscretions personifies the crusader-like confidence of the Moralistic Inquisitor. Despite the lack of evidence of Father Flynn's conduct, Sister Aloysius is determined to topple Father Flynn with nothing but her convictions. She is willing to ruin Father Flynn's career and reputation to satisfy her disgust at his accused moral lapse.

The film is an excellent meditation on morality, conviction, and of course, doubt, but the most striking character in the movie is Aloysius. She sublimates her moral idealism and righteousness into behavior that most categorize as immoral and deceitful. The Moralistic Inquisitor justifies all of their behavior (no matter how vile) so long as they can maintain their internal sense of rightness. And with narcissism present, they are inevitably, always right.

Some people of this subtype can be incredible snobs, and there is an interesting dichotomy between their moralistic orientation and the flagrant display of their wealth, status, or social capital. They may take their success and privilege in the world to indicate that they're entitled to the best because they are good people.

As narcissism increases, this subtype demonstrates increasingly less inhibition around their penchant for punishment and admonishment. They are often attracted to legal, religious, or ethically focused careers where they can locate and punish people who are not following stated laws, doctrines, or protocols. If sadism or psychopathy are present in their psychological structure, this subtype relishes shaming and penalizing transgressions. As with most narcissists, the power they wield in these positions and the opportunity to claim moral or ethical high ground is intoxicating.

> I enjoy expelling students. It's thrilling to me because they deserve to have their academic careers ruined if they do something as stupid as cheating. I have no tolerance for academic misconduct, and I have expelled over 150 students. I would expel more if our code allowed it, but there's nothing more enjoyable to me.
>
> —Trent, 57, college dean

If empathy is sufficiently degraded or nonexistent, this subtype may resort to gross displays of abuse. The atrocities of the Spanish Inquisition, the systematic and widespread murder of women and other marginalized people during witch trials of Europe and colonial America, the violent colonialization of Africa and the Americas, and gay conversion therapy are examples of the principle of this narcissistic subtype's energy at work. Indeed, not all who participate(d) in these atrocities are Moralistic Inquisitors. Still, I would be surprised if the architects of these cultural events aren't peppered with narcissistic ideologues convinced of their moral superiority. The conviction of this subtype allows them to justify their abuse of others through moral reasoning and the often-held belief that their punishment is improving or correcting perceived wrongdoing.

## When Dealing with a Moralistic Inquisitor:

1. Do not engage them in philosophical, ethical, or moral debate. They take pleasure in proving others wrong through sheer force of their certainty, and even if you're correct, they will never concede. If they grant legitimacy to your position by some miracle, they will seek revenge by demonstrating their correctness later.

2. This subtype has a powerful punitive streak. Depending on how strong their psychopathic or sadistic tendencies are, they may construct elaborate scenarios, arguments, or situations to prove a point. Humiliation or repentance is the desired outcome for their punishment.

3. It is tempting to find opportunities to point out this subtype's hypocrisy, errors, or indiscretions, but this is inadvisable because it will trigger their narcissistic rage. They will unleash their shame (via a judgmental tirade) upon you or find any and every opportunity to discover and expose any vulnerabilities or errors in your behavior or conduct.

4. Be aware of baiting, gaslighting, or other emotional manipulation tactics designed to enroll you in a drama whereby they can prove their moral or ethical superiority.

## SEXUAL ONE

Sexual Ones focus their drive for perfectionism and moral and ethical purity in interpersonal relationships with chosen intimates. They want to ensure that they are the ideal mental, emotional, and physical partner, friend, and family member to the people they hold near and dear. They focus on the romantic/intimate arena and, like all Sexual types, constantly search for the perfect connection with the ideal mate. Sexual Ones believe that relational perfection is attained if both parties strive for internal and external excellence.

Sexual Ones are fierier and are more likely to demonstrate their anger than the Self-Preservation or Social subtypes. They can be reactive and even explosive if something comes into their awareness that they find objectionable. Like all Ones, they have high internal standards, but they focus a great deal of that attention toward themselves and their partner. They can seem Eight-ish by asserting their opinions and are bold and forceful if someone violates their convictions, morals, or standards.

Sexual Ones are deeply fearful that they will not measure up to their chosen others' ideals and are relentless with themselves about constant inner and outer improvement. They expect that the special people in their lives will put forth the same effort to become their ideal. They believe they have a divine right to their partners, children, or other close relations and that if they don't get the same time, energy, or consideration from special people, they feel intense anger (and shame rise). Their anger is evident in romantic relationships, where jealousy becomes the predominant emotion accompanying their outrage around having their intimate relationships threatened.

I have always been a jealous person and felt a lot of shame about it. I hate being jealous because I can't shake the feeling that the person I've worked so hard to become perfect (inside and out) might be looking elsewhere. The silliest things can arouse my jealousy. However, I figured out in therapy that I do think given the amount of work and time I put into being the person I am for my husband gives me a bit of entitlement over his time and attention.

—Carrie, 29, teacher

The focus on idealism is also channeled into other projects aside from romantic relationships. The Sexual One is intense and focused when they have chosen a passion, and their passions are typically idealistic and principled. They can be magnetic, albeit very serious, crusaders and will relentlessly strive to ensure that they accomplish their mission.

Sexual Ones are afraid that if they thoroughly let themselves unleash their passion and fire, they will disgrace themselves and the people they care about because they will misbehave. They always feel constricted and struggle with the pull between their intense and passionate desires for freedom, expression, and the need to be appropriate and measured. They quickly become inflexible, particularly regarding errors, missteps, and mistakes. As a result, they may channel their criticality and exacting standards toward others they believe aren't working as hard as they are.

## THE ZEALOUS CRUSADER

When narcissism, Type One, and the Sexual instinct combine, it creates the archetype of the Zealous Crusader. This narcissistic subtype primarily focuses on the righteousness of their convictions and their entitlement to exact their standards onto other people. They are drawn to positions of power and authority to see their influence on others.

At the lower end of the narcissistic spectrum, this subtype displays contempt and disdain toward anything that doesn't meet their standards. They are more overtly disapproving than the other two Type One narcissistic subtypes and are generally more visibly arrogant. They take pride in their appearance and spend a lot of time, energy, and effort ensuring they are physically and sexually desirable to their mates or a potential mate. However, they hide their preoccupation with their beauty more than other narcissistic subtypes because they typically view vanity as a superficial or plebeian preoccupation. At first, they can appear quite austere yet meticulous about how they dress, behave, and project an air of moral elitism. Some may adopt intentionally average, shabby styles to demonstrate their focus on inner development, while others may enjoy expensive, well-tailored (but "tasteful") clothing that communicates the image of being "put together." The peacocking evident in the Sexual instinct shows through intellectual, moral, or ethical prowess. Of course, they want others to find them desirable but are reluctant to admit this to most people, except perhaps their intimate partners.

All narcissists in the romantic phase of relationships can engage in love bombing.[1] However, the Zealous Crusader views potential love interests as opportunities to prove their worthiness (and superiority) through demonstrations of moral fortitude. They are incredibly aggressive in their romantic pursuits and know quickly who and what they want, and stake claim to their desires in a way that a non-narcissistic One might find inappropriate.

> When I saw my wife, I knew that I was going to marry her. However, I needed to ensure that she could be the strong woman I knew she could be, so I walked over and started quizzing her about her religious and moral ideals. After 30 minutes of her fielding my questions, I told her that she would be my wife, but only after courting for three months. She rejected me, but sure enough, two days later she called, and the rest is history.

> —Akente, 53, government contractor

**The Zealous Crusader.**

The Zealous Crusader feels entitled to whatever they've deemed worthy of their attention. The strong superego of the One mixes with their narcissistic traits and the fiery passion of the Sexual instinct, and the result is a simultaneously rigid yet extreme personality. Like the other two Type One narcissistic subtypes, they are incredibly inflexible in their positions, beliefs, and standards. This subtype, however, will more readily show their rage if someone questions their moral or ethical authority. Because the arena of their narcissistic fear most acutely presents itself in the Sexual arena, their partners, children, or close friends often bear the brunt of their impressive tempers. They may fly into fits of rage over the slightest indiscretion, error, or mistake, all the while insisting that their rage is warranted due to the other person's inattentiveness to pertinent details.

People with this subtype, like many narcissists, are often charming, albeit there is frequently an unsettling or restrained wildness that can be off-putting (for a good snapshot of the disquieting nature of this subtype, research Rasputin). However, the defense strategies of the Sexual instinct increase their prowess in ensuring their immediate gratification needs are met, particularly in the domain of creative endeavors, personal projects, or close relationships. They often understand the value of charm and finesse and can, for a time, demonstrate those qualities to get what they want. However, their frustration, chronic disappointment, and rage are so close to the surface that they quickly shift their emotional expression and drop the appropriate facade quickly. They can be destabilizing forces for others because of their emotional lability. Often swinging between the poles of rigidity and explosiveness, people learn quickly to walk on eggshells to avoid upsetting them or transgressing their standards and expectations.

At the higher ranges of narcissism, this subtype can be incredibly cruel and vindictive under the guise of perfectionism. They may insult, berate, or humiliate people out of a pious belief that they are helping to improve others' lives. This propensity toward correction is particularly true of their intimates. People outside their inner circle may be surprised to learn of the abusive tactics this subtype uses to maintain control over their significant others, families, and loved ones.

He was the most upstanding, ethical, and responsible man I had ever met. About one year into the marriage, things began to turn sour quickly. He began insisting I dress less provocatively. He then began controlling my food, telling me when and how to exercise, and insisted I keep a journal of my self-defeating or negative thoughts so he could check them. He would fly into rages about the smallest things out of place in the house. I was completely terrorized. After his rage fits, he would always say to me: "I'm just trying to help you improve. It's because I love you."

—Danielle, 47, stay-at-home mom

This subtype's intensity is frequently too much for most people who encounter them. They demonstrate an air of moral superiority and generally exhibit a lack of boundaries for those they consider under their control. Many proclaim that others would fall into a rabbit hole of amoral or sinful debauchery without their watchful guidance and intervention strategies. Ironically, however, this subtype is the most prone to hypocritical trapdoor transgressions. Some may blatantly engage in behaviors they harshly judge while seeing no problem with their hypocrisy. Others will hide their misdeeds, particularly if they are well-known or hold positions of power or authority in their professional lives. A client shared with me an example of her father's trapdoor tendencies.

> We were Pentecostal, and [my father] was the pastor of our church. He was vehemently against extramarital affairs and was particularly obsessed with preaching about the sins of homosexuality, as he saw it. It was shocking when we found out he'd been having an affair with an 18-year-old teenage boy in the congregation. He justified his behavior claiming that God ordained his relationship and that, somehow, it wasn't a homosexual affair because of his special relationship with God. It was devastating, but that kind of "do as I say, not as I do" mentality was quite common for my father.
>
> —Marisol, 33, therapist

This subtype's fiery demeanor and moral justifications can make them dangerous as they are frequently unrepentant for their behavior. All Ones loathe (and deeply fear) criticism. Still, when narcissism is present, they reject all criticism (even the slightest or most valid suggestions) and lash out against anyone who questions their moral or ethical authority. If particularly psychologically compromised, they can justify even the most horrific acts. Cult leader David Koresh was very likely this subtype. His dedication and belief in protecting his congregation that led to the showdown at the Branch Davidian compound in 1993 exemplify this subtype's zealous grandiosity. The horrific tragedy that resulted in seventy-nine deaths was widely publicized but it was only later that the public learned of Koresh's psychological and religious abuse tactics.[2] Convinced of his own divinity as a prophet he could admittedly be quite kind. However, he favored female congregants, and allegedly raped and molested some underage women claiming that their obedience was ordained by God. He believed in a primitive existence and was staunchly against modern conveniences and luxuries.

Koresh indoctrinated the children of the congregation against their parents and was notoriously hypocritical regarding sex and pleasure. He was allowed to indulge in sexual activity with his many brides, while other members were often restricted or shamed for sexual desire or activity. The Branch Davidian compound lacked running water and other conveniences, however Koresh, paranoid about the impending apocalypse, stockpiled advanced weapons and firearms. Even after some of the remaining children were rescued from the compound, Koresh's indoctrination was still firmly in place, whereby they conceptualized the world in stark terms of good and evil.[3]

In all cases, this subtype's lack of empathy, fiery and zealous convictions, and jealousy can make them quite challenging to deal with due to the overall psychological resistance to considering that they could be wrong. Ones, as a rule, are afraid of making mistakes, errors, and most of all being fundamentally bad, but if even a twinge of narcissism is present within the One's psyche, admitting error or mistakes is virtually impossible. Their resistance or inability to take responsibility for their errors makes reconciling any differences of opinion or conflict unlikely because (like most narcissists), they struggle to recognize their role in problems.

**When Dealing with a Zealous Crusader:**

1. It's vital to have a strong sense of who you are when around this subtype because they easily infiltrate people's superego and self-conceptions and elicit feelings of unworthiness due to their criticism. Develop a safe relationship with a mental health professional who can help you hold onto yourself when the Crusader flares up and attacks your character.

2. This subtype can be confusing because they are by turns charming and punitive. They can be incredibly passionate and loving one minute. Still, you quickly realize that their love is conditional based on how much they believe you're matching their expectations, effort, and ideals. Be prepared for the roller coaster of feeling as though you're a disappointment or failing them.

3. Notice whether you're developing compulsive or unhealthy tendencies to keep this subtype happy. Eating disorders, extreme exercise routines, excessive cleaning, or feelings of guilt or shame around ordinary human desires are prevalent because this subtype's judgment is always just below the surface.

4. Their jealousy can be overwhelming, particularly if you're romantically involved with this subtype. It's not uncommon for people to feel like even speaking to someone else is a transgression to their relationship with the Crusader. Try to keep a realistic perspective about appropriate and acceptable relationship behaviors. If the Crusader becomes abusive, seek professional help and resources to help free yourself from increasing abuse as this subtype, if severely compromised, can be prone to violence.

# 10

## Type Two

### The Charming Supporter

Narcissistic Subtypes:
*Self-Preservation Two: The Entitled Caregiver*
*Social Two: The Flattering Networker*
*Sexual Two: The Manipulative Seducer*

#### SELF-PRESERVATION TWO

The Self-Preservation Two is a bit of an outlier because while they are focused on their impact on others and whether their help and attention are appreciated, they focus on their immediate needs and concerns. The Self-Preservation instinct makes this subtype slightly more direct about their expectations and requirements than the Sexual or Social Two subtypes. Claudio Naranjo called this subtype the "me first" Two because while they still focus on others' expectations, desires, and needs, they offer their support and care, hoping that they will have their needs met. However, they often expect that others meet their needs first before they're willing to tend to the needs of others. Hence the term, "me first."

Self-Preservation Twos excel at anticipating and tending to others' basic needs. They naturally track people's preferences and attempt to earn their right to be cared for through their caretaking endeavors. They believe that if they attune themselves to people's favorite foods, comforts, preferences, and desires, they are paying into a proverbial account that will afford them the right to be cared for. They are quite adept at taking care of themselves, but they feel more loved and supported if someone is willing to take care of them. Because Twos are transactional, they don't necessarily trust that others will help and love them unless they do things for others. Self Pres Twos love to feed others, and they are like archetypal mothers constantly monitoring whether people have everything they need to be happy, healthy, and comforted. They make excellent caretakers, and they take immense pride in their ability to care for other people.

> I always know what other people want and need. Even if I don't give it to them, I have always intuited what's needed. When I was a little girl, I learned everyone's favorite foods, and I loved cooking for people. I still do this today with my own family. It's always made me feel warm and fuzzy when I can give people I care about what they want and need. Not to sound egotistical, but I'm just really good at it!
>
> —Paulina, 34, stay-at-home mom

Self-Preservation Twos are simultaneously assertive and sweet. There is a palpable pushiness to their suggestions, offers for help, and prescriptions for others. They are prideful and confident about their caretaking abilities and, with healthy self-esteem, are sure of their innate worth and value to others. They are often proponents of self-care and occasional pampering but feel guilty for focusing on themselves too much. They can become slavish to the demands and desires of others for a period and then grow resentful and insist that others acknowledge and pamper them. Depending on their level of extroversion, they may not always directly express their displeasure. They are masterful at subtle hints, clues, and nonverbal signals to let people in their spheres know that they aren't pleased (sighing, slamming dishes, the silent treatment).

They are militant about their homes and how chores and tasks are executed. If they are parents, they are often excellent home managers, instilling their children (and partners) with a sense of responsibility and care toward their obligations and duties. They are always worried that their basic needs at any given moment will be overlooked, so they may work tirelessly to ensure that they're tending to others, so other people don't forget about them. Many harbor fears about being homeless, hungry, or destitute if other people forget their influence and necessity in their lives.

The Self-Preservation Two is personified adeptly in Disney's *Cinderella*. Oddly enough, Cinderella, the wicked stepsisters and stepmother, and the Fairy Godmother are all Self-Preservation Twos. It makes me wonder if Walt Disney didn't have a Self Pres Two in his life and intuitively wanted to show all the various faces of the subtype. Cinderella is the long-suffering, sweet, and obedient daughter whom her stepmother and stepsisters abuse to meet their needs. Finally, she is rewarded through the magic of the Fairy Godmother, who bestows her with a beautiful gown and, of course, the magic slippers so she can go to the swanky ball with Prince Charming.

Most Self-Preservation Twos harbor a secret desire of being whisked away from their service to others by a proverbial Prince Charming. The feeling of having to earn their keep through hard work and attention to others is met with a corresponding sadness and fear that they're not loved simply for existing. Conversely, the Fairy Godmother represents the benevolence and loving, motherly desire to make someone else's dreams come true. While Cinderella represents the long-suffering martyrdom, the Self Pres Two can't escape. As for the wicked stepsisters, we'll explore in the next section how narcissism and entitlement can subvert the Self Pres Two's generosity and focus on others into an almost exclusively selfish and demanding character.

## THE ENTITLED CAREGIVER

While researching this subtype, I looked for healthy and well-adapted representations of this subtype in films and literature. Of course, they exist, but this subtype's narcissistic subversion abounds in media, perhaps because the characteristic generosity, warmth, and nurturing qualities of the non-narcissistic Self-Preservation Two become strikingly discordant when narcissism is present. This subtype is demanding, entitled, difficult to please, and often petulant. Fascinatingly, the Entitled Caregiver is still highly aware of others' needs and desires. They are keen to fulfill others' desires and expectations as a means of seduction. This subtype believes, like other Twos, that they must earn their keep. However, they also overestimate their contributions and believe that others would not survive without their attention.

This subtype can be incredibly materialistic and may be highly acquisitive. However, because the Two superego defense mechanisms still tell them that they mustn't be selfish, they hide their materialism through displays of generosity. If they are only mildly narcissistic, they may break from their selfishness and have moments where their desire to support, care for, and help others is genuine. Most Twos, narcissistic or not, are unaware of their expectations for reciprocity. Pride prevents them from naming and owning that they indeed harbor feelings of resentment (however slight) because they are so attuned to others' needs, while others don't seem to be as adept at tracking theirs. However, narcissism's inherent self-centeredness and egocentricity make it virtually impossible to recognize their expectations.

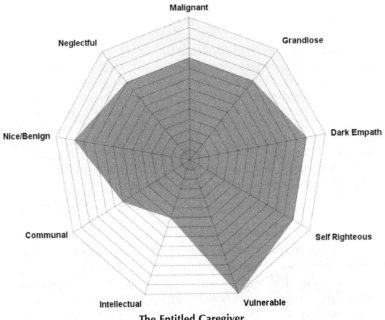

**The Entitled Caregiver.**

Their egos are entrenched in the belief of their altruism, indispensability, and kindness. They may be grumpy, cantankerous, and never tangibly help or support anyone, yet still believe that they are positive, loving, and kind to others. If their narcissism is pervasive, they believe their presence is the gift they give others and that because of their mere existence, they deserve pampering and spoiling. All Twos take great pride in their ability to anticipate others' needs. Still, because they are so egocentric and self-involved, they often filter other people's preferences through their lens and impose their will, gifts, and prescriptions on others based on what they want, rather than what the other person needs. This can be a problem for all Twos, but the gap between their intuition about others' needs and what others need can be significant with this narcissistic subtype.

They insist on having the best and are openly demanding, pouty, or even rageful if others do not satisfy their desires. Some are less overtly angry and may display their displeasure through the silent treatment or passive-aggressive displays. Cinderella's wicked stepmother and stepsisters also illustrate this subtype's potentially punitive and sadistic nature. They can become so convinced of their entitlement, and when mixed with their propensity toward militance and temper tantrums, they can be harsh and unfair and justify their punishment of others for not recognizing their obvious contributions, love, and support:

> My mother was a bit of a tyrant. She could be incredibly generous at times. She tended to buy me lavish gifts. She bought me a nice car when I turned 16, and then one day, when she was angry with me for not doing something she asked properly, she sold it back to the dealership and got me a cheaper, used car. Her generosity was always followed by punishment. She would wake me up in the middle of the night to do odd things like clean the kitchen or reorganize the pantry, but it didn't matter how I did it; it was never right. I spent my whole life trying to please my mother, but she couldn't be pleased. I get the feeling she wanted me to thank her for giving me life; in fact, one day she told me that I should be grateful that she kept me alive all those years.
>
> —Violet, 40, real estate agent

If their empathy is severely limited or nonexistent, this subtype can be unreasonable, emotionally sadistic, and chronically unsatisfied. The Entitled Caregiver very frequently functions by a "do as I say, not as I do" mentality and can be judgmental and controlling of other people while expecting that they have the freedom to do whatever they want, whenever they want. They are particularly careless with other people's money and have difficulty denying themselves whatever they want. They may resort to cheating, lying, or even stealing to ensure that their survival needs (or frivolous luxuries) are satiated. They may buy themselves only the best clothing, food, vacations, and luxury items and be shockingly frugal or cheap when acquiring these things for other people (even their children or partners).

They often oscillate through friends and intimates and can at times sadistically shower attention on one friend, child, coworker, or family member while blatantly ignoring or snubbing others, only to change their focus in a few months, weeks, or days. They focus their attention on those who pay attention to them and have little use for anyone else. Typically, the object of their current affection is anyone who will indulge their desires, whims, and demands.

The Entitled Caregiver is convinced about their entitlement and truly believes that they deserve the royal treatment. However, most appear as supportive, helpful, or generous while simultaneously taking credit for others' successes and triumphs. They believe that their influence (like the Fairy Godmother) is the magical ingredient to other people's good fortune. The following interview snippet illustrates the grandiose self-importance of this subtype perfectly:

> Me: "So tell me how you tangibly help other people?"
> Levitra: "I don't help people unless I want to. I choose whom I help and who fails honestly."

Me: "How do you decide who gets your attention?"

Levitra: "I know how to pick a winner. I chose my husband because I knew I could push him to become successful, and then I would never have to worry about anything again. I would never be with a man who was a loser or didn't know how to make money. I require a lot, and I'm a prize. I know that about myself."

Me: "So, how do you help your husband?"

Levitra: "I took care of his children and kept this house running for 30 years. I was lucky enough to have help, but I managed everything and everyone. He would probably be working at a gas station somewhere if it weren't for me. So yes, I deserve the best. I earned it."

—Levitra, 63, socialite

## When Dealing with an Entitled Caregiver:

1. Be prepared for various forms of pouting, tantrums, and passive aggression. Some people of this subtype may overtly express their displeasure, but more frequently, they will demonstrate their disappointment through childlike tantrums and a very loud withdrawal of their attention, praise, or help. It's best to ignore these tantrums because it can reinforce their belief that bad behavior will engender desirable results.

2. Remember that this subtype, on some level, wants to please you. However, they have difficulty focusing on others for too long because of their compromised empathy. Have patience and consider that because of this subtype's desire to please others, they can be sensitive to rejection or disapproval, which displays through entitlement and pushiness.

3. Do not be reticent with praise or compliments if they're genuine. They grow more frustrated and angrier if bereft of attention. Often, however, they will go to great lengths to get attention when they're feeling insecure or deprived.

4. It's important to let them know when they've been unkind, selfish, or self-centered in such a way that you feel violated, railroaded, or overlooked. Constructive behavioral shame may trigger a temper tantrum or angry outburst, but it helps define your boundaries and limitations. If they still defy your limits and relational expectations, be very clear about what you will and won't tolerate. They can be aggressive and fierce when challenged but showing them you won't be bullied is crucial.

5. The Entitled Caregiver can be amenable to empathy modeling more than other narcissistic subtypes. They want others to see them as empathic and loving. While they may not *feel* empathy to any significant degree, they can learn to model and emulate compassion, so others view them favorably.

# SOCIAL TWO

As a card-carrying Millennial child of the nineties, I am not too proud to admit that as a thirteen-year-old middle schooler, I knew every line of the 1995 film *Clueless* starring Alicia Silverstone. My cousin Kimberly and I watched the movie on repeat during sleepovers and dreamed of the days when we too would become affluent Beverly Hills kids with mansions, limitless credit cards, tons of friends, and convertibles. (I'm still waiting for that dream to materialize.) While my still intact memory of the film's ridiculous dialogue might make for an exciting read, I will spare you. However, what is worth reflecting on is a familiar trope that appeared in many teen movies of the 1980s and 1990s. A gregarious, attractive, popular, and affluent kid (usually a woman) befriends the unpopular, unattractive, lowly nerd, or homely kid. They introduce this poor, slovenly charity case to a world of friends, beauty, dating, and a high school life worth living. Without analyzing these messages' problematic cultural and social assumptions on young impressionable minds, it is worth recognizing the archetype of the Social Two.

Professor Higgins in *My Fair Lady*, Glinda in the musical *Wicked*, Elle Woods in *Legally Blonde*, and Lisa Turtle in *Saved by the Bell* are all iterations of the same archetypal role. This character often relishes assisting the socially deprived, aesthetically challenged wretch find their confidence by improving their lives (in the way that the helper sees appropriate). While not all Social Twos are concerned with increasing others' popularity, nor are they all women focused on money, clothes, or aesthetics, the impulse to be of assistance to people as a means of being socially desirable and valued exemplifies the focus of the Social Two.

As we learned in chapter 4, people with a dominant Social Instinct believe their survival depends on tracking inclusion/exclusion, politics, norms, power structures, and how to best serve the group at large without being alienated. The Social Two focuses their instinctual survival energy on the social world and becomes a connector of people. The Social Two wants to be the glue between others to feel worthy of the love and attention that they crave. Overall, the desire to be consequential to the group helps create a gregarious, charming, and ambitious variation to the Two's overall need to be pleasing and loving.

Claudio Naranjo said the Social Two was "seducing the world," and if you've ever seen one in action, you'd know that their considerable charm and interpersonal intelligence are impressive. The Social Two needs to see their willpower and influence reflected in those around them. So, while Cher Horowitz in the film *Clueless* may have been an over-the-top caricature of a spoiled, bratty, Beverly Hills teenager, her desire to "do well" by her school and family is indicative of the genuine desire of all Social Twos. They are often well-meaning and want to "do good" in the world. Many glean great pleasure out of playing matchmaker to others because, as my friend Jenny told me years ago about her propensity for matchmaking, "being the impetus for two people's love is the greatest feeling in the world." At that time, she was five-for-five on successful love connections; I can only imagine how many other lives she's touched through her interpersonal warmth nineteen years later.

Being someone who connects people who need or want each other helps the Social Two hold power in the world and affords them immense importance and significance in the lives of those they touch. Would you forget the person who introduced you to a great love or a teacher or counselor who taught you to your potential? Their social service helps feed their identity as consequential and needed and staves off the anxiety of their core fear of being irrelevant to others.

In *Clueless*, Cher spent much of the film playing matchmaker to her classmates and teachers. Her character arc centered on her journey of coming to terms with her self-interested, obnoxious behavior and arrogant willfulness so she could become worthy of love. Her pushiness was the character's most "toxic" trait causing others to feel railroaded, disregarded, and manipulated. Meanwhile, Cher was often perplexed by people's reactions to her well-intentioned efforts to help. Many Social Twos report feeling blindsided and hurt when others misunderstand or misinterpret their attempts to help others.

Overall, Social Twos are excellent advocates for others in need. Because of their innate understanding and sensitivity to the feelings and desires of others, they often utilize their coercive and persuasive charm to "do good" for the world around them. Twos' social engagement can take many forms, from being a schoolteacher who shapes the lives of young children, to political activism fighting to feed the hungry, to a small business owner who develops unusually personal relationships with their customers. They can also be like my friend Jenny, who became a choir teacher to mentor budding classical vocalists after pursuing a career as an opera singer. Whatever their chosen discipline, talents, or skill set, Social Twos thrive when in a service relationship with the group. In undergrad, I was involved in campus leadership activities and spent much time in the Student Affairs office. During that time, I developed relationships with many Twos who were caring, engaging, and sometimes even a little nosy yet still charming. Most were student advisors who relished dispensing their advice, expertise, and attention to budding students. Many of them are still there today as they realized they found their calling working in roles where they can mentor, advise, or manage others toward a common goal.

John, a Social Two, youth minister and finance manager, who participated in my research study, perfectly articulated the othered-focus of the Social Two: "I give to others hoping that what I put out will eventually come back to me. It's what I do for the kids I mentor and the people I manage. I love it; it's why I do what I do." Social Twos need to be significant to the group and derive their identity from what they can offer the group. They measure their effectiveness by how much others appreciate and acknowledge their contributions. The hope is that the more they give, the more love they will receive in return. They often enjoy working with young people or youth as they can shape the minds and paths of their young minds, or they enjoy being the power behind the throne and find significance in helping others become successful.

## THE FLATTERING NETWORKER

What happens when self-awareness and empathy are eroded in a person whose self-conception rests on their role as someone who services the needs of others? You end up with a personality type that can have a tough time recognizing why their efforts to help, support, or nurture others engender anger, hostility, or abandonment.

The Flattering Networker has a grandiose vision of themselves that often overestimates and overvalues their importance in the lives of others. As we saw with the Entitled Caregiver, there is a propensity with narcissistic Twos toward inflated entitlement masked by false humility or exaggerated martyrdom. They not only hope that they're indispensable in the lives of others (as is typical in all Twos), but also insist they are integral to the lives of others. They believe that others wouldn't survive or thrive without them. The characteristic core fear of the Two of being worthless or inconsequential has devolved into blind self-assurance that others could not function without the help, support, guidance, or other gifts they provide. The dominant social instinct adds a healthy dose of prideful judgmentalism to the otherwise sympathetic psychic structure of the Two. This creates a character who may become convinced that whatever they do for others is for the best, even if it is cruel, undermining, or selfishly motivated. They may become arrogant and boastful about their ability to "know what other people want" and often give people gifts or perform deeds that are simply their projection of what others *should* want rather than what they want.

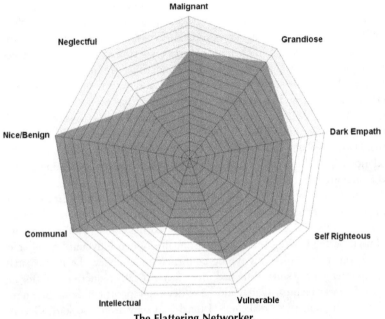

**The Flattering Networker.**

Ironically, the Flattering Networker has a nominal amount of cognitive empathy and social awareness. The Flattering Networker's intuitive understanding of others' wants, needs, and desires remains intact. It increases their propensity to flatter or even lie to others to get what they want. Unlike other narcissistic types, the Flattering Networker can appear interested in other people because of the Two's natural effusiveness and interpersonal intelligence. Nonetheless, they often have little else on their mind except ensuring the satiation of their immediate needs. They always have an agenda, and their ability to conceal their plans will depend on their relative social skill and awareness.

The Flattering Networker is primarily triggered in the social arena, so considerable gossip-mongering, backbiting, and angry jealousy are directed at those they believe are getting the attention, admiration, praise, or recognition they want from their group. When narcissism is present in the Social Two, their natural propensity toward aspiring to popularity and likability as a means of being significant to others devolves into a callous lack of concern for others, over-focusing on their reputation, over-the-top flattering, or gossiping in this narcissistic subtype.

The Flattering Networker typically displays histrionic or theatrically dramatic behaviors to garner attention from others. The inability to care about the concerns or welfare of other people is a primary feature of anyone with empathy deficits. However, for the Flattering Networker, the incongruence between their self-image as someone caring, loving, and kind combined with their social ruthlessness, selfishness, and single-minded focus on what they want or need makes it difficult for them to maintain healthy relationships with others.

Most Social Twos have a wide social net and can move between social circles, adopting a slightly different mask depending on what pleases each group. Healthy Social Twos often develop warm and lasting connections with many people because of their often-keen interpersonal intelligence. However, the Flattering Networker usually has a trail of failed or abandoned social relationships behind them, representing their difficulty in maintaining deep connections with others.

Billy is an upbeat, rosy-cheeked, and gregarious twenty-three-year-old man who recently graduated with a degree in communication. He wrote the adjectives "Nice," "Kind," "Anxious," "Loving," and "Fun" to describe himself on the Lexical Analysis Questionnaire. When Billy and I finally met via Zoom to complete his typing confirmation interview, he immediately complimented my shirt. Billy had uncharacteristically seductive ease (for his age). The way he immediately moved to develop rapport before we began the session—he wanted to make sure I liked him right from the start. Overall, Billy was warm, albeit slightly effusive for someone I had just met. As is customary in a typing interview, I asked him to describe himself a bit more after reading to him the five adjectives he used in his original questionnaire:

> So basically, I'm amazing! Just kidding . . . I guess I see myself as fun, funny, sympathetic, popular, and charming. I absolutely love people, and people love me. And I love all kinds of people. So yeah, I'm a people person. People generally like me because I'm friendly and try to be nice to everyone. I grew up doing talent shows, so I know how to lay on the charm. Don't take advantage of me, though, because I can take my attention away really quick; I'll treat you like royalty if you treat me the same way! My biggest pet peeve is when people are ungrateful or unkind. I always say, "If you can't say something nice, don't say anything at all." I'm a true southern boy in that respect. I have a fierce papa bear vibe, and I have a way of getting what I want when I really want something. I guess that's me in a nutshell.
>
> —Billy, 23, student

It became increasingly more apparent as the interview continued that Billy's self-conception, albeit falsely humble at the outset of the interview, turned out to be far more grandiose than his immediate presentation would suggest. As we continued, I wanted to know what made Billy upset as he kept referring to "resentments" he sometimes carried for others.

Me: "So what happens when you become resentful?"

Billy: "I generally get what I want, so I don't have to be resentful, but there are occasions when someone who shouldn't have gotten something gets something I want. . . . so like when Curtis got the party chair [position] over me Junior year, I was super pissed. I mean, I love Curtis; he's one of my best friends. But he didn't deserve it. I make better grades than him, and I know way more people than him and plan better parties. Everybody knew it. So I couldn't understand when everyone voted for him over me. I was the obvious choice. . . . I told a few people what Curtis told me about our Chapter President . . . I mean, I kept the secret long enough, but he told me that he reported our President for this specific violation of a national standard, which made our President get in a lot of trouble. I just didn't see any need to keep that secret anymore. I mean, I smiled to Curtis's face, but I just planted the seed and watched it spread."

Billy went on for a bit longer, justifying the vengeful divulgence of his "friend's" secret without the emotional micro-expressions or verbal cues that typically accompany remorse or guilt. The more he talked about his revenge on Curtis, the more irritable and righteous he became. When I asked if he felt like the punishment fit "the crime," he arrogantly retorted, "That's what happens when you mess with me," shrugged and laughed. There was, however, a great awareness of what he believed might have been my judgment of his behavior. After divulging a particularly unsavory emotion or action he had taken against others, he would issue recovery statements such as, "I promise I'm not as mean as I sound," and "You must think I'm terrible." In my estimation, his recovery statements had less to do with what he did to Curtis and more to do with my *perception* of what he did to Curtis.

It is not uncommon for narcissistic Twos to believe that they "never say anything bad" about anyone when, like Billy, they harbor many grievances toward others that they frequently discuss with others. The narcissistic Two is incapable of accurately assessing their behavior in the eyes of others. They often appraise all their behavior as charitable and kind and others as ungrateful, rejecting, or opportunistic.

Superficiality is a classic component of narcissistic behavior. People are a means to an end. Twos, however, must contend with the added layer of their type-specific fear of uncovering their less than altruistic motivations for fear of being revealed as a "terrible" or "bad" person. Pride functions overtime in the Flattering Networker to prevent them from becoming aware of the impact of their interpersonal carelessness because they cannot imagine that they could be interpersonally careless. Dr. Claudio Naranjo contended that pride blocks self-reflection even for non-pathological Twos' therapy and self-analysis. Thus, for the narcissistic Two, superficiality is a thick armor against intense fears of worthlessness.

Flattery can be compulsive for many Twos, but it is a manipulative strategy designed to garner more power for the Flattering Networker. All Social Twos enjoy being the "power behind the throne," but the Flattering Networker typically positions themselves to overthrow it. If others like them and trust them enough to divulge their confidences, they utilize that trust as social capital to reinforce their significance and gain clout or standing in their respective groups.

For the Flattering Networker, the instinctual social fear of being cast out of the group is coupled with the Two's core fear of being inconsequential and then further distorted by an empathy deficit resulting in cutthroat ambition and a propensity toward superficial and shallow relationships. It is not surprising that most of their relationships end in a perceived betrayal or simply in the discarding of others if they do not provide the positive, altruistic, or generous mirroring that the Two craves.

The psychospiritual structure of the narcissistic Social Two also allows their empathy deficits to remain more hidden than the other narcissistic subtypes. The social desirability of someone charming, helpful, and seductive also makes it difficult for them to seek treatment that may help them develop greater empathy for others. Pride and the need to see themselves as generous often prevent them from embarking on the work of uncovering their self-defeating qualities.

The Flattering Networker can be immensely successful, garnering considerable cultural capital and political or social power. In a culture obsessed with reality-show drama and salacious gossip, their most challenging qualities have found a stage in cheap and easy cultural entertainment. However, if their narcissism is extreme or accompanied by other psychological or emotional disorders, they are wildly inflated and entitled, believing that any treatment of others is justified. They can be cruel with their rebukes of others when people don't behave according to their prescriptions. They may engage in frequent dramatic, histrionic displays designed to manipulate others into consenting to their needs or hatch elaborate plans of revenge to avenge their pride.

## When Dealing with a Flattering Networker:

1. State your boundaries. This subtype can be incredibly aggressive because they believe they indeed must be involved in even the most minor details of every decision. If they're being pushy or overbearing, tell them, with as little emotional energy as possible, and ask that they give you some space to re-engage with them again if it's appropriate.

2. Their pride can sometimes be frustrating, mainly if they've made a miscalculation, error, or improperly judged a situation. Rather than calling them stubborn, prideful, or overbearing, suggest alternative ways to approach the problem and the individuals involved. They are highly

interpersonal, and while their empathy may be somewhat compromised, they still want to be effectual.

3. When stressed, this subtype is duplicitous, conniving, and vindictive. If they begin demonstrating these behaviors, try "gray-rocking," a technique where you divulge as little emotional content or personal information as possible during communication (thereby appearing a bit like a gray rock, hence the term). Disengaging with them altogether may prove difficult because they can be very pushy, but limiting your emotional involvement may save you both energy and grief.

## SEXUAL TWO

The 1988 animated film *Who Framed Roger Rabbit?* was a technological marvel that combined live actors and animation to create a fantastic film-noir-mystery heralded by audiences and critics alike. The dopey yet endearing main character Roger Rabbit was no genius, but from the moment we saw his voluptuous, redheaded wife, Jessica Rabbit, you knew she was trouble and that he was no fool. She was beautiful, mysterious, slightly dangerous, and oddly scandalous for a children's movie character. Jessica Rabbit, voiced by actress Kathleen Turner, was a perfect animated representation of a Sexual Two. In the film, Jessica is a complex character that you're never quite sure about because she is simultaneously sweet and vicious, loving and a little sadistic, devoted to Roger but also slightly shady. Roger suspects she may be cheating on him with the CEO of Toontown, Marvin Acme.

Okay, I know, the plot's ridiculousness is a bit distracting (not to mention Roger is a literal rabbit and Jessica is a human being). Still, the characterizations perfectly satirized the campy mysteriousness of the 1940s film noir setting. The archetype of the femme fatale is a staple throughout film-noir history and almost invariably a caricature of the Sexual Two. They channel the desire to be needed, consequential and special in the lives of others in the sexual arena and make it their business to become irresistible to their chosen mates. Like Jessica Rabbit, Sexual Twos, are often highly desirable because they recognize the inherent power available through seductiveness and embodying the object of their desire's fantasies.

No matter the gender identification, this subtype approaches intimate relationships, friendships, and even work relationships to become everything the other person would ever need. They are attentive, generous, loving, effusive, accommodating, and sensual. They are masterful at flirting and are often accused of flirting even when they don't intend to seduce. The Sexual Twos energy goes toward becoming someone impossible to reject.

Sexual Twos desperately want to be loved and valued simply by being human, but like all image types, they believe they must become someone else to be loved. Therein lies the dilemma. The Sexual Two, like all Sexual subtypes, crave intimacy, connection, and the security of an unbreakable bond with their chosen intimates. However, because the Sexual Two often molds themselves into what they believe the other person most desires, they feel insecure that others love them truly for who they are.

Claudio Naranjo taught that this subtype displays palpable aggression and can assault others with pushiness and seductiveness.[1] They can be incredibly forward and very rarely, if ever, take no for an answer. They believe that by sheer force of their willfulness and determination, they can plow through any obstacle and make anyone like or even love them. They are more aggressive than Eights because their identities are contingent upon other people's attention, praise, and approval.

> As much as I hate to admit it, I want certain special people's approval. So I become whatever they want. I know how to be a fantasy. If you want someone assertive, I'll be assertive. If you want an intellectual, I'll learn all about whatever you're into. If you want someone sweet and subservient, I can be that too. I don't usually have to ask what people want me to be; I typically just know. But if I can't figure it out, or if I've miscalculated, I'll just ask them point-blank: what kind of man do you want. And boom. I'll be that man.
>
> —Curt, 26, law student

This subtype's desire to be desirable mimics the Sexual Three; however, with the Sexual Two, their emotional warmth and genuine desire to be of service to their chosen intimates differentiates them from the Three's typically colder presentation. Their devotion, however, comes at a cost. They, like all Twos, can become frustrated and dissatisfied if others don't recognize their efforts. In this case, they may quickly help, support, or guide others that aren't in their intimate circle of care. Work colleagues, peripheral friends, or family may never see the Sexual Twos resentment. However, those they've deemed their "special people" may be all too aware of the consequences of overlooking, taking for granted, or discounting the Sexual Twos feelings, needs, or efforts. Because they are adept at becoming the ideal partner both internally and externally, they eventually feel they deserve the same special attention and care in return. They then grow despondent, sullen, or angry and can lash out at partners or intimates whom they believe aren't recognizing the great lengths they think they've traversed to give others the world.

Sexual Two's are afraid they are unworthy of love, attention, and affection and believe they must be the ideal lover, partner, and friend to earn others' devotion in return. They are outwardly often very confident and seductive, while inside, they feel an immense sadness that they must earn love. There is a considerable cost for both themselves and others for their tendency to mold themselves into the ideal. When healthy, they recognize the immense expectation they place on themselves, and subsequently, others, to appreciate and recognize their efforts to become the ideal intimate.

Suppose this subtype has moderate to high empathy. In that case, they can be incredibly listeners, empathetic and supportive confidants, and will put in the necessary time and work to nurture their relationships (which are everything to them). They want others to feel loved, supported, and protected by them and take great pleasure in their ability to ascertain and meet others' needs. They are typically more emotionally self-aware than the other Two subtypes. Many are reflective, original, and very emotionally expressive.

> I love being a therapist because it allows me to channel my ability to resonate and attune to others healthily and helpfully. I feel honored to share my clients' lives, struggles, and triumphs. I make myself available to my clients whenever they need to talk because I truly love being able to help them in real-time with issues. Of course, I've had to learn how to set boundaries, but I just can't turn people away in need. It's my honor to hold the space for people in therapy. I definitely know I'm in the right profession.
>
> —Kaleb, 43, psychotherapist

## THE AGGRESSIVE SEDUCER

> Once he hears to his heart's content, sails on, a wiser man.
> We know all the pains that the Greeks and Trojans once endured.
> on the spreading plain of Troy when the gods willed it so—
> all that comes to pass on the fertile earth, we know it all!
>
> —*The Odyssey*, 12.188–91[2]

In Greek mythology, the Sirens (a bird/woman hybrid creature) might have been the classical world's first introduction to the archetype of the Aggressive Seducer. The siren's song hauntingly danced across the sea before enticed sailors sailed to their deaths toward the dangerous cliffed island homes in the Mediterranean Sea. Legend says that none could resist the sirens' melodies and that the promise of wisdom, power, and beauty was all-consuming for the weary travelers. Yet the siren's promises come at the steep price of death. The myth of the Siren, a questionably sexist cautionary parable to young men about the dangers of beautiful women, recognized that what is alluring and seductive is not always good for us.

The Aggressive Seducer is almost invariably some mixture of grandiose, vulnerable, and self-righteous narcissists. Like all Sexual Twos, they strive to become the ideal object of their chosen interest's desire. However, the Aggressive Seducer has difficulty ascertaining how much seduction, aggression, and pushiness is too much because of their empathy deficits. They can be extraordinarily charming and adaptable. This ability affords them the ability to be masterfully manipulative. They focus almost exclusively on their own needs but sublimate this tendency into an apparent over-focus on the other person. They are just as transactional as the other Type Two narcissistic subtypes yet are the most adept at concealing their motives.

Their ability to mold themselves into different people to match the other's ideal is a strategy for meeting their insatiable attention needs. They may present as wildly different personas to different people in their lives to suit the other's expectations and desires. When stressed, Naranjo observed that the Sexual Two's aggression could be a bit like a cat playing with a mouse. This subtype has a predatory and relentless approach to getting what they

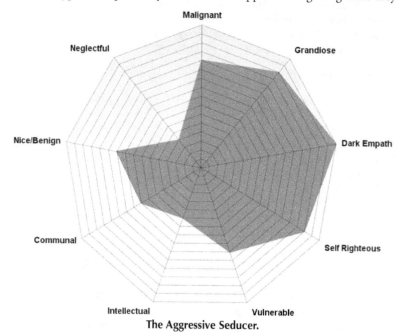

**The Aggressive Seducer.**

want. They also believe that no one should ever deny them anything they want or need. However, because Twos adjust to others' desires and fantasies, this subtype leaves a trail of broken hearts and lives in their wake. Their entitlement is demonstrated in the sexual arena, as they believe that they should always prevail in matters of love and lust.

Sexual aggression is common with this subtype (no matter the gender identification). They can be persistent and pushy beyond the point when someone has denied or rejected their advances. They cannot imagine why everyone doesn't want them, and rejection is unacceptable and a punishable offense. An interview with this subtype reveals the seductive hubris of this subtype and the potential callousness and exploitative tactics that the Aggressive Seducer displays:

> Blake: "I always get what I want. Sooner or later. I know I'm attractive, and I have no problem using my charm or sexuality to get what I want. I seduced my math teacher in college when I was failing. I'm not even gay, but I flirted like you wouldn't believe to guarantee my 'A'. I even 'accidentally' texted him a racy picture. Of course, I acted sufficiently mortified when he feigned outrage. But I knew the image would forever be burned in his mind. He asked me out once the class was over, and I got my 'A' and didn't respond. The whole thing gave me a sense of my power; I feel like I deserve attention. I haven't been rejected yet. But if I ever am, I would be angry."
>
> Me: "Why?"
>
> Blake: "Because I know I'm irresistible. I guess I wouldn't believe it if someone rejected me. I kind of feel like I'm everyone's type (laughs). There was a girl in college who said that I assaulted her, but you know how women can tease."

It's of the utmost importance to maintain power in their relationships. They strive to become the only person in the other's lives and, in the beginning, can seem sympathetic, kind, and over-the-top generous. They are the kings and queens of love bombing and can make someone feel immensely special until their subsequent potential love interest or favorite person comes along. Then they become impossible to please, disappointed, and blaming if they think the object of their once laser-focused attention deviates or wavers in any way.

Admiration and attention are of paramount importance for this subtype, and they need other people to bolster their feelings of desirability and significance. Much like non-narcissistic Sexual Twos, they diligently embody their chosen target's fantasy. They alter their clothing, voice, hair, and interests to reflect the other's tastes. However, unlike non-narcissistic Sexual Twos, the Aggressive Seducer rarely shares genuine emotional content. They are masterful at focusing on the other person, their interests, fantasies, and innermost thoughts to hopefully get the other person to fall in love with them. Their heightened ability to make people fall in love or lust with them bolsters their image as irresistible. They are unconcerned with deep feelings of love or connection because they aren't in touch with their emotional depth. However, they may fabricate emotional content, family histories, or additional relevant information to mirror the other person's expectations. Once they feel they've hooked their prey, many enjoy seeing what distances the other person will traverse to keep them engaged and satisfied. When the other person fails to meet their expectations or demands, they quickly turn spiteful, guilt-tripping, and belittling. They easily play the victim and often claim their deeds as selfless and devoted to the ungrateful others who took advantage of their generosity and love.

The Netflix hit *You* is a compelling and high-drama television series depicting the narcissistic Casanova (and incidentally a whole host of other narcissists). The show dramatizes the obsessive love cycle of a seemingly mild-mannered bookstore clerk Joe (played by Penn Badgley). The show chronicles Joe's propensity for stalking and subsequently becoming romantically involved with women he has never met and the shenanigans that ensue due to his dark hobby. Joe learns everything about his prey; their interests, past relationships, family history, sleeping and eating habits, and mirrors their interests to construct the image of being the perfect boyfriend. The thrill for Joe lies in the chase; he is predatory, albeit loving and even reverent toward the object of his obsession. Joe's romantic sensibilities and extreme jealousy eventually led him to increasingly more intense crimes to keep his beloved close.

Of course, once Joe's infatuation wanes (or they die), he shifts his attention to a new obsession and begins the hunt again. Joe represents how extreme narcissism, sociopathy, and Type Two merge to create a character that is simultaneously romantic, loving, and protective, as well as aggressive, violent, and pathologically jealous. His tendency toward elevating his love interest to goddess-like heights sets his partners up for an inevitable fall from grace, intensifying his rage and subsequent psychopathic, violent need to capture and isolate his love(s) to prevent them from leaving. Joe lies at the end of the spectrum for this subtype and their propensity toward crimes of passion (a feature they share with the Tempestuous Diva and Reactive Rebel narcissistic subtypes).

**When Dealing with the Aggressive Seducer:**

1. Boundaries are essential. This is the most boundary-crossing of all twenty-seven narcissistic subtypes. They do not take no for an answer, which can be helpful in some situations but can become problematic when they're not considering your feelings or boundaries. Stating your limits and keeping them firm is crucial to avoid being railroaded by this subtype.

2. Be aware of their ingratiation tactics. This subtype is immensely flattering and will utilize those techniques to get what they want. While their compliments may be genuine at times, there is frequently an ulterior motive. Asking them directly what they want or need can help fast-track the process and may save you some time and grief when you're feeling manipulated or used.

3. Remember that this subtype is transactional (as are most narcissists). They most certainly want something in return if they do something for you. What they want will vary situationally, but they often crave attention, praise, or admiration.

4. If they become aggressive, violent, or immensely jealous, seek refuge from a trusted friend, counselor, or safe person who can help. They are often apologetic and seemingly remorseful after their outbursts, but they are sure to repeat the behavior without intervention strategies because of their emotional dysregulation. However, they rarely seek help for their behavior because of their pride and will blame you for the problem.

# 11

---

# Type Three

## The Successful Achiever

Narcissistic Subtypes:
*Self-Preservation Three: The Ruthless Workaholic*
*Social Three: The Disingenuous Opportunist*
*Sexual Three: The Untouchable Star*

### SELF-PRESERVATION THREE

American culture personifies success, ambition, and the importance of a winning image. America's focus on hard work, dedication, drive, and grit has remained a central part of its cultural zeitgeist. The United States is a Three-ish culture. We reward the basic tenets of the puritanical work ethic, instill aspirational ideals in our children, and harbor an inherent exceptionalist belief that success is for the taking if you work hard. Self-Preservation Threes are the workhorses of the Enneagram. They are slightly less focused on cultivating a shiny image and more focused on ensuring that their wealth, security, and material comforts are abundant. Self Pres Threes are workaholics and believe that through the constant and insistent pursuit of one's goals, they can earn value, recognition, and praise from other people. Like most Threes, this subtype believes their worth hinges on their production and output. Goals are determined by what other people deem as valuable, impressive, and worthwhile. In that way, Threes imbibe American cultural values unlike any of the nine types. The Self-Preservation Three understands the importance of wealth and, more importantly, the independence and freedom that money and material security provide. Self-Preservation Threes seek money and security to help them assuage doubts about their value to others.

> I love working. I don't necessarily have to love my job; it just needs to be something I can excel in. If I can't move up or be recognized, I don't care. Everybody is so focused on working in their passion. I couldn't care less about that. I got into this industry because I'm good with money, and honestly, I love money. I just want to make sure I always have enough money to never rely on anyone else. It helps, of course, if I can look good while doing it [laughs].
>
> —Thomas, 53, financial analyst

The finance industry abounds with this subtype due to their innate understanding and appreciation of money. The fast-paced, glossy, and high-stakes energy of the banking and finance industry are well suited for this ambitious subtype. Of course, not all Self-Preservation Threes work in the finance industry. No matter what line of work they find themselves in, it must be lucrative and potential for growth, visibility, and preferably aspirational.

Self-Preservation Threes are pragmatic, efficient, and constantly aware of their energy output and reward input. They hate to waste their own time, which as Self-Preservation types, is very important. They often harbor palpable anxiety about achieving their goals and report a nagging feeling of constantly running a race. They feel that other people will catch up to them if they relax, and they'll feel like losers. Failure for any Three is "not an option"; however, failure is gauged by their material success rather than their public persona for the Self Pres Three. Both are important, but this subtype often prides themselves on being "straight shooters" and factual, making them appear like Eights to other people. The difference, however, is that the Self-Preservation Three is still highly aware of their image. No matter how brusque, blunt, or straightforward they may appear, they always stop short of behaving in ways that could ruin their image or reputation.

> I can be pretty blunt. I like to tell it like it is, but yes, I'm always aware of how I'm coming across. I don't like to waste time, which is why I like to get straight to the point. I can unintentionally offend people, so I've learned to be kind of "white paper" like in my business interactions. I'm friendly, but not so much that I lose credibility. I always say the best image is the one that works. But I couldn't care less about designer labels and Cartier watches. I want to be presentable, but who has time to shop for all that stuff!
>
> —Brenda, 49, real estate agent

Unlike the other Three subtypes, the Self Pres Three is less focused on living up to other people's ideas of success and prestige. Tiger Woods extols the value of being self-directed: "One of the things that my parents have taught me is never listening to other people's expectations. You should live your own life and live up to your expectations, and those are the only things I really care about."[1] This subtype is constantly competing with themselves first and foremost. Competition is a mindset rather than an external necessity in the life of the Self Pres Three:

> I compete with myself all day long. I love my Apple Watch because I will time myself to see how long it takes me to do the dishes, or the laundry, run errands, or pick up the kids from school. First of all, it keeps me fit and active, but most of all, I love the feeling of beating my records. I was a track athlete in school, and I guess I never lost that desire to go quickly and measure my success.
>
> —Carrie, 32, stay-at-home mom

Success for this subtype is more self-defined than the other two Type Three instinctual subtypes. However, it is still somewhat contingent upon what their respective cultural values dictate. Because they work hard early in their careers, Self-Preservation Threes can often afford to retire early. This allows them to pursue less lucrative passions in the second half of their lives.

Once upon a time, when I worked in the glamorous world of shopping mall retail, I had the pleasure of observing the legendary work ethic of the Self-Preservation Three. "Paige" was always working; when most nineteen-year-olds were busy partying, drinking, and trying to get out of work, Paige picked up any extra shifts and worked through her breaks. She was reliable, hardworking, professional, and was generally well-liked, although she could be unintentionally brusque or dismissive. Her work ethic wasn't due to necessity. She came from an affluent family and had a doting and generous father. She often refused his financial assistance and insisted that she wanted to be "self-made." Because of her financial discipline and need for independence, Paige bought herself a Mercedes-Benz, started a stock portfolio, and saved up enough money to pay for her breast augmentation by nineteen. I have lost touch with Paige. She attended a prestigious law school, but her social media portrays someone living a lifestyle that most young professionals only dream about.

With average to high-level empathy, this subtype, while admittedly focused on success, money, and security, often sincerely wants to support others in the pursuit of their dreams. Many find meaning in empowering other people to become financially independent, physically fit, and focused on their dreams and goals. Threes, in general, enjoy motivational speaking because once they've reached a level of success, they want others to enjoy the same satisfaction and independence they do:

> I love helping young women (and men, for that matter) arm themselves with the knowledge and confidence to manage their financial futures. I teach seminars for free to young professional women on managing their money. It's my way of giving back because I wished I had someone to show me how to become successful. If I can help fast-track someone else toward their dreams, I'll do it.
>
> —Adiké, 50, entrepreneur

## THE RUTHLESS WORKAHOLIC

Not all Self-Preservation Threes are as enthusiastic about helping others achieve success or freedom. If narcissism is present, the strong work ethic and pragmatic orientation of the Self-Preservation Three morphs into workaholism and a cut-throat orientation to win at all costs. The inherent sociopathy of Wall Street due to its focus on accumulation, wealth, and power makes it a breeding ground for narcissists in search of success. I'm not suggesting that everyone on Wall Street is narcissistic. However, those traits pay handsomely in that world. There is no shortage of exemplars in popular media of greed and power. Still, perhaps no film personifies this like the 1982 Oliver Stone film *Wall Street*. The film's iconic villain, Gordon Gekko, played by Michael Douglas (a likely Sexual Eight in real life), embodies the Ruthless Workaholic. Gekko's character, most famous for his iconic line "greed is good," was a proponent of attaining money, power, and status at any cost. Gekko is intensely transactional, ruthlessly competitive, and unapologetically exploitative. The film introduced audiences to the corporate psychopath and revealed the dark underbelly of America's white-collar elite.

The Ruthless Workaholic focuses on amassing wealth and power, not unlike the Cynical Tyrant discussed in chapter 16. However, unlike the Tyrant, this subtype is more adept at adapting their image to get their immediate needs met. Threes, in general, are disconnected from their authentic emotions. Still, with narcissism present, they are almost entirely disconnected from emotion at all. This subtype is cold and often appears calm and collected under pressure. They are very confident, grandiose, and assertive. While they invariably harbor feelings of entitlement, they maintain their work ethic and enjoy the "grind" of moving up the ladder. They all claim to be "self-made," but depending on their level of sociopathy, they may consider swindling or conning other people to be hard work. And, honestly, deceiving and finagling other people is a full-time job.

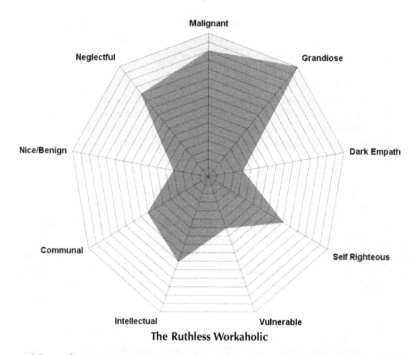

**The Ruthless Workaholic**

My academic interest in sociopathy and psychopathy was certainly piqued when I fell down the rabbit hole of a television series called *American Greed*. The docuseries chronicles the exploits of con artists, sociopaths, and white-collar criminals in their pursuit of money. Forgive me for not recalling the specific psychological profiles. It was 3 a.m., and I was half asleep during my impromptu binge. Still, I remember being struck by the sheer number of Ruthless Workaholics. The allure of get-rich-quick, Ponzi and multi-level marketing schemes is attractive to this subtype because they promise quick returns with minimal effort. This subtype greatly values their time and energy over other people. They would prefer to exploit someone else's time and energy if they can arrange it.

Not all Ruthless Workaholic's antics rise to the *American Greed* level of malignancy. Many Ruthless Workaholics work in business, upper-level management positions, or other professions that value efficiency and a laser focus on the bottom line.

> I am a good boss, but I don't abide laziness or complacency. I'm out there doing my best every day, and if someone doesn't have the same winning values I do, I have no use for that kind of person on my team or in my life. I don't care if

you're sick . . . work from home. I did it. I'm glad I'm moving out of middle management to corporate now. It's where I've always belonged. Plus, I'll finally reach my six-figure salary goal.

—AJ, 43, sales manager

In the Enneagram community, it's common to refer to Threes' propensity to conceptualize themselves as "human doings" rather than "human beings." The term is apt for the type as it speaks to their tendency to confuse what they produce in the world with who they are. However, the phrase is more appropriate for the narcissistic Three, who truly believes their production measures their worth. Because they judge themselves this way, they view other people through the same reductionistic lens. The Ruthless Workaholic truly believes someone has little value if they don't have an impressive resume or a bank account worthy of the *Forbes* list. Of course, not all people of this subtype are rich or work in high-powered jobs. Ruthless Workaholics are working in grocery stores, gyms, insurance companies, and still, some are in jail or otherwise unable to work. Whatever the case, all of them aspire to associate with the high rollers in any community. They desperately want to be associated with those they've identified as having power, money, and status.

Most Threes are adept at managing their image, but this subtype becomes less conscious of how they're coming across. They can be gauche, peacocking, and garish in their desire to demonstrate their wealth and status. If they can afford it, they will want the most expensive cars, homes, jewelry, and have stock and investment portfolios to match. They can be incredibly judgmental about people's possessions and wealth. They may quickly decry people's lack of wealth as laziness or complacency. If they aren't economically privileged, they still value wealth, material possessions, and status and strive to appear as though they've "made it."

This subtype is relatively straightforward because the goal is invariably the same: to amass more money and resources. Their single-minded focus makes them feel more mechanical and colder than other subtypes. They have difficulty expressing vulnerable emotions and are unapologetically uncomfortable with intimacy, emotionality, or introspection. They only find usefulness in bringing more cash, resources, or security to their lives. If they are parents, they will be largely unavailable due to the likelihood of spending excessive amounts of time at work. They are frequently inattentive partners but may try to compensate for their romantic deficits by providing their partners with material security or luxuries. This, however, also makes them feel entitled to treat those they financially support in whatever manner they see fit. They will proverbially throw money in people's faces and use money and security as a form of control over people in their lives. Some may even hide their ruthlessness, lack of empathy, or concern for others from their partners. They can present a thoroughly different image to their partners than they present at work. A client shared the following about her ex-husband, whom we believed to be this subtype:

> I had no idea my husband was stealing money from the company he worked at for 20 years until the police showed up at my door. He knew why the police were there, and he came downstairs fully dressed and went quietly. He said nothing to me. It was like I was living in a bad Lifetime movie.
>
> —Caroline, 54, retired teacher

## When Dealing with a Ruthless Workaholic:

1. Try to remember that their workaholism and focus on performance is their value and masks deep insecurity that they are only as good as what they produce. You are more than your production, efficiency, or earning potential, as are they despite their tendency to mechanize their existence to avoid emotion or vulnerability.

2. It is difficult to maintain compassion for this subtype because they are so hardened and robotic much of the time. However, remembering the pressure they put themselves under can help understand the motivation behind their relentless striving. The Ruthless Workaholic believes their identity is their work and vice versa, which creates immense pressure to perform optimally.

3. Professionally this subtype can be demanding, harsh, or have unreasonable expectations. If this is the case, it may be time to find a new job. Typically, they don't change this behavior because it is intrinsic to their self-conception. They've likely been highly rewarded for their production-oriented ideology. You won't change it, so it's best to change your situation.

4. Getting this subtype to recognize, name, or value their emotions is often an uphill battle. They don't value intangibles like ethics, feelings, or even spirituality generally. However, if you can appeal to their desire for efficiency, success, or effectiveness, they may consider integrating some habits or techniques to improve their bottom line.

## SOCIAL THREE

In the early 2000s, I was an unabashed fan of the hit singing competition show *American Idol*. The chemistry between Paula Abdul, Randy Jackson, and Simon Cowell was endlessly entertaining, and the excitement of the contestants made for great television. I was also fascinated by Ryan Seacrest's smooth and flawless ease while hosting the series. At that point, Seacrest was a relatively unknown DJ-turned-television host. He later became a mainstay of American primetime television. Seacrest was always well-coiffed, polished, appropriately quippy, and gracious to the contestants and judges alike. Like his idol and later mentor, Dick Clark, he personifies the slick polish of the Social Three. There were few, if any, errors in his performance. Ryan Seacrest was masterful at the post-performance interview. Like all Social Threes, Seacrest fully embodied his role. He initially hosted the show with comedian Brian Dunkleman (whom virtually nobody remembers). It quickly became apparent that he didn't need Dunkleman to carry the show. Seacrest still hosts the show and has become a significant network television force. He went on to host the iconic New Years' Rockin' Eve, replacing his idol and fellow Social Three, Dick Clark. He went on to sign multimillion-dollar production and hosting deals with E! and NBC Universal and, in true Three fashion, become one of the richest men in television programming.

Social Threes make it their business to live up to the roles they've adopted. They are adept at image manipulation and circumvent the fear of being a loser, incompetent, or worthless. They want others to see them as the model person in their chosen field. Social Threes constantly calculate and gauge people's reactions and makes micro-adjustments to their personas to achieve maximum results. They want to look, act, dress, speak, and walk the part, whatever the "part" is—being the best means not only being successful but looking successful as well. They are aware that success is in the eye of the beholder, and they're determined to captivate others with their impressive performances.

All Social subtypes struggle with shame, and the Social Three attempts to manage their fear of exposure and embarrassment by cultivating a winning and impressive image. They often lead with their resume and understand that "it's not what you know, it's whom you know." They strategize to ensure that they place themselves near or around the people that can help them advance their goals. However, they can harbor fears about having some aspect of their past, personality, or identities unmasked. As a result, they are prone to fabricating, concealing, or burying parts of themselves that don't match the winning persona they've constructed. If, for some reason, they can't hide an element of their identity that others may reject, they skillfully spin negative publicity into positive buzz.

I am very image-conscious. I have used it to my advantage in my life. I
remember when I came out in high school. I was terrified because I was running
for student body president. I was afraid people would find out I was gay and not
like me anymore. So, I used it to my advantage. I leveraged my sexuality into
a campaign marketing strategy, and I got 80% of the student vote. I'm good at
spinning things, which is why I want to work on a presidential campaign one day.

—Trent, 22, student

In addition to being the most image-conscious type, the Social Three is
also status-conscious. They intuitively understand that you must know the
best people to be the best. Others can at times find their propensity for
upward social mobility disingenuous. However, they are intimately aware of
the adverse effects of a poor reputation. At times they can sacrifice accuracy for
efficiency because, like all Threes, they believe that practicality and efficiency
are more important than perfection. That said, Social Threes strive to be "the
perfect person," according to Katherine Chernick Fauvre, and want to appear
ideal in every way. Contrast Three's external perfectionism with Ones, who
value accuracy and moral integrity over expediency. This doesn't mean Social
Threes are without integrity, just that *appearing* perfect is more important than
*being* perfect.

Most Threes identify with being aspirational, but the Social Three most
embodies the spirit of ambition. They are generally very positive and state
that they need positivity to continue to reach their goals. The term "dress for
the job you want, not the job you have" was most certainly coined by a Social
Three who understood that looking successful was half the battle of being
successful. The high-stakes million-dollar real estate industries in New York,
L.A., Dubai, and other cities filled with wealth and affluence abound with
Social Threes highly skilled in selling a lifestyle. This subtype is plentiful in
the marketing, PR, and advertising industries, where image management is
paramount to success. Self-help guru and ultimate motivational speaker Tony
Robbins exemplifies the upbeat, high-energy "success is a lifestyle" attitude of
the Social Three.

## THE DISINGENUOUS OPPORTUNIST

When narcissism and Social Three intersect, it creates the Disingenuous Opportunist. Recognizing this subtype in the wild can be tricky because of their
ability to adopt various images that suit their needs. Threes are already predisposed to higher narcissistic traits due to the psychological necessity of having

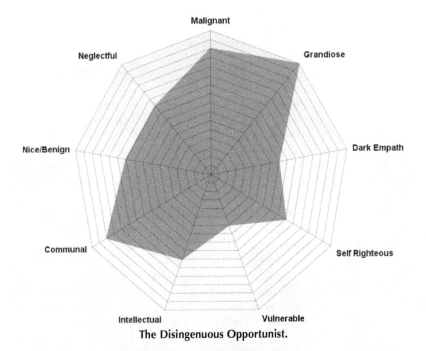

**The Disingenuous Opportunist.**

high self-esteem and confidence to achieve one's goals. However, with higher narcissism, this subtype is incredibly adept at spinning the truth to its advantage.

The Disingenuous Opportunist measures their own and others' worth by their social capital. They are immensely impressed with wealth, fame, and social power. They will often stop at nothing to attain and maintain whatever image they've adopted. They are duplicitous, superficial, and often quite snobbish. They believe that only well-known and well-connected people are worthy of others' attention. Thus, many people of this subtype are obsessed with fame. Social media has afforded this subtype an avenue to fame that, at one time, only a tiny percentage of lucky hopefuls could attain. Instagram, Facebook, and TikTok are now fertile ground for anyone desirous of mass public attention to capitalize on creating a curated personal brand. Because this subtype is innately gifted with image manipulation, they often see quick avenues to status, fame, and fortune as irresistible.

> I am not at all concerned with what is real. I mean, sure, if someone looked at my Instagram or TikTok, they'd think I was ballin', but in reality, I work for my dad part-time (but nobody needs to know that). I'm obsessed with becoming

famous and will make it happen. I've already gotten some endorsement deals
and some free stuff. You gotta' look aspirational, or people won't want to see
you.

—Davanté, 24, social media influencer, rapper, part-time pharmacy
technician

It's difficult for people of this subtype to care about anything more than
their image and success. While some are benign, others can be ruthless and
cutthroat in their pursuit to become the best of the best. If their narcissism is
particularly advanced, they will think nothing of lying, cheating, or stealing to
advance their goals. They lose touch with all semblances of integrity. They can
easily gravitate to the quickest and most efficient route toward their dreams
(even if it means taking advantage of other people).

It's not uncommon for the Disingenuous Opportunist to adopt multiple
personas for varying occasions. They may be the perfect image of a mild-
mannered, church-going boy by day and shift into a smooth-talking, club
promoter by night.

Yeah, I can be whomever I want to be. I'm good at putting on any kind of face to
get whatever I'm going for. I can even change my accent. Around my family, who
is Chinese, I am the picture of a good Chinese son. I even have two jobs, my day
job at a mortgage firm and my night job as a club promoter. Sometimes to get
girls, I'll make up a new persona just because it sounds fun or is interesting. I've
gotten good at managing the different identities. The hard part is keeping people
separate who could compare notes.

—Zhao, 27, mortgage lender/club promoter

For this subtype, the ends justify the means. If they successfully project
their chosen image and it catapults them to their next goal, they consider it a
successful performance. Gaining attention for a false image, however, rarely
satisfies for long, and they eventually search for increasing avenues of validation.

Matt Damon plays an iteration of this subtype in the 1999 film *The Talented Mr. Ripley* (based on Patricia Highsmith's 1955 novel of the same title)
that is chillingly apt. Tom Ripley, a young pianist of modest economic status, is approached by the rich Herbert Greenleaf. Greenleaf assumes Ripley
is an "Ivy man because he's wearing a Princeton jacket." Tom doesn't correct
Greenleaf and invites Tom on a boat trip to meet his son Dickie. Tom, a
closeted gay man, becomes enamored with Dickie and his lifestyle. His envy of
Dickie's social status, money, and popularity becomes all-consuming. Dickie (a
Hedonistic narcissist) enlists Tom to keep a dark secret, empowering Tom
with leverage. The film simmers with tension as Tom slowly assumes Dickie's

identity and enjoys a lifestyle that would otherwise be inaccessible. The film illustrates the descent into more profound and darker levels of psychopathy and grandiose delusion. It's also an important reminder that narcissism can worsen over time and quickly devolve into violent or otherwise destructive territory.

Tom's ability to mimic the voice, mannerisms, and attitudes of Dickie point to this subtype's propensity toward mimicry and fabrication. As empathy erodes and narcissism takes a greater hold of the psyche, this subtype can become incredibly duplicitous and fraudulent. Christian Bale played another chilling example of this subtype in the film *American Psycho*. Bale's campy depiction of Patrick Bateman is a cult classic. Still, it demonstrates the reality of this subtype's obsession with image, competition, and success. If you haven't seen the film *American Psycho*, do yourself a favor right now and Google the "*American Psycho* business card scene" and watch the simultaneously hilarious, disturbing, and realistic drama of Bateman's selection of the perfect business card.

This subtype's cutthroat and occasionally deadly ambition easily inspires the big screen. Another fictional example is Nicole Kidman's depiction of Pamela Smart in the 1995 Gus Van Sant film *To Die For*. Smart is a highly ambitious, intelligent, up-and-coming television producer, news anchor, and psychopath who convinces her underage boyfriend to kill her husband and then enjoys the media coverage because it grants her more notoriety and success. The film is based on the book of the same title, which was a "ripped from the headlines" true-crime story with similar features.

## When Dealing with a Disingenuous Opportunist:

1. Be prepared for shifting images and personas depending on who they're around. You may never see their other faces, but don't be alarmed when people know a completely different iteration of their personality. This is a method utilized to help minimize their anxiety about being rejected. They believe it helps them reach their goals.
2. This subtype can be snobbish and elitist about popularity, designer labels, trends, and other external markers of success. Remember to hold onto your values and sense of worth when around them when they're either overtly or covertly denigrating or judging your interests, friends, preferences, or pedigree.
3. This subtype comes alive in a social setting and quickly turns on their persona. They can be charming, gregarious, and entertaining and may at times be exciting people with whom to socialize. However, their need for attention can cause them to steal other people's spotlight, which can be

infuriating and demoralizing. It can sometimes be easier to exclude them from big moments (as painful as that may be) to avoid having them use your accomplishment as a stage for their attention-seeking.

4. If you're in a romantic relationship with this subtype, it's vital to remember that you are not only in a relationship with them but also their image and their social circle. They will expect you to be present at their events and favorably represent them. If you can't do this, you may need to find another relationship where your social capital doesn't measure your relationship.

## SEXUAL THREE

In the 1990s, a sudden barrage of impossibly beautiful, tall, and almost ethereal supermodels exploded onto the world stage. The elitism and fantasy inherent in the beauty industry manifested a new breed of enviable, larger-than-life celebrities that nicely personifies the archetype of the Sexual Three. The intimidating external perfection of this subtype makes them highly desirable. Like the Social Three, they too are masterful at constructing an image that others want. However, the focus shifts to the sexual/intimate arena, focusing their energy on being a desirable partner or mate. They are simultaneously slick and soft, unapproachable yet receptive, and always mindful of others' gaze upon them. They struggle to balance their desires to be successful and aspirational in the world and being devoted and available to their chosen intimates.

Australian director Baz Luhrmann's visual feast *Moulin Rouge* starring Nicole Kidman (a real-life Sexual Three) and Ewan McGregor personifies the inner struggle of the Sexual Three adeptly. Kidman plays Satine "the sparkling diamond," the most captivating Moulin Rouge performer. She is intelligent, beautiful, seductive, and indebted to the exploitative club proprietor Harold Zidler. Zidler keeps Satine safely locked away in the walls of the Moulin Rouge because he knows that his bread and butter is Satine's riveting, crowd-pleasing performances. Satine's untouchable persona is hardened by her business acumen and the seedy Rouge nightlife. Ewan McGregor plays the romantic, bohemian Christian who falls instantly in love with Satine after watching her performance.

The film chronicles their star-crossed love story as Christian desperately tries to prevent her from marrying the narcissistic Duke of Monroth. She's been promised to the Duke by Zidler as an intended investment in the future sustainability of the nightclub. Satine agonizes between her rising professional career, her loyalty to Zidler, the promise of a loveless but lavish lifestyle with the Duke, and the love of her soulmate Christian. She agrees to marry the Duke. Throughout the film, we see the Sexual Three's commitment to their performance, whatever that may be. She resigns to marry the Duke, explaining to a heartbroken Christian that she could never entirely give herself over to love. She is, after all, "the sparkling diamond" meant for public consumption. Despite her love for Christian, her public persona proved a significant roadblock to achieving authentic happiness.

Like Satine, Sexual Threes are acutely aware that others desire them. They typically have worked very hard to ensure that they are universally attractive. Claudio Naranjo taught that this subtype was trying to embody the masculine/feminine ideal. They adopt an image that affords them significant relational and social capital. Even if they don't have the raw materials of attractiveness, this subtype will put in the time, effort, and money to maximize their assets. I've encountered more than a few bodybuilders, personal trainers, models, and actors that are this subtype. Dylan was an impressive specimen, tall, jet-black hair with piercing blue eyes and a svelte, muscular build. He shared that his ability to turn heads has always been an asset in his life. He's paying his way through law school through bartending, fitness modeling, and personal training. His ambition matches his physical prowess, as is the case with most Sexual Threes:

> It sounds ridiculous, but I want to be everybody's type. I've always gotten attention for my appearance, and people underestimate my intelligence. I have a double degree in mathematics and political science. I'm not a dumb guy. But I have gotten a lot in my life by using my appearance, and I'm fine with it.
>
> —Dylan, 27, law student

Dylan shared that he's always looking for his soulmate and is secretly despondent that he hasn't met her yet. He's known for being a player. He enjoys the attention he receives from both men and women and capitalizes on that attention to satisfy his intimacy needs. He shared that he wants to communicate untouchable, raw sexuality but is uncomfortable letting someone see behind the curtain.

> I feel nervous when I genuinely like someone because I am deathly afraid they won't like the real me. Hell, I don't even know if I like or know the real me. I'm afraid I'm nothing more than this person I've created. I want someone to peel back the layers, but what if there's nothing under those layers. . . . It's a constant struggle to decide whether I want people to appreciate the image I've constructed or break the mirror and find the real me.

This subtype is more prone than the Social or Self-Preservation subtypes to play with their image. The other subtypes typically find a winning image that works and stick with it. They always make micro-adjustments to their presentation depending on the audience, but the primary persona remains static. However, Sexual Threes, because of the natural mercurial energy of the sexual instinct, makes them more prone to trying on different personas. No matter how they mold their presentation, it will always maximize their appeal and desirability. This subtype has a smooth, cool, and untouchable mystique that is often intriguing to others.

In addition to the pressures of maintaining an external image of perfectionism, this type is adept at mirroring others' interests, preferences, and tastes. Unlike the Sexual Nine, the Three's transformation makes them strive to be the perfect complement to a particular relationship rather than to become like the other person (as is common with Sexual Nines):

> I try to figure out what kind of partner, employee, friend the other person wants, and I want to be the perfect companion. I try to maintain my flavor and style, but if someone wants a strong, assertive partner, I become that person; if they want a more submissive or emotionally available partner, I can do that too. Still, friends or family will know, particularly when I'm in a new relationship. I subtly change my clothing and speaking style and try to immerse myself in the other person's world to become what that person most wants.
>
> —Kira, 35, store manager

The pressure to maintain a pristine and desirable image creates grief for this subtype. While they desperately want to be loved for who they are, the anxiety of dropping their chosen persona feels overwhelming. The more people they feel they must impress, the more anxiety-producing life becomes, and they can retreat from relationships, work, or social relationships. This contrasts with the other Type Three instinctual subtypes whose focus on production and efficiency rarely gives them a break. The Sexual Three can retreat to avoid the terror of disappointing the people they look to provide their feelings of worthiness and identity.

With intact empathy, this subtype can be unusually supportive. Due to the Three's focus on efficiency and pragmatism, they frequently offer their assistance to their intimates. They can be incredibly motivational and very loving partners, parents, friends, and coworkers . . . and they look great while doing it.

## THE UNTOUCHABLE STAR

"Amazing" Amy Dunne is a chilling psychopathic representation of the Untouchable Star's decline into increasing levels of madness. Amy, played by Rosamund Pike, is the narcissistic antagonist in David Fincher's adaption of

*Gone Girl*, a novel by Gillian Flynn. Amy was the inspiration for children's books her parents wrote titled *Amazing Amy*. Amy was the gifted, cherished, and mythologized perfect child. Amy is portrayed as beautiful but icy, very intelligent, and self-important, and falls for writing teacher Nick (Ben Affleck). Nick is below her status, but the two fall for each other and eventually marry. Their marriage is externally perfect and funded by her wealthy parents but feels sterile and superficial. When both lose their jobs due to the recession, the marriage slowly disintegrates.

Nick pulls away from Amy and becomes distant and, in her estimation, "lazy." She increasingly belittles, emasculates, and berates him as her desperation to recapture his attention (and kindle his ambition) has the opposite effect of creating closeness. Nick cheats on Amy, which triggers Amy's psychopathy and malignant narcissism. She stages her disappearance (and apparent death). She embarks on an unhinged campaign to seek revenge against her husband for withdrawing his attention. In the end, we learn, from Amy's admission, that the whole intensive drama that ensues was all a performance to test her husband's love, devotion, and admiration.

Amy is an extreme psychopathic example of this subtype. Still, Pike's steely portrayal and chameleonic ability to shift from a beautiful polished intellectual to a raging malignant narcissist is stunning to watch. Most Untouchable Stars don't devolve to this level of violence and sadism, but the emptiness and focus on maintaining the slick ideal image of the "perfect" relationship represents how narcissism manifests in this subtype. They are even more image-conscious and vain than non-narcissistic Sexual Threes. They channel their grandiosity (and rage) into maintaining unattainable flawlessness. They spend very little of their inner resources developing emotional depth or interpersonal skills. Instead, they become masters at cultivating an elite, beautiful, and powerful image.

The Untouchable Star commands others' attention and is hyperaware of other people's perceptions of them. They guard their personas fiercely and become angry and vicious if they believe someone tries to tarnish their image. They are exceptionally protective of their romantic/sexual prowess and place great importance on physical attractiveness as social capital and sexual power. If they aren't physically attractive, they strive to earn enough money, power, or status to attract a desirable mate (although this is true of all Sexual Threes). Still, the Untouchable Star focuses almost exclusively on external beauty, status, or power. They find it difficult to connect with other people emotionally. For all Sexual Threes having the right partner helps them feel valuable by extension. Still, when narcissistic, they channel their superficiality, elitism, and relentless obsession with looking good onto their partners, which can result in toxic relationship dynamics:

> My husband was completely obsessed with the way I look. It was very flattering at the beginning of our relationship. He used to say we were the most beautiful couple in the room, and honestly. He loved to call us a "power couple." There were some red flags, like the fact that on our 5th date, he bought me a ton of expensive designer clothes and used to make me do these weird photo shoots dressed up like his own little personal doll. After I had our child, he was fixated on me getting back to my pre-baby weight. I had trouble losing weight due to some complications with the birth and some post-partum depression. He became irate when he'd find out I hadn't worked out. He started fixing my meals and watching me eat them to make sure I wasn't "eating junk." At the worst of it, he would call me "fat" and talk about how "loose" I was.
>
> —Ophelia, 33, yoga instructor

They are exacting perfectionists and demand that almost everything in their lives appear impeccable, including their children, spouses, friends, and families. This subtype is typically grandiose, which hides deep insecurities

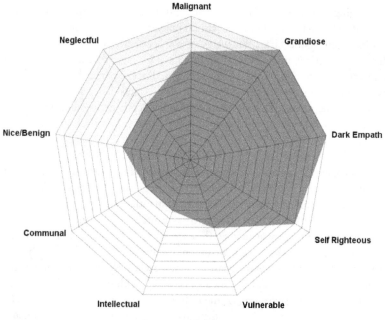

**The Untouchable Star.**

about their attractiveness and desirability. They can present as excessively cold and unapproachable or dynamic, charismatic, and boasting. They want others to acknowledge their greatness and believe that they will be shamed and humiliated if they don't perfect the performance. If their narcissism is prevalent enough, they begin to lose control of their image as outbursts become increasingly frequent. They may rage at partners, coworkers, or family for not giving them the attention and admiration they crave. However, they can be highly dangerous because of their slick charm and excellent ability to lie, gaslight, and diminish others.

A discussion of the Untouchable Star would not be complete without mentioning this subtype's extreme sadistic, psychopathic iteration. Ted Bundy, one of the most infamous serial killers in American history, was likely this subtype. Bundy's trial mesmerized and horrified spectators. Known for his dashing good looks, undeniable charm and charisma, and penchant for beautiful young women, Bundy was at once monstrous and attractive. Bundy represented himself in his murder trial and entertained and charmed the court, much to the disgust of his victim's families. Many forensic psychologists have commented on Bundy's seeming likability and undeniable allure, increasing his murder success rate. Unlike other people of this subtype, Bundy saw his victims as possessions. The sadism and distorted object-relations of the serial killer and this overall subtype points to their conceptualizing people as possessions "as one would possess a potted plant, a painting, or a Porsche. Owning, as it were, this individual."[2]

## When Dealing with the Untouchable Star:

1. This subtype has the unique ability to make you feel exceptional once their attention fixes on you. While it is flattering when they focus on you, be aware that being involved with them as a friend or partner can quickly become tiresome. You will be expected to shower them with attention, admiration, and validation to keep them happy.

2. Try to maintain your style, boundaries, and identity because this subtype is notorious for molding others to their ideal vision of the perfect partner. If they start to insult you with their improvements, draw a firm boundary and let them know that you feel disrespected by their attempts to change or alter your image.

3. This subtype can be insulted if you reject or ignore their advances or attention. If you end a relationship (whether professional or romantic), they may try various techniques first to woo you back and then shift

to attempting to discredit your reputation or image. Bear in mind that this comes from deep insecurities of being worthless. For this subtype, rejection feels like death to this subtype.

4. If romantically involved with this subtype, clean breaks are the best because their propensity toward emotional manipulation, stalking behaviors, and rage can be overwhelming. If you need assistance breaking free of a toxic dynamic with this subtype, seek the help of a trained professional to help you strategize ways to create and maintain healthy boundaries.

# 12

## Type Four

### The Intuitive Romantic

Narcissistic Subtypes:
*Self-Preservation Four: The Fussy Masochist*
*Social Four: The Entitled Outcast*
*Sexual Four: The Tempestuous Diva*

#### SELF-PRESERVATION FOUR

Self-Preservation Fours are tenacious, insightful, sensitive, and self-contained. Like all Fours, they believe that they must be unique, suffering, and exceptional to receive love, attention, and care from others. Self Pres Fours describe themselves as fiercely independent and painfully sensitive. While they value the freedom of autonomy, they also crave the attention of others to ensure that they are loved, valued, and appreciated for their unique contributions. They feel, not unlike Twos, that they must earn the right to be cared for. However, while Twos focus on how they can be of service to others, Fours focus on their emotional insight, creativity, and woundedness to secure others' attention. This subtype often prefers expressing themselves through an artistic medium where they can reveal their innermost thoughts and feelings without risking too much exposure:

> It's easier for me to express myself if I write my feelings down. I get so flustered when I'm asked to express myself directly. Words fall so flat when trying to express

my emotions at the moment. If I have time to write them down, I can add color, texture, add heft or remove weight to my experiences. It's more beautiful when you can craft your reality. I don't know what I'd do without the ability to write.

—Leona, 29, writer

They possess a fierce tenacity paired with a palpable sense of being too sensitive for the harshness of this world. This creates a deeply sensitive, occasionally shy, yet impassioned crusader for emotional authenticity. They are often focused on alleviating suffering, and eliminating whatever they deem unjust, unfair, or imbalanced. Their focus on unfairness, a quality they share with Types Six and Eight, comes from their belief that they have gotten the short end of the stick in life. They become convinced that the universe, God, or some unseen force is punishing them for an unknown past deed and that enduring their pain is the only way to redeem themselves and earn their way back into proverbial paradise and happiness.

Self Pres Fours are willing to suffer for an ideal, beauty, or art. They, like all Fours, see suffering as an almost religious experience. The Four's identity is intrinsically tied to suffering, pain, or alienation. This subtype wants to be known for what they create and is a true artisan. Their chosen medium: songwriting, singing, pottery, art, dance, or just the unique way they live, demonstrate to others their specialness, and ideally invites people into their world so they can be known.

The desire for this subtype to express themselves through a medium is common. One famous, albeit tragic, example of this subtype is celebrated poet Sylvia Plath. Plath was a precocious child. She spent a great deal of time on her own and found it challenging to connect with other kids. She was intellectually gifted, enjoyed school and learning, and felt the other children were concerned with silly superficial things. Plath's beloved father died when she was ten years old, and she began keeping a journal and experienced her first major depressive episode. Plath's struggles with depression and her first suicide attempt inspired her first and only novel, *The Bell Jar*. Her mastery over metaphor, symbolism, and unusual turns of phrase are well documented in both her book and voluminous poetry catalog. Plath's copious journaling gave readers an intimate peek inside of her inner world. *The Unabridged Journals of Sylvia Plath* reveals an incredibly introspective, mercurial, and quietly competitive woman whose simultaneous insecurity and conviction in her giftedness indicate the Self-Preservation Four. Plath was notably dauntless at times and could flout her security in surprising ways. This tendency arises out of the Self-Preservation Four's need to feel their emotional aliveness through undermining their security:

I want to taste and glory in each day, and never be afraid to experience pain, and never shut myself up in a numb core of nonfeeling, or stop questioning and criticizing life and take the easy way out. To learn and think: to think and live; to live and learn: this always, with new insight, new understanding, and new love.

—*The Unabridged Journals of Sylvia Plath*[1]

Their dauntlessness can create situations where their financial, physical, or emotional stability are undermined. This is often unconscious for this subtype because, as Self-Preservation types, they crave security. Still, the Four energy creates a competing need for emotional intensity and destabilization drama.

This subtype has a unique way of viewing the world and their relationship to others and frequently reports feeling alienated from other people. The self-preservation instinct within the Four ego structure makes them crave connection and mirroring from others (as is common with all heart types) and avoids relying too heavily on others for their basic needs. All Fours exhibit a push/pull orientation to relationships, but the Self Pres Four is always ambivalent about how much they want or need other people in their lives. They often disdain managing the mundane responsibilities of life (working, cleaning, bill paying, etc.). Ironically, however, they can be adept at managing day-to-day necessities. They would much rather spend their time and energy creating, daydreaming, or focusing on the analysis of their emotional world.

They are highly aesthetic and focused on the emotional atmosphere of their surroundings. They may be particular about lighting, colors, textures, and design. They are often proponents of natural living and prefer organic, tasteful, or minimal aesthetics. Self Pres Fours feel aggravated and discontent when forced to endure environments they find aesthetically objectionable. They can be simple or patrician in their style yet insist on luxury or elegance in their homes.

> I absolutely abhor overhead lighting. I have checked out of hotel rooms and refused to stay at family members' homes because they didn't have the right lighting. I'm not trying to be snooty. It doesn't have to be overly fancy, but certain design elements are so offensive that I can't relax if I have to be in them for long.
>
> —Gerald, 47, interior designer

This subtype can be tireless champions for injustice and is willing to suffer and endure great pain to uphold their ideals. Their "passion for protest," as Claudio Naranjo noted with Fours overall, is surprising when it comes from the normally reticent, isolated, and withdrawn Self-Preservation Four. Their typically hypersensitive persona can suddenly become fierce, biting, and for-midable in the face of injustice or unfairness. It's not uncommon to see this subtype protesting for children or animal rights or taking up causes where human rights are violated. Their tenacity and identification with suffering make them effective and vocal advocates of humanity.

## THE FUSSY MASOCHIST

With the withdrawn Enneagram types (Four, Five, and Nine) finding blatant examples of this narcissistic subtype in literature or film is challenging because the extent of their narcissism typically goes undetected due to their vulnerability and seeming insight into their own process. The Fussy Masochist believes that their lives are more difficult and emotionally challenging than those around them. They are convinced of their specialness as well as their loathsomeness. The aesthetic focus of the self-preservation instinct is heightened in this sub-type as they channel their frustration and anger into a pervasive discontent of everything and everyone around them. They believe that people have chroni-

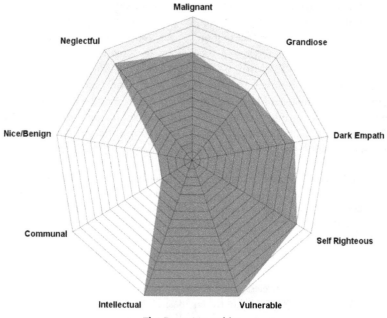

The Fussy Masochist.

cally disappointed them throughout their lives and have failed to recognize the extent of their brilliance, creativity, or insight. However, instead of directly voicing their discontent, it's displayed passive-aggressively and through indirect displays of spitefulness and eruptions of hateful judgment. This subtype can be tyrannical and demanding to those around them which creates a multitude of interpersonal issues.

Julie, a twenty-seven-year-old unemployed artist, reached out to me and wanted to contribute to my research on empathy. She claimed she was an "extreme empath" (a claim more than one participant has made) and wanted me to understand what it was like for her to live with this overwhelming empathy that she claimed was "debilitating":

> People irritate me. I'm too independent and sensitive and can't really deal with other people's emotions. Most people are babies about the stupidest stuff and it's hard enough dealing with my own issues. I just want to write and draw. What would make life easier is if I had a rich benefactor to help me pay for my life. I have a hard time keeping jobs because I hate people telling me what to do and all the jobs I'm qualified for are peasant jobs. I didn't finish my degree because I got headaches too much and had to leave school. If my parents had invested a little more in my future I probably wouldn't be here. I flunked out of college and never went back. My professors didn't get it anyway. [My parents] support me right now. They don't understand me either. They think I'm spoiled but they don't understand what my depression is like. Last week I had to ask Dad for $900 so I could repaint my living room because the color was wrong and was making my depression worse. He said no. So I guess if I end up committing suicide you'll know who to blame.
>
> —Julie, 27, artist

It will come as no surprise to you I'm sure that Julie scored quite low on empathy. However, her belief in her special empathic abilities is the manifestation of her grandiosity. Many narcissistic Fours are convinced of their specialness typically through their empathy, spiritual, or intuitive abilities, or their impressive or misunderstood intellectual or artistic skills. Indeed, some Fours are intuitively gifted, creative, and spiritually astute, but when narcissism is present, they use their specialness as a justification for their exemption from living as mere mortals.

The Fussy Masochist typically exhibits some hypochondriasis and mild factitious tendencies.[2] Type Two in both its narcissistic and non-narcissistic forms is more prone to using physical illnesses to garner attention, love, and to justify getting their needs met. However, Fours utilize mental or emotional conditions (depression, anxiety, OCD, bipolar, etc.) to garner pity and thus justify being above the rules or responsibilities. This does not mean that these conditions don't exist, however, they inflate or exaggerate their severity or worsen them by not properly managing their emotional or physical health.

Some people with this subtype will purposely make poor financial or romantic decisions that they are relatively sure will spin them into emotional or economic turmoil so that they can justify their sullen withdrawal from responsibility. Many will feel, like Julie, that they are above regular work and refuse to support themselves. They often make other people responsible for their basic survival needs, whims, and desires and easily guilt trip or punish others through tempestuous temper tantrums and emotional withdrawal or isolation designed to control others. A client shared her experience growing up with this subtype as a parent and demonstrates how their emotional manipulation and obsession with beauty and aesthetics manifested in her household:

> My mother would get angry with me for the stupidest things. She thought I was embarrassing because I wasn't overly concerned with the way things looked and beauty, art, and culture as she was. So, if I came home with dirt on my clothes or wanted to play with the boys outside, she would punish me by not speaking to me. Sometimes for days! I remember when I was 14, she didn't talk to me for a whole week. Not one word. She was angry because I used my allowance to buy these Garbage Pail Kids trading cards. They were purposely disgusting animated characters with snot, farts, and boogers. So, she didn't talk to me for a week. She didn't fix me dinner or even acknowledge I was alive.

> —Lori, 43, fitness instructor

The Fussy Masochist's need to control their emotional experience and those around them can be particularly frustrating. They potentially have a natural aptitude for understanding the inner world as Fours. Healthy Fours are particularly skillful at articulating their emotional experience and helping others embrace and express their own. However, when narcissism is present, they become emotional bullies and prefer telling other people how they should feel and why they should feel that way. They cannot separate their own emotions from those around them, and they can be incredibly callous and harsh in service of telling others "The truth." There is considerable anger and rage that runs with this subtype, and without a proper outlet like a cause to protest or an art medium, they will lodge their insults and frustration at those around them. It can be challenging to maintain relationships because they can be vicious and somewhat sadistic if envy rises.

They frequently disown their envy and instead belittle and diminish others, utilizing whatever intellectual or creative resources are at their disposal. They can be biting and sardonic to others and lash out at others who have gifts, talents, resources, or qualities they lack. However, their lack of accurate self-appraisal makes it difficult for them to recognize their disdain as envy and instead assume the problem is the other person. Because this subtype is withdrawn instead of incessantly engaging in conflict with others, they periodically retreat into their worlds where they can reinvigorate their damaged self-esteem through fantasies of fame, beauty, or wealth.

This subtype may fantasize about having more meaningful friendships, more money, or meaningful romantic relationships but expects others to seek them out and can be incredibly judgmental and dismissive if others don't live up to their very high standards.

Their intolerance of others' sensitivity manifests as a loss of subtlety and sensitivity in the presence of narcissism. They expect that others treat them with compassion, respect, and consideration as they frequently react to others with disdain, vitriol, or dismissal. As narcissism increases in this subtype, they can become reckless and impulsive with their material security and expect others to pick up the pieces. Spending exorbitant amounts of money on themselves, missing work, risky sexual or social behaviors, and substance abuse are typical when this subtype is stressed. Their engagement in activities that undermine their self-preservation security is intended to help them drum up emotional content and, often, to punish themselves and others for their discontentment and self-loathing.

### When Dealing with a Fussy Masochist:

1. This subtype is prone to dependent behavior and will often have fundamental limitations that prevent them from taking care of themselves or manifest an emotional disaster through which they may expect your support. Be clear about your boundaries and set limits or timelines so you don't end up draining your resources and develop resentment.
2. If they become cutting, blaming or cold, and dismissive, remove yourself from their presence. They hate to be ignored, but it's crucial that you don't endure their vitriolic attacks. Remember, the silent treatment is still an attack.
3. Avoid sharing how or why they've hurt you unless you're sure that they can handle the truth of your experience. This subtype is particularly sensitive to criticism and may be wholly unable to accept any responsibility for their role in a conflict or disagreement. Discuss your feelings with a trusted friend, therapist, or loved one who can create safety and validation around your emotions.

4. Suppose they become particular about comfort, aesthetics, food, or other aspects of their lifestyle, and those preferences are at odds with your own. In that case, it's best to avoid trying to convince them that their priorities are unreasonable. If you are financially supporting them, tell them that since you help pay for their lifestyle, you'd like to have an opinion when appropriate. If they insist upon specific standards because they financially or domestically support you, it's essential to communicate your preferences as firmly as possible to maintain your autonomy.

## SOCIAL FOUR

Writer, cultural critic, poet, and playwright Oscar Wilde once said, "Most people are other people. Their thoughts are someone else's opinions, their lives a mimicry, their passions a quotation."[3] Wilde's aptitude for biting social commentary, beautiful prose, and his advocacy of individualism exemplify the Social Four's societal role. Wilde was an aesthete. His love of beauty, art, and culture reflected his desire to beautify and refine the world around him. He was outspoken through his art and notoriously aloof in person; Wilde was a man of privilege and, by some accounts, a fantastic snob. Nonetheless, his often-provocative writings and advocacy for a luxurious, beautifully curated, and leisurely life made him a larger-than-life figure in society and literary circles.

Wilde reportedly wanted to be painted or photographed lounging and languishing, so it didn't appear he worked too hard. His aristocratic sensibilities and criticisms of mainstream hegemonic masculinity were often the subjects of social ridicule. Wilde was convicted of sodomy and gross indecency in 1895. The charges were common penalties for men suspected of being gay. Oscar Wilde is a fascinating figure. I considered discussing him as the narcissistic variant of the Social Four because the literary criticism of Wilde focuses so much on his sexual proclivities for young men. Thus, it's difficult to parse the homonegative accusations from what could have been a narcissistic spectrum disorder.

Social Fours want to see themselves and need to be seen by others, as above the typical crowd. Their fears of being mundane, ordinary, and average manifest in the social arena. They then focus on ways they are alike and different from those around them. They are often painfully aware of feelings of alienation or deviation from "normal" people. Social Fours simultaneously celebrate, accentuate, and defend how they're different from other people. They then envy, deride, and resent the ease with which other people seem to navigate the social world. Often shy, withdrawn, or at least self-conscious, this subtype is the most shame-sensitive of all twenty-seven instinctual subtypes. They are terrified that they will make a social faux pas that invites criticism, judgment, or hatred. Some Social Fours deal with their fear of social shame by becoming critical of the culture at large. They may take pleasure in provocatively challenging social norms, customs, or rules. They can adopt a subversive dress style or embrace counter-culture movements to navigate their social insecurities.

Some Social Fours are painfully shy and prefer to stay away from the potentially judgmental eye of others. They can be compassionate, insightful, and understand others' pain or tribulations. Many are attracted to helping professions like mental health counseling, teaching, or other jobs to connect with people who feel isolated, different, or cast out from society. Like all social subtypes, they want to be appreciated, noticed, and valued for their contributions. However, they are frequently misunderstood due to their often critical and piercing opinions about societal norms, popular aesthetics, or trends.

Most Social Fours feel a desire, and in some instances, an entitlement toward being accepted into an elite class of people. Those born into or privileged enough to be accepted into elite societies may feel empty, forlorn, or reject their social affiliations. To many people, it can seem as though the Social Four is destined to feel alienated and dissatisfied with any group with which they affiliate. This is because the fundamental identity of the Four rests on their differences from those around them. It is common for Social Fours to long for inclusion and acceptance and then reject the very people they've sought out.

This subtype's love/hate relationship with the group often characterizes their subtype's orientation to the social world. A former client, Asheesh, illuminated it beautifully:

> I feel like an ugly monster most of the time. I've always felt painfully different from everyone around me. I wanted desperately to be accepted and loved. And honestly, to be cool. But there was always something awkward about me. I get so shy just having a conversation with someone I don't know, but for some reason, I can go out on stage and perform as my life depended on it. The crowd's energy and belief in me make me feel like I can do it. But as soon as I walk off stage, I want to hide. One time after a play, a former castmate told me a group of people was waiting backstage to congratulate me and get my autograph. Me! I couldn't do it. I didn't want to ruin their perception of me and see how weird, ugly, and awkward I was in real life.
>
> —Asheesh, 30, actor

Despite their self-consciousness, this subtype can be deeply soulful, incredibly sensitive, and make valued and interesting contributions to whatever groups or communities in which they position themselves. Even on the periphery of the group, their insights into the emotional dynamics, potential injustices, or contradictions at work in the group's process of cultural identity are astute and, despite their criticality, often correct.

## THE ENTITLED OUTCAST

Hands down, one of my favorite dramedies is the 2006 film, *The Devil Wears Prada*, directed by David Frankel. I've long been a sucker for a movie with a solid female villain. With the added star power of Meryl Streep and her exceptional acting ability, it was an instant nominee for my top ten favorite films of all time. Streep plays Miranda Priestly, a dramatized characterization of *Vogue* editor-in-chief Anna Wintour (a real-life Social Four). The film, based on the book by Lauren Wiesberger, chronicles a young journalist's (Andrea "Andy" Sachs, played by Anne Hathaway) experience working at a prominent fashion magazine, *Runway*. Wiesberger's book chronicles her brief experience working for Wintour at *Vogue*.

Priestly is demanding, haughty, unempathetic, cold, and brusque. Her singular control over the fashion industry is unparalleled. Andrea's sharpness takes

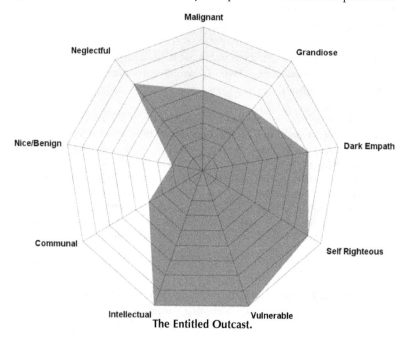

**The Entitled Outcast.**

Priestly by surprise upon meeting the homely yet ambitious career hopeful. However, Priestley's narcissistic plan sought to transform Andy from the fashion-clueless, intellectual, and thoughtful journalist into a aesthetic-obsessed, elitist, cutthroat businesswoman, like Priestley. It's not long before Sachs integrates into the high gloss, luxurious, fast-paced world of high-fashion publishing. Like most people who have the misfortune of working for a narcissist, Sachs suffers from constant stress and anxiety, striving to live up to Priestley's ever-changing and impossible standards. Priestley's disdain for Andy (and everyone) is displayed through her snobbish and vitriolic monologues about fashion, beauty, success, and the importance of taste. Everyone around Priestley enables her narcissistic abuse by justifying her behavior because of her position. She is constantly disappointed in everyone and has notoriously gone through hundreds of young assistants who have inevitably failed to live up to her expectations.

Streep insisted that the screenwriters include a scene to reveal Priestley's human side in a stroke of acting genius. Sachs shows up at her home. In a moment of apparent vulnerability, Priestley is visibly upset, crying about her impending divorce and its possible effect on her image. The vulnerable break in Miranda Priestley's usually steely and intimidating demeanor aptly demonstrates the insecurity of the Entitled Outcast, who has managed to become the ultimate insider. This subtype's propensity toward snobbery and a mixture of intellectual elitism and aesthetic superficiality can be disorienting if narcissism is present. They are often highly judgmental of others' tastes in everything from fashion, literature, music, film, food, art, philosophy, or décor.

They believe themselves to be the arbiters of good taste, and they are more than happy to let others know they are aesthetically or intellectually superior. The Entitled Outcast is confident in their superiority and grandiose in their expectation of special treatment due to their refined and highly curated tastes. However, they still harbor a fair amount of self-consciousness, which they attempt to hide. Many Entitled Outcasts will develop a larger-than-life persona that makes them appear intimidating and unapproachable. Their persona helps to cover their shyness, shame aversion, or social insecurity. Other people of this subtype simply retreat and become remote, inaccessible, and create an aura of untouchable mystique. In either case, this subtype often pairs with avoidant features.

I believe I am supposed to be rich. I have always known I deserve to be around beautiful people. Ever since I was little, I felt like it was my destiny to be in luxury. I got an internship at a design house, but all I did was get coffee for people and answer phones. It was below me. I quit after a week. I'm too talented to start at the bottom. I need to find someone rich who will pay for my interior design line. I fully believe that the right person will just come along. I know I have something special.

—Alain, 27, fashion student

Entitlement is characteristic of virtually all twenty-seven narcissistic subtypes. Because Fours generally harbor a sense of entitlement due to the conviction that they have suffered more than others, they are especially demandingly when narcissistic. Typically, there is a characteristic denial of weaknesses or flaws with narcissists. Even vulnerable narcissists deny their shortcomings and prefer to blame other people for failures or problems. Fours are intimately aware of their faults and inadequacies; the Entitled Outcast is no exception. However, their inadequacies become reframed into strengths. "Well, I'm not good at cleaning the house because I'm too intelligent and can't focus on such a menial task." Or, "I just can't be around ugly things or people, I'm too sensitive, and it assaults my senses." They often find a way to demonstrate to others their exceptionalism in both its positive and negative manifestations.

The Entitled Outcast often sees themselves as a tastemaker. No matter their aesthetic or intellectual sensibilities, they are confident about their preferences. I encountered this subtype as an undergraduate creative writing major. "Jack," an advanced poetry classmate, always sported a perfectly well-worn motorcycle jacket, impossibly skinny jeans, dyed black hair, and black combat boots. As is customary in many poetry workshop classes, we would go around the room weekly and read our work and receive comments from our classmates.

While the occasional critical comment or strong reaction wasn't out of the question, for the most part, we were all supportive, encouraging, and complimentary. Jack, however, rarely had a kind word to say about anyone else's work. Predictably Jack would wait until everyone had finished their critiques. Jack eviscerated even the most brilliant prose written by us or published celebrated poets. Nevermind that Jack's poems weren't all that compelling, and the other students would gladly seize opportunities to criticize Jack's poems. Jack seemed unfazed by our criticism of his work as he was quite confident in his. He evaded facing his work's inadequacy by going into self-righteous rants about how he needed the course to hear "bad college poetry" because he wanted to be a literary critic. By doing this, Jack positioned himself above the rest of the class and justified his scathing critiques through his burgeoning role as a critic. He was entirely in his element as "Lord of the Poems." I noticed that my classmates began to pander to his expectations and critiques. Those who couldn't stand the weekly derision thought it easier to try to please him.

I ran across Jack one day in the student union, the only time I ever saw him out "in the wild." He was withdrawn, hiding his face behind his shaggy black hair, staring down at the ground. He appeared far less objectionable out of the classroom, where his literary sensibilities weren't a prime social currency. I felt terrible seeing him so uncomfortable amidst the crowd, so I said hello. He snubbed me and refused to speak and walked right past me as though he had never seen me before.

Later, I learned from a classmate that he went to various boarding schools throughout his life. It seems his wealthy parents didn't know how to deal with his anxiety and depression and instead opted to send him away. I'm speculating that along the way, he discovered that contributing to the world through the cultivation of a sophisticated, critical, and judgmental image was better than people rejecting the awkward, unhappy, depressed kid underneath. Rejecting others helped him have a sense of power and control in a world where he otherwise may have felt disempowered, flawed, or deeply inadequate.

## When Dealing with an Entitled Outcast:

1. Remember that their snobbery or elitism overcompensates for feelings of inadequacy, hurt, or shame. This subtype can fabricate aspects of their history to cover over class-shame or other biographical details that they believe would cause others to reject or ridicule them.

2. This subtype can be famously arrogant and condescending. This flares with heightened envy brought about by feelings of inferiority or inadequacy. If they become condescending or rude, it's best to remember the origins of the behavior. With this subtype pointing it out may bring about angry reactivity or further insult. If you can, walk away or try "gray-rocking" to emotionally detach from their behavior.

3. Suppose you catch this subtype lying, fabricating, or embellishing an aspect of their lives, talent, or experience around others. In that case, it's best not to call them out at the moment. Arousing their shame can incite their rage, and they may seek revenge or opportunities to undermine you later.

4. At times it can be helpful to communicate to this subtype if you feel they have been insulting or disrespectful. They are highly shame-sensitive. While they may be angry or resentful about you voicing your opinion, they may back off to avoid further shame. However, if they become volatile, overly reactive, or abusive, tell them that you will not endure abuse and leave the situation.

## SEXUAL FOUR

Anne Sexton was a feminist confessional poet known for exploring deeply personal and socially taboo subject matter. Sexton was famous for her raw emotional style and bold, audacious, and self-revealing personality. Sexton professionally came of age when many women poets and artists (including fellow Four, Sylvia Plath) were garnering public attention. Sexton, a housewife-turned-Pulitzer-Prize-winning poet, represents the gold standard in poetic emotional vulnerability and explicit honesty. Her work, frequently banned from public readings, explored masturbation, menstruation, female pleasure, sex, suicide, rape, and mental illness. Sexton was severely bipolar and was transparent about her struggles in managing her disorder while meeting societal expectations as a wife and mother. Sexton was an admittedly challenging woman, not simply because of her bipolar disorder but also because of her high expectations for enduring deep connection with her intimates. Biographer Diane Wood Middlebrook wrote about Sexton's simultaneous emotional volatility and profound ability to nurture and support her family and friends.[4] She was, by all accounts, an incredibly complicated woman.

Sexton's mixture of emotional capriciousness, deep insight, and relational demandingness exemplify Sexual Four. This subtype's desire for uniqueness and avoidance of emotional flatness channels into their desire for union with someone who will mirror their insight, depth, and specialness. Sexual Fours are passionate champions for everyone's divine right to live authentically. They want others to feel safe and free to express their emotional truth no matter how beautiful, ugly, inappropriate, or taboo. Their identities are contingent upon being regarded as emotionally transformative to others. Their ability to intuit and voice their own and others' emotional experiences is finely tuned. Their innate understanding of the human psyche allows them to quickly build intimacy and rapport with those whom they choose to connect. They, like all Fours, fear their inadequacy. However, the Sexual Four's inadequacy fears are most evident in the intimate arena. They are terrified that partners, best friends, children, and other intimates will abandon them for someone more interesting, beautiful, insightful, and creative. This subtype can be strong, audacious, bold, and opinionated (much like Eights). They are also emotionally vulnerable, insecure, self-doubting, and focused on building relationships and rapport to avoid abandonment.

The Sexual Four is most acquainted and comfortable with their envy. Envy arises when others threaten their uniqueness or their exclusion connection with others. They attempt to quell their instinctual anxieties by becoming irresistible to the object(s) of their affection, much like Sexual Twos and Threes. However, unlike those types, they prefer to seduce by demonstrating their depth, wisdom, and originality. If this subtype senses a threat to their creative or intimate security, they become competitive. Self-hatred fuels their competitiveness. They hate themselves for being inadequate. They also loathe competing for the other's attention. This cycle makes them hate both the object of their affection and their competitor. By the end of this process, the Sexual Four has become angry, resentful, and disappointed in the person or project they once found redeeming and satisfying. This can confuse intimates who recognize their fall from proverbial grace as the Sexual Four becomes increasingly more emotionally demanding, competitive, and dissatisfied. If not careful, this subtype has a high propensity toward relational drama. The desire to keep emotions heightened helps stave off core fears of emotional flatness and mundanity.

The use of the word hatred may seem strong to some of you. However, research has shown that Fours frequently utilize the word in their everyday lexicon. Claudio Naranjo wrote about the propensity of the Sexual Four toward hatred.[5] He saw the hatefulness of the Sexual Four as paramount to the personality structure overall. Their internal perfectionism (not unlike Ones) and shifting emotional identity create a very self-critical character. Their criticality and self-hatred are often the engines behind their passionate immersion in whatever they view as representative of their identity.

Ironically, for the Sexual Four, despite their focus on authenticity and emotional rawness, they're prone to suppress their authentic expression to present a more refined or curated image. They do this because of fears that others (particularly those they find desirable) would reject them once they discover their insecurity and emotional volatility.

> I feel like I'm always walking a bit of a tight rope. I want to be seen as emotionally honest and authentic. Raw even. It's weird because I worry about people thinking I'm gross. I don't want to seem overly rehearsed or fake at all, but I feel like people will be able to see my insides. It's probably because I can see easily into other people, so I assume people are doing the same to me. I do want certain people to notice me, I want to make them pay attention. I try to balance seeming vulnerable and open with being fierce and beautiful.
>
> —Shovonne, 43, theater professor

Sexual Fours are uncomfortable if people have lukewarm or, worse yet, no feelings toward them. They strive to make an impact on people positively or negatively and feel that to make no impression on others around them is a curse of the dull, bland, or banal. When psychologically healthy and with normal to average empathy, the Sexual Four is profoundly empathetic and intuitive about others' emotions. They believe deeply in the value of emotional expression and creativity as a means of spiritual and psychological emancipation. They can be transformative for others simply by being themselves and encouraging and supporting others to do the same.

## THE TEMPESTUOUS DIVA

At ten years old, I vividly remember seeing the trailer for Francis Ford Coppola's 1992 film adaptation *Bram Stoker's Dracula* and immediately being mesmerized and intrigued. It wasn't simply the incredible special effects and gothic horror sensibilities of Stoker's classic vampire tale. The emotionally resonant tone of the film spoke to me as a young Four. Dracula is a seductive and complex character. Coppola, likely a Four himself, added a prologue to Stoker's classic gothic novel. The prologue acted as a motivational backstory to Dracula's life as an immortal blood-sucking, supernatural monster. In Coppola's imagining, Dracula, a fearsome knight known as "Vlad the Impaler," returns victoriously from the Crusades. He finds his beloved wife Elizabeth dead from suicide because she feared he died in battle. The grief-stricken knight rages at the church because they have dammed her soul and refuse to bury her body. Dracula, in turn, renounces God and vows to rise from the dead to avenge her death.

Dracula's anger at God is so intense it imbues him with immense dark supernatural powers, lust for human blood, and immortality. Four centuries later, Dracula summons Johnathan Harker, a British solicitor, to visit his Transylvanian castle to facilitate a real estate purchase. He glimpses Harker's fiancée Mina in a photograph and believes she is the reincarnation of his dead wife. His passion awakens. His hatred and envy for Harker fuel his decision to terrorize and attempt to murder Harker so he can travel to England and reunite with his long-lost love. Dracula travels to England and assumes the image of a wealthy, elegant count. He seduces Mina, kills off her friends, and wants nothing more than to make Mina his bride again.

Hatred and envy animate Dracula. He can only remain undead by literally sucking the life out of his victims. The vampire archetype is quintessentially Sexual Four. The necessity and penchant for seducing, manipulating, and eventually murdering other people is an appropriate metaphor for the Tempestuous Diva narcissistic subtype. Vampires have long captured our imaginations as dark, enchanting, supernatural figures that stalk the shadows.

This subtype is prone to stealing other people's creative accomplishments, romantic partners, friends, or diminishes others' happiness or successes out

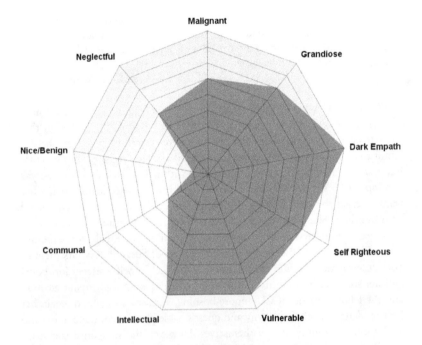

**The Tempestuous Diva.**

of spite. They can also easily feel exempt from the rules that govern "normal" people's behavior. Their entitlement is often so bold and unapologetic that other people do not challenge them. Their propensity toward grandiose entitlement can sometimes land them in legal trouble or situations where their lack of respect, reverence, or concern for protocol, rules, or formalities bring about consequences.

Many people of this subtype covet and disdain healthy, happy relationships. They can often take it upon themselves to seduce or undermine others' relationships, accomplishments, or goals as an expression of their hateful envy toward others' contentment.

It wasn't until middle school that I cared more about my appearance. I noticed that men's attention was directed at me for the first time in my life. But for some reason, they never chose me. I wanted to be chosen. My friend Claire was the total opposite of me, blond, cheerleader, popular. I was this sort of witchy, dark emo-girl, and I liked it like that. She started dating this football idiot, Blake, and I was pissed because he was hot (even though he was dumb). It just wasn't fair that she always got everything she wanted. Long story short, I ended up getting [Blake] to fall in love with me. He broke up with Claire, and I dated him for a few weeks before I got bored. I just wanted her to know she couldn't have everything she wanted. It was the first time she probably realized life wasn't fair. Ever since then, I've kind of had a thing for married guys. Happy marriages make me sick because I don't believe in happy endings.

—Anya, 27, makeup artist

When interviewing Anya, I sensed no remorse or guilt for her treatment of Claire. She revealed they never spoke after she began dating Blake but that she felt no real feelings about the end of the relationship. However, she did admit that part of what caused her to undermine Claire's relationship was that her best friend would be spending less time with her because of a man. Anya's fixation on life's unfairness paired with her chronic dissatisfaction makes her want to exact the same feelings of disappointment, insecurity, and emotional pain in others. She is an emotional sadist, a common feature of this subtype.

Angelina Jolie masterfully played another skillful fictional representation of the Tempestuous Diva in the film adaptation of Susanna Kaysen's memoir *Girl, Interrupted.* The film chronicles Kaysen (likely a Self-Preservation Four) and her stint in a mental institution after an overdose of aspirin and alcohol, and the fellow patients at Claymoore hospital. Kaysen's struggle to regain her independence and the misogyny and questionable practices of the doctors and staff are interesting in and of themselves. However, the antagonist sociopath Lisa Rowe, played by Jolie, truly makes this film electrifying and chilling. Lisa is intelligent, charismatic, manipulative, and emotionally violent.

Lisa has been in the institution since she was twelve years old and is the unofficial leader of the ward. The other patients look to Lisa for permission, guidance, and protection. She is a dangerous figure because of her innate understanding of the psychological issues of each of the patients. As a long-term resident of Claymoore, she develops leverage over the other patients. Lisa initially likes Kaysen, believing she can control her as she has the other wards. The two become embroiled in a complicated relationship where Kaysen fights to maintain her autonomy and sanity despite Lisa's narcissistic abuse.

Like the Sexual Eight, Lisa demands loyalty and devotion from the other women. She gains power by cultivating pseudo-deep personal relationships with each of them. Despite her occasional sadism, gaslighting, and verbal and emotional abuse, they all feel like Lisa cares for them.

A heartbreaking scene shows Lisa convincing a fellow ward, Daisy, an OCD sufferer, incest victim, Self-Preservation Two, to commit suicide. Lisa feels no remorse for her emotional manipulation and abusive treatment of the other girls. As Kaysen reveals, she keeps all of them in her proverbial clutches to ensure they don't leave, believing that if she must suffer in the institution, they all must suffer.

In the final scene of the film, Susanna challenges Lisa's psychological domination. Only then can we see her vulnerability and the true extent of her despair, feelings of inadequacy, and abandonment fears arise. It's difficult not to feel empathy for Lisa. She's been institutionalized most of her life and frequently receives electroshock therapy and other punishments for her antisocial, rebellious behavior. However, she is a malignant emotional bully. Her envy and hatred of the other women's goodness forces Lisa deeper and deeper into her sociopathy and eventually, by the end of the film, a complete psychotic break.

If empathy is sufficiently absent, this subtype is notably cruel, outwardly hateful, and emotionally manipulative. The Tempestuous Diva subtype is often the dark empath and vulnerable narcissistic variant because of their intuitive understanding of human emotions and the ability to appear emotionally resonant, pseudo-empathetic, emotionally revealing, and seemingly interested in others. They are adept at trauma bonding with anyone who will validate their sad stories or reinforce their need to be regarded as a rare orchid. However, the propensity of the non-narcissistic Sexual Four to seek validation of their uniqueness through empathic mirroring of others' innate specialness is degraded in this subtype. The goal is almost exclusively to exact their misery, disappointment, and rage at their inability to connect with others due to their narcissism.

## When Dealing with the Tempestuous Diva:

1. This subtype is emotionally intense and can be prone to dramatic emotional displays. These often elicit others' attention for something they perceive is unfair. Ignoring this subtype is dangerous because it will usually increase the volatility of their reactions. Offer to listen to their experience and emotions but with the caveat that they try to minimize their reactivity.

2. Do not try to relate to their emotional experiences. Their feelings of being misunderstood, invalidated, or mundane activate when people describe their experiences to this subtype's experiences. Instead, validate their experience's uniqueness and then ask if they want you to share your interpretation or similarities with them from your perspective.

3. Emotional manipulation is common with this subtype but may be subtle. Notice efforts to undermine your security, happiness, accomplishments, goals, or dreams through negativity, disdain, or expressions of doubt. They engage in these behaviors out of the erroneous fear that if others are happy, healthy, and independent, they will leave them. Of

course, if their behavior is problematic enough, it is often inevitable that people leave them.

4. If they become violent, leave. This subtype can be prone to crimes of passion, physical expressions of frustration (breaking glass, punching walls, screaming, hitting, etc.) If they become emotionally dysregulated, seek shelter away from them and consult with a licensed therapist qualified to treat narcissistic abuse. Breaking free from this subtype can be challenging due to their ability to oscillate between hatefulness and genuine emotionality.

# 13

## Type Five

### The Remote Investigator

Narcissistic Subtypes:
*Self-Preservation Five: The Miserly Misanthrope*
*Social Five: The Intellectual Elitist*
*Sexual Five: The Dark Voyeur*

#### SELF-PRESERVATION FIVE

When Barry emailed asking if he could contribute to my research on empathy and personality, I was thrilled. Fives rarely want to be interviewed due to their high need for privacy and anonymity. Barry initially asked to speak on the phone because he hated video conferencing. However, I told him that I needed to correctly confirm his Enneagram type, Trifix, and instinctual subtype by observing him speaking and talking. He reluctantly agreed if I could ensure his anonymity, which of course, I did. Barry shared that he was excited to participate in the study because he's long been a student of the Enneagram and recently developed an interest in the supra-marginal gyrus's role in the experience of empathy. I assured him I'd be unable to contribute meaningfully to a substantive neuroscientific discussion. Still, I'd be thrilled to listen to what he'd found out.

Initially, Barry unintentionally obscured himself during the video chat. He was flanked by massive bookshelves behind him and sat in a poorly lit study. I told him I needed to see him more, and he turned on a tiny desk lamp which revealed a multitude of scattered magazines and books. He wasted no time telling me we had to conclude our interview in an hour because that's as long as he can typically handle socializing in one day.

> I tend to study one topic for a long time. I would go to the library every day after school and read about rare butterfly species in middle school. I even signed up for a butterfly collection group, but I hated capturing them. It was cruel. I wanted to collect them, but it seemed wrong. So I settled on studying them. At other times in my life, I have been into 1930s British warplanes, phonetics, archaic and early dynastic cuneiform, the Enneagram, respiratory pathogens, and, most recently, brain stuff. I read a lot about coronaviruses before we even entered the pandemic. I like to research things that scare me a lot. It helps me feel more in control of the fear.
>
> —Barry, 58, computer programmer

Barry's interests indicate the Self-Preservation Five, who enjoys delving deeply into specialized topics. As a fundamental feature of their personalities, Fives hoard information, and data. The Self-Preservation Five is the most prone to accumulating books or other collections that center around their interests. They can spend hours poring over their interests. Many say that their intellectual interests are just as (if not more) enriching than relationships. Barry also pointed to the Five's tendency toward researching or exposing themselves to whatever scares them. As a Self-Preservation Five, Barry's fears constellate around self-preservation concerns.

> I have a pervasive fear of people watching me or trying to invade my privacy. It's ironic, though, because I enjoy watching other people and observing their habits. People are fascinating from afar, but I want them to stay away (for the most part). I feel like when people know things about you, they can manipulate you, and that's another one of my fears. I am terrified of someone trying to manipulate me. So I stay away from them.
>
> —Barry, 58, computer programmer

Fears of invasion are common for Fives, particularly Self Pres Fives, who are the most private and remote of all the Five subtypes. Their avoidance of entanglements and relationships often helps them manage the anxiety of others' expectations. Self-Preservation Fives amass resources to afford them the ability to maintain their independence. For this subtype, autonomy and independence are matters of life and death. Other people typically perceive Self-Preservation Fives as miserly due to their characteristic frugality and the propensity to minimize their desires and needs. Some Self Pres Fives will even challenge themselves to live in spartan and reductionistic ways as a means of feeling safe. They believe that the fewer attachments they have, the less likely they will be beholden or indebted to other people.

Not all Self Pres Fives suffer from OCD, but all report that their fears of invasion and contamination amplify their avoidance of relationships, activities, and environments that could be uncomfortable. Many avoid emotional entanglements and relationships because they believe that either they or the other person will contaminate the relationship and ruin it. They place high regard on purity. Unlike Ones, who focus on moral and ethical purity and perfection, Fives concentrate on the purity of ideas, data, information, and theoretical constructs. They avoid interpretation because they view it as a form of contamination. For many Self Pres Fives their intellectual interests, hobbies, and imaginations are the only realms free of obligations.

Self-Preservation Fives with regular to high empathy are deeply sensitive and profoundly respectful of other people's boundaries, limitations, and personal preferences. They are not usually emotionally expressive but can be astute listeners and offer sage wisdom won through their years of observing and cataloging life. Other people may be struck by their sudden generosity, demonstrations of emotional sensitivity, or compassion.

> I don't have many relationships on purpose. I amicably divorced at 35 and decided that married life wasn't for me. We have one child whom I love very much. She's a lot like me, and we don't have to talk much to feel connected. Honestly, I think we both prefer it that way. However, I am very close with my sister, who is blind. When I was in my 20s, I wanted to understand what it was like for her to be blind, so I behaved as though I were blind for two months. I would blindfold myself every day using a blackout eye mask I constructed that mimicked total blindness. I wore dark glasses over the mask to make sure. I would go to class, cook dinner, and do everything sightless. I learned braille even. It was humbling. I would only take the mask off for ten minutes at the end of the day to ensure that my eyes still adjusted properly to light. She knew nothing about my experiment. I recorded my observations and thoughts on a voice recorder. I sent her the recording one day as a gift . . . I was honored to have seen the world through her eyes.

> —Barry, 58, computer programmer

For Barry to abdicate his ability to read books or construct his highly detailed dragon figurines is a massive act of generosity for this subtype. They view their independence, time, energy, and resources like gold and can become fierce if their boundaries are breached. They often compartmentalize their relationships and commitments to deal with the anxiety of too many potential demands. Many Self-Preservation Fives find it challenging to commit to anything because of the fear of being overwhelmed.

*Chapter 13*

# THE MISERLY MISANTHROPE

Daniel Day-Lewis won the Oscar for depicting the ruthless oil tycoon Daniel Plainview in Paul Thomas Anderson's epic western period drama *There Will Be Blood*. The film chronicles Plainview's ascent as an oilman in the late nineteenth and early twentieth centuries. Plainview is a man of few words and seems singularly focused on building an empire from oil prospecting. Soon, he establishes a drilling site near Los Angeles and adopts a child orphaned by an accident on his oil site. However, Plainview does not adopt the boy simply out of empathy for losing his father. At first, it seems Plainview felt responsible for the child but later saw the boy (H. W.) as an asset in helping him acquire oil rights to various properties. He views H. W. as more as a business partner than a child and even refers to him as such. Plainview is approached by Paul Sunday, who tells him of potential oil underneath his family's land. Much of the film illustrates his complicated relationship with Sunday and his pious, preacher (and narcissistic) twin brother Eli (refer to chapter 9 for an analysis of Eli). Plainview's primary objective throughout the film is to amass more

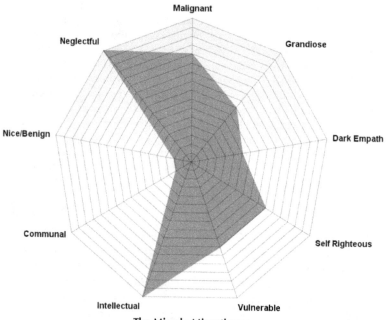

**The Miserly Misanthrope**

wealth. Daniel views all relationships as transactional and disposable once they no longer serve him.

*There Will Be Blood* boasts two narcissistic characters (Plainview and Eli). It nicely reveals the differences between the Miserly Misanthrope and the Moralistic Inquisitor. Plainview remains dry, unemotional, and remote throughout the film. He is sinister due to his lack of empathy, misanthropy, and sudden and explosive violent temper. Plainview admits to being profoundly misanthropic and cynical about people stating, "I look at people and see nothing worth liking." His disdain for people, relationships, and singular desire to acquire more and more oil rigs, money, and power are hallmarks of the Miserly Misanthrope. The film is a detailed character study showing greed's corrosive dangers. It is also a parable on narcissism and the origins of corporate psychopathy in the United States.

This subtype is greedy and almost entirely unconcerned with relationships of any kind. Their narcissism augments their fears of being without their basic survival needs. They channel their greed into a stark, emotionless acquisitiveness. Like non-narcissistic Self Pres Fives, this subtype fears that they will be depleted of their energy and resources. However, they believe other people are obstacles to meeting their needs. They develop a profoundly cynical and avoidant attitude toward all relationships. They have no use for emotions, sentimentality, or kindness. They often reduce other people to mechanistic, animal-like motivations and believe that others are profoundly ignorant and clueless.

The Miserly Misanthrope focuses on stockpiling information and resources as a means of security. However, the knowledge they seek is frequently dark, anti-humanistic, and exploitative. This subtype may still minimize their basic needs, preferring a simple life with few possessions. They will fiercely hoard their time, energy, and attention from others. The Miserly Misanthrope sees other people's emotional needs as a nuisance and makes no qualms about dismissing, belittling, or chastising others for legitimate emotional needs.

They can be quite neglectful of others. If they have any meaningful relationships, they resent intrusions on their time, money, or energy. As is common with most Self-Preservation types, they believe that others will drain their resources if they don't protect them. When narcissistic, they eliminate the possibility of others' demands intruding on their needs. They do this by building emotional (and sometimes literal) fortresses around themselves to prevent anyone from appealing to their sensitivities, lest they manipulate them. The compartmentalization tendencies of the Five are amplified with this subtype. People in their lives may not even know the other exists if they've chosen to keep their worlds separate.

Ebenezer Scrooge of Charles Dickens's novella *A Christmas Carol* is the quintessential exemplar for this subtype's cantankerous greediness. Scrooge, a London businessman, is miserly, reclusive, cold, and unempathetic. As is typical with most of Dickens's writing, the novella meditates on the moral price of greed, industrialism, and classism. Scrooge disdains Christmas and derides its merriment and the expected generosity and graciousness the Christmas holiday elicits in others. His infamous refrain "Bah, humbug!" is a representation of his exasperation at others' Christmas tidings of good cheer: "If I could work my will, every idiot who goes about with 'Merry Christmas' on his lips should be boiled with his own pudding and buried with a stake of holly through his heart. He should!"[1] Scrooge's hostility was so deeply embedded in his psyche that he wished death upon anyone who expressed genuine happiness. The miser found nothing redeemable in human beings and instead sought refuge through the hoarding of money. His lack of relationships and avarice rendered him emotionally brittle and sadistic like Plainview.

The Miserly Misanthrope can become violent when paired with psychopathy in extreme cases. They can begin to disidentify with their humanity and see other people as empty sacks of flesh undeserving of life. They're often embittered from a lifetime of ridicule due to their awkwardness, remoteness, or emotional deficits. This subtype can abstract people into concepts and ideas to justify their hatred and mistreatment.

> People are just bugs to me. They are no better than roaches or beetles, and honestly, they should probably all die. I wouldn't last in jail so I couldn't kill anyone. But human beings are greedy flesh bags, and they deserve all the pain and horror they get. I stay to myself, mostly because if I'm around anyone, I feel so sickened by their opinions, emotions, and blah blah blah. Just leave me alone. I'll watch my horror movies by myself, and everybody else can run around and act like any of this matters.
>
> —Curtis, 22, student

The ability to abstract people into ideas or concepts and divorce themselves from being human is common among Fives. However, the Miserly Misanthrope's abstraction can have dangerous effects on others as they begin to see people as obstacles or tools to achieving their dreams of total isolation.

Ted Kaczynski, colloquially known as the Unabomber, is this subtype. Kaczynski, a former mathematics professor, and prodigy, retreated to the woods to pursue a naturalistic lifestyle. He rejected modern conveniences and wrote a detailed manifesto. The 35,000-word essay denounced leftism, industrialization, the destabilizing effects of technology, cultural superficiality, and made other critiques of contemporary culture. In response to what he believed was the decline of humanity, he sent mail bombs with the goal of alerting the masses to the dangers of their materialism and consumerism. Kaczynski harbored a deep disdain and mistrust for people. He believed because of his superior intelligence and ability to see the truth, it was his job to wake up the idiots of the world. The grandiosity and egocentrism of this subtype manifest in their isolation and cold abstraction. They dissociate themselves as geniuses and others as mindless cogs waiting for intelligent intervention. Whether it's greed or stark minimalism, this subtype seeks refuge from their fears of annihilation through exploiting or minimizing others' needs, perspectives, or experiences for their security.

**When Dealing with a Miserly Misanthrope:**

1. Try to eliminate any expectation that someone with this subtype will be generous with their time, energy, money, or resources. This will help mitigate your disappointment with their stinginess. Without expectations, you may be pleasantly surprised if they offer their help or resources.

2. Their need for alone time and privacy may seem excessive to you. Remember, the more you push for interaction, emotional expression, or communication, the more grumpy, resentful, and cold they become. If you give them space, they may occasionally decide to emerge and connect for short periods.

3. If they become excessively miserly, hoarding, or frugal, remember that their survival fears have been activated. They may need some form of reassurance that there are enough resources to be had. Suppose there is a shortage of some vital resources. In that case, however, they may grow increasingly anxious, and their paranoia will increase.

4. At times this subtype can be relentless about finances or incredibly petty about money and maybe convinced that other people are exploiting their resources. They then justify their attacks and aggression toward others out of fear of being depleted. If they become abusive or begin obsessing about these issues, it's best to remove yourself from the situation.

## SOCIAL FIVE

Social Fives seek security by being valued as knowledgeable, competent, and respected for their contributions to society. Academia is a perfect environment for this subtype. They thrive where they can learn, teach, and disseminate their hard-won knowledge. This subtype is slightly friendlier than the other two Five subtypes and finds the energy of a group of like-minded thinkers invigorating. Like all Fives, they want to gather enough information before sharing their findings with the world. Still, like all social subtypes, they need validation from the group to feel valued.

The Social Five professors I encountered in my doctoral program had a robust knowledge in different theoretical areas of communication. They could be assertive and almost Eight-like in the proclamation of their opinions. However, unlike Eights, they were decisively focused on the information itself rather than asserting their power. Once they finished teaching or discussing data, ideas, theories, or postulations, they retreated and became almost ghost-like. Despite their relative sociability compared to other Fives, excessive socializing is draining if it doesn't have an intellectual purpose. The appearance of extroversion and social amicability can be confusing for others because they can, like turtles, quickly retreat into themselves. Some Social Fives may even enjoy parties, clubs, or other highly stimulating social atmospheres and then leave once they've gotten their fill.

The Social Five holds the archetypes of the wizard, the shaman, or the scholar archetype because they often endeavor to become the seekers and holders of arcane knowledge. They are frequently attracted to information that is difficult to gain or highly specialized. They want to carve a niche for themselves and dispense wisdom based on their findings.

The Social Five wants to be the keeper of knowledge since this is the way they garner respect from the group. To be part of the group and avoid rejection, they must become experts.

> I have always had a love/hate relationship with people. I don't like people very much because I think they say some pretty stupid things. However, I think the right people can help foster intellectual growth. I'm a lifelong learner. That's why I wanted to be a professor. Being an expert in something gave me a sense of purpose.
>
> —Peter, 53, professor of economics

Social Fives equate their value with their knowledge. They can be moralistic and Oneish, particularly around their core values of education and the value of critical investigation of meaningful topics. They believe that others would not respect them without their extensive specialization in a particular area(s) of interest. As a result, they often seek positions of intellectual power (hence why academia is so attractive for this subtype).

Social Fives view other people and groups as a sort of necessary evil. Like all Fives, they fear intrusion or becoming enslaved to others' expectations and losing their autonomy. However, if they aren't at the top of the intellectual hierarchy, they strive to reach that level of authority:

> My biggest pattern is always [becoming an] intellectual authority or becoming higher up as a teacher of some sort. Even in high school, people would come to me for academic help or objective advice. Online I'd always gain knowledge and become a [personality] typist or source of knowledge, so people would always come to me for that, . . . but it is also a curse in a way. I realized after reflecting that I can never be a normal person in a group. I always need to espouse knowledge of some sort . . . I've gotten into conflicts because people have thought I was too inaccessible, arrogant, or high-standard seeking. I get paranoid about keeping my position because I've realized that people can get threatened by my authority. I can dismiss people a lot, so it angers people, and I've had people rally against me because of my approach.
>
> —Salomé, 21, student

Being rejected or misunderstood by their chosen group is painful. It can reinforce their belief that human relationships and humanity are not worth pursuing or saving. If healthy and with average to high empathy, this subtype can be generous with their time, energy, and insights. They will gladly share what they've learned and take the time to help others who are genuinely interested in learning what they have to say. They often have a high value of being meaningful contributors to conversations in their spheres of interest. They will revere other experts who have proven their competence. They are mindful not to tread on others' boundaries. Many try to be polite to conceal their discomfort with social interactions. However, they can suddenly become animated and uncharacteristically loud or expressive if they begin talking about a subject that fascinates them.

## THE INTELLECTUAL ELITIST

If people were less idiotic, I wouldn't have to tell them what to think. I know that I'm smarter than most people I meet. I have an IQ of 157, which is way above the average intelligence. I have two master's degrees, a Ph.D. and a Postdoc. I am also one of the leading researchers in my field. I know what I'm talking about.

If I don't, then I don't speak. I wish other people would do the same. The world would be a lot quieter.

—Dierdra, 44, clinical director

Dierdra is the epitome of the Intellectual Elitist. Confidence in her expertise and intellectual aptitudes is arguably warranted due to her academic achievements and intellect. However, her disdain for seemingly everyone around her indicates an intellectual narcissist. This subtype believes that their value in the world comes not just from their scholarly contributions like other Social Fives, but their intellectual superiority over others. They can be snobbish about intelligence and prefer to only associate with those they've deemed competent and learned.

Compared to the non-narcissistic Social Five subtype, the Intellectual Elitist is more interested in their public image. All Social Fives can pursue advanced degrees, specializations, or other scholarly distinctions to feel a sense of value. However, the Intellectual Elitist wants to wield power over others. They try to reach the top of the pecking order in whatever group they choose and may undermine others to reach the top of the heap. They sabotage by publicly challenging other people's thinking or the depth of their knowledge. They may take

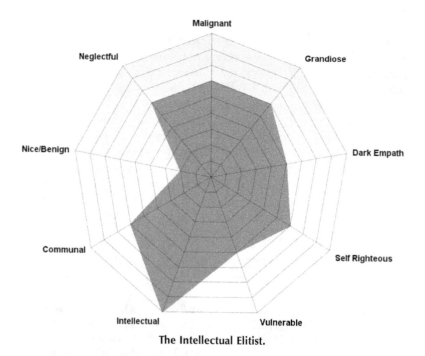

**The Intellectual Elitist.**

cheap shots at others to help bolster their sense of intellectual superiority—the more people who witness their jabs, the better.

This subtype, like all Fives, can easily dissociate people from their emotions. They do not value others' emotional experiences, mainly because they don't make sense. They are disinterested in navigating feelings and will quickly shut down others who want to discuss emotions out of their incompetency fears. Frequently their abstraction of others allows them to justify inhumane, insensitive, or callous treatment toward others. They believe that most people are thoughtless lemmings who need to be told what to think.

People of this subtype (in addition to being convinced of the inherent stupidity of almost everyone around them) also enjoy creating chaos because of their innate cynicism about humanity:

> I have been in the IT world for some years. It's dull primarily because it's programming stupid dating apps, for I think people need to be told how to think. I feel like steering the focus of the masses is a necessary evil. So, I started working for a troll farm during the 2016 election. I kind of enjoyed creating disinformation because it's funny to see what ridiculousness people will believe. Some of the things we populated on social media were absurd. Honestly, I just wanted to see everything go to shit. And it did. I don't have any allegiance to any political party or ideology because I think they're all dumb.
>
> —Chet, 34, content creator

The desire to create chaos and undermine the security of the ignorant masses is a theme among this subtype. It's a feature of their lack of empathy, grandiosity, and megalomania. They believe that dismantling people's inherent security, happiness, or identities is a kind of philanthropy.

The 2019 film *Joker*, directed by Todd Phillips, is an excellent character study of a classic comic book villain. However, Phillips' Joker, played by real-life Five Joaquin Phoenix, is perhaps the darkest and most realistic iteration of Batman's diabolical arch-nemesis. Phoenix's Joker is the epitome of the "evil genius" type of madness that can characterize the Intellectual Elitist. Joker serves as a backstory for the supervillain's ascent to, well . . . supervillainy. Arthur Fleck, Joker's actual name, is depicted as an awkward loner with the condition that causes him to laugh uncontrollably at inappropriate times. He works as a clown but is assaulted by bullies on an increasingly crime-infested Gotham city street. The attack is the beginning of Fleck's spiral into madness. Fleck fantasizes about being a stand-up comic and fantasizes about appearing on the *Late Night with Murray Franklin* show to deliver a comedy set that will catapult him into notoriety. However, Fleck descends further and further into madness after being fired from his job as a clown and assaulted by three

Wayne Enterprise businessmen on the subway. Fleck snaps and shoots one of the men in self-defense and flees the scene. The murder unlocks Fleck's psychopathy. He experiences himself as split between the mild-mannered, sensitive, and socially awkward Arthur and the growing power of his violent, grandiose alter-ego, Joker.

As the chaos and tension of the film mount, we witness Fleck's total descent into psychopathy as he assumes the identity of the Joker. The menace of his narcissism is palpable. Fleck finally makes it to the Murray Franklin show to perform his comedy set in the film's final act. Murray had previously mocked Fleck's jokes, awkwardness, and overall discomfort, and Joker wants revenge. Dressed in full clown makeup and a purple suit, Joker derides, shames, and terrorizes Murray with an unhinged tirade to avenge his public ridicule. Finally, in an act of spectacular violence, he shoots Franklin on air.

The film is bleak, nihilistic, and a fascinating psychological study. Fleck doesn't start the film as a psychopath. He is gentle, if a bit odd—a man with legitimate economic, mental, and physical limitations. However, by the end of the film, Fleck believes he must exact his revenge on a society that scorned and rejected him. He does this by splitting off from his former identity and inhabiting the role of his alter-ego, Joker. Because Joker, within the context of the Batman universe, is inherently an agent of chaos. Thus, his desire to sow fear, confusion, and despair reveals the depth of his antisocial sadism.

### When Dealing with the Intellectual Elitist:

1. When they are talking about their area of expertise and become arrogant, condescending, or patronizing, it's best to back off to avoid the potential for insults or a battle of wits.
2. This subtype values intellectual pedigrees. They may dismiss your education or knowledge because it doesn't meet their standards of excellence. Or, if they're the more anti-social variation of this subtype, they may deride your formal education, believing that their self-taught knowledge is more valuable. Hold on to what you are sure of and take their criticisms with a grain of salt, remembering it stems from deep-rooted fears of incompetence.
3. Having any emotional discussion can be difficult with this subtype. They can be exceedingly cold and overly rational if defended. If you feel emotional, it's best to remove yourself from the situation because showing them your emotional vulnerability will trigger their hostility.
4. Some people of this subtype can be emotionally dysregulated and may exhibit more chaotic and antagonistic features in some instances. When they feel threatened or incompetent, they may resort to uncharacteristic

emotional displays of anger, insults, or even physical violence to regain control over a stressful situation. If possible, leave immediately if they become aggressive because they can be unpredictable and dangerous when triggered in this way.

## SEXUAL FIVE

Sexual Fives focus their fear of depletion, contamination, and the desire to be competent and knowledgeable into the intimate arena. Like all Sexual subtypes, they desperately crave union with a desired other. However, due to their inherent discomfort with initiating, building, maintaining relationships, they prefer to keep their intimates at a distance. Sexual Fives idealize love and intimacy and believe that they will contaminate the purity of their connections if they are too engaged in them. They are also terrified that their partners and loved ones will ultimately drain them, so they retreat from their primary pair bonds. The struggle to maintain the purity of the love or connection while desperately desiring to be close to and near those they love creates a complex inner struggle.

This subtype believes that if they can gather enough information about those they care about, they will feel competent and confident in their relationships. Ultimately, they want someone with whom they can share their inner worlds. However, this is often an area of considerable anxiety for the Sexual Five. They can be like steel traps for information. At first, they gather information about the object of their affection. They may learn everything they can by observing a potential love interest for weeks, months, or years before gathering the courage to engage in conversation.

> When I saw my wife for the first time, it was love at first sight. She worked at the student union restaurant, and I would go there every day and just watch her. I just wanted to see how she interacted with others. I observed her mannerisms. I eavesdropped on her conversations with other patrons. I didn't even think about it as creepy; it was like research. I imagined our life together. I talked about her all the time to my best friend, and he kept telling me I just needed to ask her out. The thought of it terrified me. She was perfect, and I didn't want to find out she wasn't (or that I wasn't what she wanted). I was afraid she'd be better in my mind because everything is better in my mind. One day, after four months of observing her and going to the restaurant every day, she walked up to my table and said, "So, are you a creepy serial killer, or do you want to ask me out." I just stared at her, which I'm sure made it creepier to her. I didn't say anything, and she walked away! I went back the next day after I worked up the courage (several panic attacks later), and I did ask her out, and I guess the rest is history. She calls me her little stalker, a term of endearment, but when other people hear it, they make some funny faces.
>
> —Bradley, 42, cybersecurity expert

The Sexual Five, in essence, conceptualizes their relationships. Many have fallen madly in love with strangers who may not even know they're alive. The potential disappointment of initiating a relationship and the person not meeting their expectations or, worse yet, the person rejecting or abandoning them makes the idea of the relationship more palatable. Ironically, however, once the Sexual Five has chosen a potential mate, it's quite challenging to sully their idealized image of the relationship or other person. They can maintain the mental purity of the relationship by creating distance between them and the other person. For the Sexual Five, distance makes the heart grow fonder. They find the obstacles of distance (whether physical or emotional) exciting and a potent aphrodisiac. Their propensity to avoid significant relationships can be immensely frustrating to their partners, children, and family.

The Sexual Five thinks that if people knew what was inside their minds, they would be repulsed, scared, or disappointed and reject them. They want to share all their innermost thoughts, desires, and fantasies. However, because Fives' mental worlds are darker, or at least unusual, compared to most others, their fears of rejection or judgment are not entirely unfounded. Ideally, they could share their inner worlds with their partner. However, they doubt they will be accepted, so they pull back instead and become elusive. They may suddenly open up, become uncharacteristically revealing and emotional, and may not share again for days, weeks, or months. However, they possess an uncanny ability to pull other people's secrets, stories, and experiences out of them. They are like intimate informational sponges, gathering data about the other which helps them feel close to them. However, they also want to know that other people will hold their innermost thoughts with the same confidence and fidelity that they do for others. James Spader (a real-life Five) plays a perfect exemplar in the 1989 Stephen Soderberg film *Sex, Lies, and Videotape*. The film is about a man who records women recounting their sexual histories and fantasies and catalogs them as a form of pleasure for himself.

This subtype is incredibly intense, and they like to express their emotions or feelings through physical expressions of love, sex, and intimacy. Because they have trouble connecting with their feelings, they can require more extreme or taboo sexual encounters to satiate their intimacy needs. This can be surprising for partners because they may suddenly become aggressive and lusty about their sexual preferences and fantasies when normally withdrawn and quiet. They want total union with their love objects. Nevertheless, they may retreat for a period (emotionally or physically) after these encounters for fear of being overwhelmed by their partner's emotional demands.

This subtype can be Fours in their love for beauty, philosophy, psychology, or art. However, they tend to focus more on the mechanics behind these areas of interest and discuss these topics in a less emotionally revealing way than Fours. The latter are seeking identity through their interests. Fives are profoundly imaginative and report always building intricate worlds in their minds.

Famous impressionist composer Frédéric Chopin was likely this subtype. His beautifully evocative music personified the romanticism of the era. His masterful understanding of composition and ability to weave haunting, melancholic, and nostalgic melodies became trademarks of his style. Chopin was a child piano prodigy and showed superior musical ability by six. He spent much of his childhood plagued by illnesses and was a small and unassuming child. Chopin's letters to intimates revealed a passionate, complex, sensual, and cerebral man who often felt uncomfortable sharing his affections with people in real life. He was much more apt to express his love interests through his piano compositions. For Chopin, it seems the notes in his music were far more representative of his emotional world than words. He became enamored with a few distant love interests in his life. Still, none captured his heart and attention like writer George Sand. Chopin and Sand shared a tumultuous but passionate relationship toward the end of his life. Chopin's impact on romantic music was massive, notably since he only wrote for the piano. His haunting and, at times, surprising piano compositions directly represent his rich inner world and beautifully define the richness of the impressionistic era.

The ending of relationships for Sexual Fives is harrowing because they so often idealize the utopian emotional experience of being in love (not unlike the Sexual Seven). The alien-like, strange, surrealistic, and iconoclastic world of Bjork personifies the Sexual Five, who often marries their detached emotionality with a clinical starkness.

## THE DARK VOYEUR

The ordinarily upbeat, gregarious, and hilarious Robin Williams received rave reviews for his depiction of Seymour "Sy" Parish in the 2005 psychological thriller *One Hour Photo*. Sy is a lonely photo technician with no friends, partner, or social life. He buries himself in his work which he enjoys because he glimpses inside of people's private worlds. Sy has tried over the years to get close to the Younkin family. Over the years, Sy has stolen copies of the family's photographs and displayed them in his own home. However, his advances are rebuffed because of his shyness and awkwardness. Sy sees a potential entry point one day when he observes the family's matriarch, Nina Younkin, purchasing a book. He pretends to be interested in the book and strikes up a conversation. Nina learns he lives a solitary life and shares that her son is like Sy in his penchant for isolation.

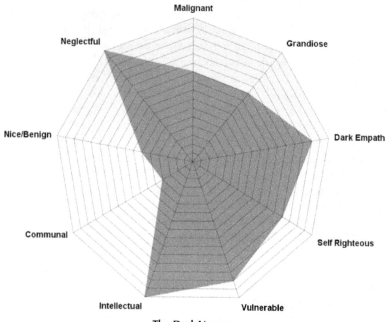

**The Dark Voyeur.**

Sy is eventually fired for various infractions. However, before he leaves his job, he discovers photos of Will Younkin, Nina's husband, apparently having an affair with another customer, Maya. To warn Nina of Will's indiscretions, he places the photos of her husband canoodling with Maya in her photos. Incensed because his romantic view of the Younkin family is shattered, Sy follows Will and photographs him and his mistress to send the photos to Nina. He becomes so obsessed with Will's indiscretions he takes candid photographs of their daughter and sends them to Will to intimidate him into confessing his indiscretions. As Sy's aggression and preoccupation grow, he follows Will and Maya to a hotel room. He forces them by knifepoint to pose in sexually provocative positions to send the photographs to Nina.

Williams is chilling in this role as a psychopathic Sexual Five seeking intimacy and closeness through stalking and physically and emotionally abusive behavior. His need to maintain an unsullied and picturesque view of the Younkins speaks to the Sexual Five's tendency toward keeping relationships as a fantasized mental conception. However, when reality doesn't match his romanticized view of the Younkins, Sy snaps. He believes, self-righteously, that it is his job to teach Will a lesson to restore his image of the perfect family.

This subtype is prone to stalking behavior and could colloquially be categorized as "creepy" to those who encounter them. They are typically isolated, secretive, and very good at concealing their motives or maintaining stealthy watch of those they're intrigued by. When higher functioning, this subtype excels at work where they're required to maintain anonymity while gathering information; thus, spy or intelligence work is often attractive to them. They're very good at adopting alternate identities or becoming invisible to acquire intimate details about people's lives. They believe that they deserve a bird's-eye view into their obsession's lives. They can be incredibly invasive both in their surveillance of others and in the way they probe for information without self-revealing.

Because this subtype often has subverted ideas about privacy, intimacy, and boundaries, they often conceal their inquisitiveness through an aloof or calm demeanor. They usually prefer to be solitary because they are often very paranoid about other people spying on them. Others may never discover the predatory way they quietly select and target people to investigate. They may employ charm or adopt personas and alternate identities to get close to different people. It's ubiquitous for people who engage with this subtype to say they feel like they don't really know who they really are.

Because they've only mentally conceptualized most of their relationships rather than engaging with them, they can become disenchanted and disappointed with the objects of their affection.

I met my ex-boyfriend online in a fetish chatroom. I was researching fetishes for a paper in my master's program. He was very knowledgeable about the history of corsets, so I found him intriguing. We talked for a while, or I guess it's more appropriate to say that I talked, and he asked me questions. Many of his questions were invasive, but I guess I found it intriguing. He love bombed me pretty hard. He was talking about how I was his fantasy woman. It was after he went home [from a visit] that the trouble started. He seemed to know where I was all the time . . . my friends suggested he'd put a tracker on my car. He swore he didn't, so I ignored it. There were other things like the fact that he wanted me to send him sexual videos constantly, but he'd never sent me any. . . . I reached my breaking point, and I texted him and told him I was done and that I wanted him to leave me alone. He said nothing, which was the most disturbing thing. I still have nightmares about him.

—Celine, 27, graduate student

Celine's experience harkens to the remote invasiveness of this subtype. She shared later that he sent her an email saying he was devastated by her leaving him and that he might not be around for much longer. Luckily, she didn't respond, recognizing his email as a manipulative appeal to her empathy. Luckily, two years later, he has yet to reach out again, much to her relief.

This subtype's dark inner world often reaches depths that most people would shudder to hear. However, it's not their thoughts that are dangerous. They often want others to satisfy their dark fantasies in real life because of the lack of impulse control common with narcissists. Their lack of boundaries is ironic, given their firm and definitive boundaries around their privacy. This subtype may be quiet, efficient, and competent in professional environments. No one would be aware of their narcissistic tendencies. Even their families may be unaware of this subtype's taboo underworld, as they are masters of concealing any thought, emotion, interest, or activity they don't want to be exposed.

If the Dark Voyeur's narcissism is advanced, they can be unpredictably rageful or violent. Their anger can be staggering because of their customarily reserved or quiet demeanor. When their psychopathy does flare up, it is often quite intense. They are frequently subtly threatening and enjoy playing mind games with people as sadistic gratification. Some may even delude themselves into believing that people are as intrigued by their mental games or abuse as they are due to their tendency toward relational idealization. They justify their attacks on others, believing that their love, concern, or care for people exonerates them.

## When Dealing with the Dark Voyeur:

1. Boundaries are crucial with this subtype. They may not honor them, but it's essential to be very clear about your privacy, limits, and preferences. This is especially important if you're in a romantic relationship. They can be surprisingly persuasive, charming, and mysterious to seduce you into their worlds.

2. This subtype can be prone to withholding personal information while prying into your mind. Play a game of quid pro quo with them to help draw out some of their inner thoughts if you begin to feel invaded by their mental examinations.

3. The Dark Voyeur can particularly struggle with empathy or relating to people. Suppose they are being particularly dry or seemingly unemotional. In that case, it's best to walk away temporarily from the conversation and return later. As you increase your emotionality, they will increasingly become less engaged or utilize your emotional revelations to manipulate you later.

4. If this subtype becomes angry or appears to be growing more agitated, they can become quite explosive and threatening. Avoid stoking their rage, remove yourself from the situation, and seek professional intervention from law enforcement if you're physically, mentally, or emotionally abused. Breaking free from this subtype can be challenging because of their propensity toward spying and stalking.

# 14

---

# Type Six

## The Loyal Skeptic

Narcissistic Subtypes:
*Self-Preservation Six: The Defensive Pessimist*
*Social Six: The Ambivalent Underminer*
*Sexual Six: The Overreactive Rebel*

### SELF-PRESERVATION SIX

Sharp, relatable, inquisitive, sensitive, and loyal are five words I would use to describe almost every Self-Preservation Six I've known in my life. And there have been quite a few. My best friend, business partner, and "ride or die" of over twenty years, my mother, and many others whom I have the pleasure of knowing have exemplified the quiet bravery and complex emotionality of this often-misunderstood type. The nature of Type Six is the variation in their own mental/emotional experience from moment to moment. This makes them the most elusive type to themselves. They often have trouble settling on their type because of self-doubt and a tendency to identify with their behaviors rather than their motivation. This is also why it isn't easy to weave a consistent thread with how each Six will present themselves since how they represent themselves in the world is variable depending on the Six. I often teach there are nine different kinds of Sixes because, depending on how they see themselves, the "flavor" will alter slightly and mimic the other nine types.

The Self-Preservation Six is an interesting mixture of warmth and suspicion. They want to trust others because forming alliances with stable, self-assured, and confident people helps them feel surer of themselves. This subtype's penchant for ferreting out the truth and exposing what they believe to be problematic, dangerous, or noteworthy are critical requirements for investigative journalism, as is the necessity for bravery. Putting oneself in potentially dangerous situations to get to the bottom of a mystery or discover what's not immediately evident is a strength this typically humble subtype proudly boasts:

> If something is going on that shouldn't be going on, I'll find out. There's a quote from a movie that I love: "the truth loves me." I love that. My friends come to me to investigate their new boyfriends to see if they're creeps or violent ex-cons; hell, I'll tell them who they hung out with in 7th grade and where they all are now. I want to know what's going on. If something is off, I feel it, and I can't relax until I find out what it is.
>
> —DeeDee, 37, bookkeeper

Not all Self-Preservation Sixes lead with their investigative skills. Many are private, admittedly anxious, but generally loving people who keep to themselves. A persistent refrain of this subtype is the desire to be left alone. Not because they all dislike people, but much like Fives, it's very easy for them to feel overwhelmed by others' demands or expectations. However, unlike Fives, they feel a duty to offer help or support. This creates a conundrum for them as they want to be regarded and appreciated for their loyalty and reliability, mainly because they hope others will reciprocate when they need it. They also strongly feel the weight of expectations and responsibility, which increases their anxiety, sadness, or frustration. Nevertheless, they are more than capable of shouldering great responsibility as they are often the stewards of anything they've been chosen or volunteered to protect or guard.

The hero Jon Snow in the popular HBO series *Game of Thrones* based on George R. R. Martin's fantasy anthology of the same name is one perfect exemplar of the modest everyman turned reluctant hero. Snow is presented as the "bastard" son of Lord Eddard Stark and raised alongside Stark's "legitimate" children. He is an outsider in his own family and decides to join the Night's Watch (a group of soldiers charged with guarding the massive wall that separates them from the "White Walker" monsters and other threats). Jon's humility and sadness are palpable as he struggles to find his identity. He wants to prove his capability to protect his community and family's honor. In typical dramatic epic-fantasy fashion, Jon is killed, resurrected, and becomes the chosen leader in restoring House Stark to its glory. Eventually, the once underestimated and humble Jon rises to become King of the North. The intricacy of the series is far too intense to discuss within these pages but suffice to say, Jon's journey is a typical trope within Self-Preservation Six.

Both Frodo and Bilbo Baggins in Tolkien's *Lord of the Rings* anthology are examples of anxious, humble (and unlikely) heroes who must rise to the occasion to defend themselves, their family, or friends' way of life. This subtype can be fierce and unyielding if threats to their security arise. The ability to spring out of their anxiety or apprehension can sometimes surprise even them:

> I am not a conflict person. I hate it. Mostly I want people to leave me alone. I don't let many people into my life because it's hard to manage the expectations of everyone. I'm susceptible to guilt, and too much responsibility can bring up a lot of guilt. I surprise myself sometimes because while many things make me anxious, I can be a badass if I need to be. Especially if people mess with my little core group of people close to me, I will stick my neck out. People think I'm this fearful little girl, but if you mess with my people or me, you'll see a whole other side.
>
> —Larsa, 24, sales associate

This subtype feels that if they support people they've deemed physically and emotionally safe, trustworthy, and reliable, they have more confidence in their abilities to overcome their anxiety. When anxiety arises, they can become rigid to manage their growing fear. Homelessness, hunger, physical harm, illness, and being deceived or lied to by someone they care about rank among their biggest fears. However, when they are in the Six style's counterphobic stance, they can be punchy, provocative, and challenging if they perceive something amiss in their environment.

The Self-Preservation Six is especially attuned to what could go wrong in a situation that could be threatening, dangerous, or simply annoying and supports others by warning them of potential pitfalls ahead. Unfortunately, their warnings are frequently disregarded or misinterpreted as negative, which can be very painful for this subtype. Their vigilance is employed to keep themselves safe or free from anxiety and as an act of love and support to people they care about.

Some people of this subtype are more creative, melancholy, and Fourish, while others are more helpful, upbeat, and nurturing—like Twos. Whatever their outward expression, their behavior mitigates the possibility of overwhelming anxiety that could render them nonfunctional, cowardly, or unable to defend or support themselves. Some people erroneously believe this subtype sits around thinking about being murdered, home invasion, or hand wringing about doomsday scenarios. This is a gross reduction of this subtype's savvy with resources and ability to challenge unfairness, abuse, or mistreatment.

Many Self-Preservation Sixes have an endearing, lovingly neurotic, and wicked sense of humor. Not typically flashy or attention-seeking, people may be surprised to hear their sometimes boisterous and biting remarks.

## THE DEFENSIVE PESSIMIST

In popular culture, the narcissistic variation of the Self-Preservation Six is often infantilized, comedic, and less threatening. While indeed their brand of anxiety can make for amusing television and movies, their brand of narcissism can be just as damaging, abusive, and problematic as the other twenty-seven subtypes. However, to illustrate the Defensive Pessimist's narcissistic traits, I would be remiss if we didn't explore two comedic exemplars. In the 1991 Frank Oz film *What About Bob?*, Bill Murray plays an anxious, dependent, and obsessive-compulsive character who becomes a nuisance for his psychologist, Dr. Leo Marvin, played by Richard Dreyfuss. Bob Wiley is a genuinely fearful character who becomes dependent on Dr. Marvin. Bob develops an unhealthy

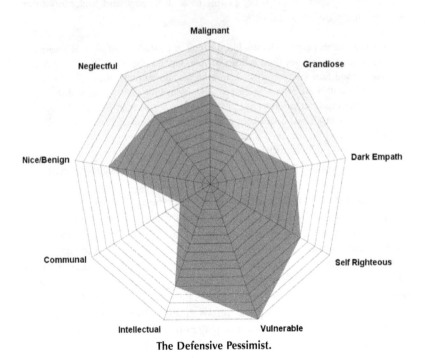

The Defensive Pessimist.

attachment to his psychologist, whom he enlists to help work through many issues. However, Bob's problems are exacerbated by Bob's hypochondria and conscious fabrication. For example, Bob is afraid he will develop Tourette's syndrome, so he intentionally screams obscenities because he believes, "if I fake it, I don't have it."

Bob remains innocuous until he inserts himself into Dr. Marvin's personal life. Bob's anxiety and obsession with Leo motivate him to charm his wife, children, and friends to the point where they all feel they must fold him into activities. Bob makes everyone walk on eggshells around his neuroses, but his manipulation and self-absorption hide behind a pleasant and endearing facade. Bob is a nice or benign narcissist, but his dependency and insistence on the attention of everyone around his anxieties make him very interpersonally challenging. While Bob isn't angrily defensive (he's relatively amicable and annoyingly friendly), he is resistant to taking responsibility for his mental health and developing healthy autonomy. Throughout the film, he crosses multiple boundaries and drives Dr. Marvin virtually insane with his refusal to leave.

In almost all cases the Defensive Pessimist, while indeed not consistently as inane as Bob Wiley, wants other people to acknowledge and preferably cater to their many anxieties and concerns.

> I used to joke that my mother was like the mom from the movie *Carrie*. She wasn't religious and didn't lock us in a closet or anything, but she was so fixated on her anxieties and fears and projected them onto us. She wasn't so much afraid of us being physically hurt. Honestly, she was too busy making sure she was healthy and safe to pay much attention to our physical safety. She seemed particularly angry with me because I was a laid-back and popular kid in school. . . . She tried to make me worry that my friends were talking badly about me or would try to plant thoughts that I think she thought might undermine my confidence.
>
> —Olivia, 33, elementary school teacher

As Olivia indicated in her interview, this subtype can be envious of other people's confidence and lack of anxiety. They believe that others should share in their anxious preoccupations and may try to push their fears, uncertainty, or propensity toward self-doubt onto others. This is one way the rage of this subtype can manifest. The effect can be subtle because their concern can at first seem supportive. However, their doubting and naysaying can have an erosive impact on others' self-confidence. Their disdain for confident, spontaneous, carefree, or happy people manifests through obstructionism. To control other people, the Defensive Pessimist may purposely try to sabotage or thwart someone else's success as a means of punishment. They have a long memory for being slighted, insulted, or otherwise disrespected than some of the other subtypes. They exact their revenge by being difficult or endlessly finding (or creating) problems for anyone who doesn't honor their anxieties, concerns, or agendas.

This subtype can be particularly pushy and uncompromising about how they want things done, mainly in their homes or work environments. This ensures that their anxiety or discomfort doesn't flare. They may demand that the dishes are put away specifically or that people follow their prescriptions for eating, cleaning, finances, and so on. They believe that others should cater to them, so they don't have to be anxious. They may even fabricate anxiety or panic attacks or lash out angrily when others don't bend to their will.

The Defensive Pessimist can also be significantly more negativistic, depressive, or angry than other subtypes. They legitimately struggle with some level of anxiety. However, they believe they are entitled to react to their fears in whatever manner they see fit. They may call others out for being insensitive to an unreasonable demand or attempt to police or alter others' language, opinions, or behaviors to whatever they find more suitable to their safety, comfort, and security.

The typically warm and supportive nature of the non-narcissistic Self-Preservation Six is sporadic at best in its narcissistic iteration. They may only support or help others out of a transactional desire to ensure that they will get their needs met down the road. They manipulate others with their insecurities to assume responsibility for things they find too anxiety-producing or difficult. It's not uncommon for this subtype to become angrily reactive, blaming, and verbally or physically abusive if something goes wrong in their lives. Their innate mistrust of themselves and their decision-making makes it impossible for them to trust other people, and they endlessly test others' trustworthiness.

This subtype is defensive, combative, and typically displays "angry" anxiety when agitated. This combination of features can make working through conflicts or disagreements very difficult. They are prone to cutting anyone off that triggers their alarm bells without explanation, warning, or justification. They often claim that they're upholding their boundaries but very often, it could merely be that a person said or did something they didn't like or refused to cater to rules of engagement. Once the Defensive Pessimist mentally positions someone or something as "dangerous," they become rigid, cold, and dogmatic in their perspectives and justify their persecution of others in the name of self-defense.

**When Dealing with the Defensive Pessimist:**

1. Be aware that when this subtype becomes reactive and angry, something in their awareness has frightened them. Their fear of impending disaster, chaos, or panic can make them react aggressively and angrily. However, responding with the same energy will typically escalate their anger.

2. The Defensive Pessimist is prone to endearing themselves to people for support and security. It can be upsetting to learn that someone has attached to you for what protection you can offer, so be mindful that if you believe you have met someone of this subtype, they may be looking for a proverbial train in which to hitch their wagon.

3. This subtype can at times appear vulnerable, scared, and helpless. While there is likely legitimate anxiety behind their reactions, they can often increase their emotional reactivity to elicit a response in others, particularly if others will handle something they find difficult or fear-inducing.

4. Find ways to encourage their independence because they can become highly dependent on others to allay their fears. Their dependency can be controlling and, at times, abusive. They can be prone to guilt-tripping or baiting others into emotional responses that they then leverage to get what they want. For example, provoking you to anger and then claiming that your anger is terrifying or dangerous. This is a subtle form of gaslighting that can be quietly erosive.

## SOCIAL SIX

The wildly popular hit television show *Friends* is filled with the rambunctious, relatable, quirky, and often playful energy of the Social Six. While not all the characters are Social Sixes, almost all are Sixes. Katherine Chernick Fauvre affectionately referred to the tendency for Sixes to band together in solidarity a "Sixpack." However, the sitcom's producers were either consciously or intuitively aware of the relatable allure of the Six. Finding an inordinate number of Social Sixes is expected when looking at the Enneagram type distribution of any friendship-based ensemble cast. Social Sixes endeavor to be loyal, relatable, dependable, endearing, and dutiful. They channel their fear of anxiety and uncertainty into the social sphere and seek security through alliances with a like-minded group, institution, or ideology they believe will provide them with the support they crave. Social Sixes love being a part of something larger than themselves and flock to environments where they can be counted on to defend and support their tribe.

Social Sixes recognize that there is strength in numbers and believe that an attack on one of their chosen tribes is an attack on the whole tribe. They are affiliative by nature, and even if trepidatious or suspicious of groups. They are almost always looking for a group (whether formal or informal) that matches their interests, ideologies, beliefs, or values. The Social Six's anxiety temporarily lessens if they feel they've meaningfully contributed to their chosen cause. Even the negatively identified Social Six that avoids mainstream groups and affiliations align with others for safety and a sense of belonging.

> I always said I hated groups. I didn't join any clubs in school and didn't have a huge friend group. I didn't play any sports because I didn't fit in with those guys. Now I can admit I always wanted to be the cool jock dude, but that just wasn't me. I'm kind of a nerd [laughs]. I had 4 or 5 friends I stuck with throughout middle school and high school. We all went to different colleges, and I felt lost after that. I tried fitting into a few different cliques in college. I even joined a fraternity for a year, but the guys were jerks, and I didn't like them very much. . . . When I graduated, I started getting into online groups. I met some other people into UFO stuff (I've always been into UFOs and aliens), and they were super cool guys. About ten years ago, I joined my UFO group, and we meet up a few times a year to go UFO hunting and go to conferences and stuff.
>
> —Cesar, 34, restaurant manager

There's significant variation in how Social Sixes can present in the wild. Some are more buttoned-up, professional, and seem Oneish, Threeish, or Sevenish in their presentation. They can be ambitious, gregarious, outgoing, and focused on gaining popularity. Others may be more reserved, intellectually focused, and Fiveish. Some are anti-establishment, countercultural, and rebellious and may seem Eightish or Fourish in presentation. And yet still, some are laidback, easygoing, and just enjoy hanging out with their friends and seem more Nineish or Twoish. In almost every case, the motivation to find certainty, security, belonging, and safety through their affiliation with their chosen group is central to the overall psychological strategy of the type.

Social Sixes typically have the most difficulty finding their type due to the variations in their behavior, personal style, and presentation. They often identify with their friends, political or religious ideologies, professional personas, or roles in society, making them mistake their behavior and group role(s) for their core motivations. It can sometimes be difficult for some Social Sixes to recognize their anxiety as they may sublimate their fears of being anxious, cowardly, or unprepared for other activities.

A former student of mine, Perry, was a textbook Social Six. He enrolled in my personality psychology class and spent the entire semester vacillating about his Enneagram type, despite receiving feedback from classmates, myself, and even questioning his family and friends on which types he "seemed like" to them. His tendency to seek others' opinions on his psychological motivations and then to mistrust, argue with or dismiss their assessments is a hallmark of this subtype. The final week of the class, he shared this revelation:

> I was completely unaware of my anxiety. You mentioned that the first week, we started studying the Enneagram, it seemed like I could be a Six, and I completely dismissed it. I didn't see myself as anxious at all. I played football and was confident in my athletic ability. I make friends easily, and I love stuff like dirt biking and skiing. Six just sounded so . . . whiny or something. But then something clicked: I always have a core group of friends. We dress alike, talk alike, like the same music, date the same girls, and like movies. I started asking myself what about that made me feel good. If the boys have my back, I feel like I can do anything. But if I'm alone and none of my friend group or extended friend group are around, I don't feel confident and like I can't do anything until I form an alliance.
>
> —Perry, 21, student

Their chosen group or affiliation provides the Social Six with a sense of purpose, identity, and security. Some Social Sixes may want to differentiate themselves from within the group, perhaps to stand out for their contributions, style, or differing opinion from the larger group structure. They may be more counterphobic or independent about their preferences but still define and track themselves and their value with the group's needs. They are typically very dutiful and feel a great sense of responsibility to support or help others who may be in danger or need.

When stressed, they can become exclusionary and fearful of anyone who doesn't fit into their conception of like-mindedness. They are simultaneously fascinated and terrified by people, groups, or ideologies that are different. If they're more counterphobic, their curiosity may cause them to seek friendships or relationships with others simply because they want to allay their fears of what they see as fundamental differences. If they're more phobic or defended, they may avoid or position others outside their comfort zone as dangerous. They often fear being ridiculed, cast out, being deviant, or otherwise rejected by their chosen group and left for the proverbial wolves should they have to go it alone.

## THE AMBIVALENT UNDERMINER

The Social Six takes their duty to protect whatever group or institution they've chosen further than all the other types. The Ambivalent Underminer takes the fears of the Social Six, being left out, cast out, or otherwise disconnected from the group, and ensures their position in the group, and the protection of the group, by becoming bullying and aggressive, passive-aggressive, and ambivalent. This subtype is prone to paranoia and typically aligns themselves with an ideological, philosophical, religious, or group-think mentality that helps them feel more secure in themselves. They have more natural confidence due to their narcissistic grandiosity and believe it's their job to protect whatever they see as their way of life.

We've all experienced the energy of this subtype if we've ever ostracized, criticized, or teased someone for being different or deviating from a particular standard. We've all felt scared or threatened by someone/something we don't understand or like. And maybe even persecuted (or wanted to persecute) or reject someone for their perceived difference in our eyes. Due to their fear and heightened paranoia, the Ambivalent Underminer feels that anyone outside

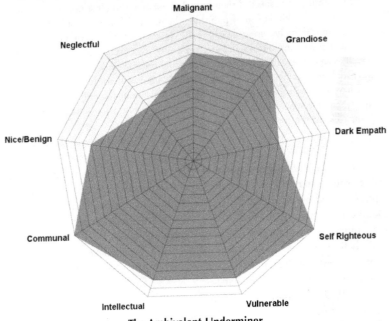

**The Ambivalent Underminer.**

their conception of safety deserves their suspicion. If this subtype is not a part of a group or affiliation, they become the authority via their identification with an ideological position (i.e., political ideologies, religion, philosophy, nationalism, race, gender, etc.). Their fear of others' varying opinions makes them reactive and feel justified in attacking or demeaning others who don't share their views.

Some people with this subtype may not be entirely focused on something as lofty as a religion or a political ideology but may find refuge in their friend group, where they believe they're superior to others. They may justify ostracizing or belittling others they think are beneath them and their group's superior position. They will also see themselves as elevated within the group. They may try to control the group by pitting people against one another or becoming dictatorial to ensure that people stay in line. This subtype's dark or sadistic side intensifies in organizations where hazing or forcing others to prove themselves through acts of bravery or endurance manifests this subtype's archetypal energy.

> I'm in charge of the pledges. It's my job to make sure they become the kind of women that our organization would be proud of. Not just with their grades and social lives but every aspect of their lives. I guess they chose me because I enjoy pushing them and kind of enjoy punishing them. If a girl steps out of line, I have no problem making her do study hall in the closet. They must learn. I don't want that girl representing our organization in a way that makes us look bad. I see myself as an enforcer. There are standards of our organization. We dress a certain way; we have specific values; we date a certain kind of man. It's just the way it is. I have no tolerance for insubordination or deviation, honestly. They can do that when they leave college, but if they live under my organization's roof, they're going to learn the correct way to be.
>
> —Lacey, 21, student

There's a Oneish self-righteousness with this subtype that is endemic to all Socials to some extent. However, unlike Ones, their standards and ideologies are typically based on outside authorities and don't come from their convictions. Despite their narcissism, they doubt their beliefs and conceptions without the support of an authority figure (or "support figure" as one Six called it). They believe that with the support of whatever they've deemed an authority, they must enforce their rules, standards, prescriptions, or ideologies on those around them, no matter how harsh.

The HBO series *Succession* is a meditation on narcissistic personality disorder as most of the characters on the show exhibit some degree of narcissism. The black dramedy chronicles the complicated in-family drama of a large

U.S. media conglomerate with a formidable malignant Rupert Murdoch–esque billionaire patriarch at the helm named Logan Roy (more on Roy in chapter 16). Roy is aging, and the show documents the shenanigans of his adult children vying to be the next in line to run Waystar RoyCo. His eldest son from his second marriage, Kendall Roy, is the apparent successor to the family's billion-dollar industry. However, his complicated relationship with his father and his narcissistic tendencies become problematic for him as he tries to navigate the passing of the torch. RoyCo is implicated in a severe abuse scandal at one of its subsidiary companies.

Logan tries to stop the proverbial bleeding by playing high-stakes chess with federal investigators, investors, and the public. He soon finds himself undermined and challenged from both inside and outside his family. The various Roy children are all scratching, clawing, scheming, and jockeying to either receive the keys to the kingdom from Logan himself or position themselves close enough to power to ensure their financial success. However, his son Kendall, played by Jeremy Strong, decides to take the heavyweight media giant head-on. Their dynamic is a master class in Eight narcissism versus Six narcissism. Kendall is the Ambivalent Underminer. He is incidentally one of the more flawed and human characters in the show. Nonetheless, he is a self-righteous narcissist whose inner war with his past addictions, deep need to be cool and relevant, and faux-moralistic objections to his father's ruthless reign are a mass of contradictions.

Kendall decided to expose his father by attempting a public coup of his father's business and thus starting a war with one of the most powerful men in the world. Kendall's methods are rarely overt. He's a master at undermining his father, leaking stories to the press, public humiliation, poaching employees and his siblings away from his father, and so on. Kendall knows he needs an army behind his revolt and is attempting to prove that he is not only the rightful heir to the Waystar throne but also that he will be more ethically responsible than his brutish father. Kendall is confusing because he alternates between a seemingly genuine desire to "do the right thing," a refrain he mentions throughout the series, and wanting the glory of overseeing the billion-dollar media conglomerate. Kendall neglects his relationships, forgets his kid's birthdays, and is endlessly obsessed with being regarded as relevant and hip.

He remains ambivalent about whether he even wants control of the company and appears wishy-washy and undermines his authority. Kendall is a reluctant leader that wants to be the top dog. He persecutes what he views as amoral behavior by his father and then throws reactive temper tantrums when people don't kowtow to his ambivalent leadership style.

The Ambivalent Underminer is often (though not always) indirect in their assaults. They often believe they're doing what's best for the greater good and thus justify their bullying or attacking others. They are often contradictory, vacillating between being agreeable, accommodating, rule-oriented, argumentative, obstructionist, and rebellious. Their egos are very fragile, and they react very poorly to criticism of their behavior. They insist that their motivations are pure as they've often sublimated them into whatever duty; they believe they must protect the underdog. They become highly suspicious of outsiders and are erratic about their choices. This subtype can often feel like superheroes in their minds and are often proponents of vigilante justice or harbor fantasies of their grandiose hero complexes. They justify their manipulation, bullying, or coercion of others as valiant attempts to save someone or something (which is more often themselves or their egoic pride).

This subtype can become very dangerous and paranoid on the far end of the spectrum, yet their cowardice often causes them to seek others who will do their bidding for them. Charles Manson is a perfect example of the psychopathic iteration of the Ambivalent Underminer. In most people's minds, Manson exists as an almost mythological boogey monster due to the gruesome and horrific Manson Family murders in 1969. Biographer Charles Guinn notes that Manson's history is peppered with infractions with the law such as burglary, sex trafficking, and assault. Manson was deemed "aggressively antisocial" by his juvenile caseworker.[1] He was erratic, fearful, aggressive, and seemingly unable to follow the rules. However, he seemingly always needed an entourage or gang around him. He preferred the company of other like-minded drifters, criminals, and fraudsters because they shared psychological commonalities, and his affiliative tendencies further emboldened his criminality. Manson was said to be very charming, persuasive, and unsettling. It is not uncommon for this subtype to maintain some of the typical relatability with the non-narcissistic Social Six.

Eventually, Manson amassed a small following of people, and his Manson Family cult devolved into a doomsday cult where he projected his anxieties about an impending apocalyptic race war. Manson's fear of blacks and other racial minorities bled into his ideology. He utilized this to rationalize why his "family" needed to "kill the pigs" and revolt against the police. The doctrine was convoluted but dangerous, and he was convicted of instructing three women to kill actress Sharon Tate in her Los Angeles home and four other women. He was convicted of conspiracy, yet maintained his innocence, and blamed the American public for the crimes because of their inherent violence and hypocrisy. Manson's abdication of responsibility, tendency to get others to do the "heavy lifting" for his crimes, fear of the "other," and twisted ideologies are common with the psychopathic iteration of this subtype. Even if they are antisocial and counterphobically disregard rules and regulations as Sixes, they fear being blamed and persecution despite their tendencies to blame and persecute others.

## When Dealing with the Ambivalent Underminer:

1. This subtype can be very controlling and militaristic about how things are done, making living or working with them a challenge. Let them know that while you respect their protocols, if their rules or ideas about the world are oppressive, you won't enforce or participate in them.
2. Their paranoia about others' intentions, ideas, or beliefs can often become exaggerated. This subtype is prone to forms of elitism, bigotry, separatism, or persecutory fantasies that can be disturbing. Tell them if you find their dialogue offensive or remove yourself when they spiral into persecutory tirades.
3. Some people of this subtype can be highly rebellious and defiant. They may have antisocial tendencies that make them resist any kind of restrictions. If they engage in illegal or risky behavior, it's best to distance yourself because if they get into trouble, they tend to blame others to avoid punishment.

## SEXUAL SIX

Fear for the Sexual Six acts as fuel for their adrenaline and a constant monkey on their back that they must wrestle to prove themselves worthy of the ideal mate. This subtype believes that surrendering to their cowardice is the worst fate, and thus they are more frequently counterphobic than the Self-Preservation and Social Six. However, like all Sixes, their relationship to fear and anxiety is complicated and nuanced. Sexual Sixes believe that by appearing strong, competent, attractive, and fearless, they will be worthy of attracting a capable mate that can help ease their anxieties. This subtype can seem Threeish in their desire to look good but is also frequently emotionally complicated, creative, and soulful like Fours. They can then alternate between being laid-back like Nines and aggressive and blustery like Eights. They are often unaware of their anxiety because as fear arises, they must barrel toward it, so it doesn't make them feel cowardly. They are afraid to be caught in their fear and unable to rise to the occasion to overcome their anxieties when necessary. More specifically, they're worried that if they appear to be cowards or afraid around the objects of their desire or intimate connections, they will lose their support and love and then become more fearful.

I hate showing my anxiety. I feel like I have to look like I have it together all the time, but internally, I'm a mess. I started doing weight-lifting at the gym in high school, and I started getting bigger, and women started looking at me more. I did my first CrossFit competition five years ago and won, and I loved how it made me feel. I have to admit I get a lot of attention from women (and men), but inside, I'm always anxious they'll find out how anxious I am. So, I feel like when I go out, my body is a kind of armor, so people don't see that underneath all of this, I'm still kind of a scared kid. I used to get into fights in college to see if I could win. I wanted to know that I could overcome my fear and do what needed to be done under pressure.

—Tevin, 27, personal trainer

The tendency for this subtype to "puff up" to seem less fearful or anxious is quite common. They believe that their posturing, whether by demonstrating their strength, intelligence, and beauty (and preferably all three), will get people to leave them alone and simultaneously attract a desirable mate that can help bolster their self-confidence.

Many people of this subtype share an attraction to adrenaline and risk-taking endeavors. Bungee jumping, driving fast cars, rock climbing, and other extreme sports and activities can help them feel as though they control their anxiety and fear. They are often big proponents of mind over matter. They can even take their propensity toward overcoming their limitations and overriding their fear to impressive lengths.

A "mind over matter" ideology is a common defense mechanism for this subtype. Intense emotions like fear, sadness, and grief can be overwhelming and create further panic and anxiety, triggering their core psychological fears. To avoid the existential terror of being controlled by uncontrollable human emotions propels this subtype to seek ways to demonstrate their strength and lack of fear. Deliberately triggering their fear through extreme actions not only helps them feel in control over their anxiety and less cowardly, but may also attract a partner who is impressed by their mastery. However, sometimes they are unaware that fear is driving the proverbial bus until they find a system like the Enneagram:

I had no idea that I was afraid of anything. As weird as it sounds, it never crossed my mind. I guess I had built up such an image of myself as being this badass that wasn't afraid of anything that I forgot that everything I've done in my life is a response to my fear. I joined the military because I was afraid of it. I learned how to jump out of planes because I was afraid. I did nude modeling because I was afraid of it. I reacted so quickly to my anxieties to overcome them; I didn't register them as fear until I started studying the Enneagram. My husband said he was interested in me because I wasn't afraid of anything, but when he got to know me, he was like, "you're anxious about everything!"

—Tatiana, 38, parole officer

This subtype frequently comes across to others as self-assured and confident because this is what they want to project to be desirable to a robust and capable partner. However, their fear of being found to be inadequate or not enough for their intimates is equally as vital. They can be difficult to chase down and often test their intimates for trust and loyalty extensively before becoming fully devoted. This subtype can be provocative, argumentative, impulsive, and reactive during the testing phase and then be sweet, placating, responsible, and conflict avoidant. Their behavior can be confusing and erratic to others, but it's representative of the ambivalence they feel about letting someone into their inner world.

The contradictions of this subtype can be as confusing as their emotional lability and characteristic reactivity. While they can have a rebellious streak and are headstrong and fiercely independent, they can also be loyal and faithful friends, parents, and partners. They want others in their lives to support and protect them, and they gladly return the favor and, as such, can be very picky about whom they allow into their lives. They know that once they commit themselves to a relationship, and the person passes their loyalty tests and can prove they aren't scared by their mercurial nature, they're deeply devoted.

## THE OVERREACTIVE REBEL

The intense energy of the sexual instinct mixing with narcissism and Six creates an intense and complicated subtype. The fear of being abandoned by their intimates produces a volatile mixture of reactivity, angry vulnerability, and potentially controlling behavior that can be difficult for others to navigate. The Overreactive Rebel is often argumentative, paranoid, domineering, and emotionally manipulative. They begin most of their relationships by being endearing, charming, and more than a little cocky. They can be highly desirable in friendships, romantic relationships, and to employers because they know how to utilize their combination of relatability and over-confident bravado to attract others. They can be highly vulnerable, emotionally expressive, and prone to violent or reactive outbursts if angry or provoked. Their bluster, sex appeal, and confidence are often very attractive to people they choose to pursue, and they're frequently good at picking relationships where they can maintain the upper hand.

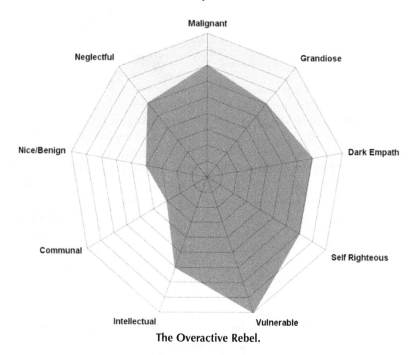

**The Overactive Rebel.**

They pledge their loyalty and protection quickly and may even be prone to acts of courage to demonstrate their strength and love. They can be like a burst of exciting energy when they first enter people's lives. If they have natural charisma (which this subtype often has), they know how to leverage their natural charms, talents, and strengths to attract people. To others, this subtype may be aggressive, provoking, and angry to demonstrate their power, virility, and fearlessness.

In the 2011 film *Blue Valentine*, Ryan Gosling (a real-life Sexual Six) plays a vulnerable narcissistic iteration of this subtype. The film depicts the often toxic but realistic love story between Dean (Gosling) and his wife Cindy (played by Michelle Williams). Gosling plays a young, rebellious, wise-talking but self-proclaimed "romantic" tough-guy who courts a vulnerable Williams (who plays a phobic Self-Preservation Six). The film is a nonlinear exploration of the couple's relationship from its beginnings to their current troubled and difficult marriage. Dean, while working for a moving company, first sees Cindy at a nursing home while she's visiting her grandmother as he's helping to move the customer into the facility. Dean is confident, charming, cocky, and won't take no for an answer as he tries to convince her to give him her phone number. She doesn't acquiesce to his advances. Some time passes, and she hasn't contacted him, so he decides to essentially stalk her by following her onto the bus from the nursing home so he can position himself to ask her out.

Cindy is vulnerable and fresh from a toxic relationship with her wrestler ex-boyfriend, Bobby. Her relationship with Gosling begins tumultuously as she finds out she's pregnant with her ex-boyfriend's child. She is reluctant to share the news of her secret pregnancy with Dean. We first see an example of Dean's emotionally manipulative behavior because he feels entitled to Cindy's secret. To push her to confess, he climbs a chain-length fence next to the Hudson River and threatens to jump off if she doesn't reveal her secret. She tells him and reveals she isn't sure if it's his child or her ex's, and he proceeds to punch the fence multiple times as she walks away from the emotionally charged scene. The rest of the movie jumps back and forth between the couple's early relationship and their present-day marriage living in rural Pennsylvania five years later.

As we flash forward, Dean, a high school dropout, works as a painter while Cindy works as a nurse to financially support the family. She wants him to try to provide more for the family. Dean feels entitled to sex with Cindy and gives various manipulative speeches about his feelings of rejection because she doesn't want to have sex when he wants. He's jealous, reactive, and emotionally needy. He swells with bluster and then dissolves into emotional vulnerability to get her to cater to his insecurities. Dean drinks frequently and refuses to get a better job or apply himself and in one scene shows up at Cindy's job drunk and belligerent to force her to pay attention to him after a fight. He's angry and confrontational, and his behavior is reprehensible, needy, and petulant. His chaotic ambivalence, emotional manipulation tactics, and unpredictable aggression are painfully realistic manifestations of the abuse of this subtype. Inevitably each outburst is followed by a tearful apology.

*Blue Valentine* depicts this subtype's emotional lability, reactivity, and emotional entitlement. They demand other people's loyalty and devotion and expect that others excuse their behavior because of their supposed love, protection, or care for others. They often hold others hostage due to their fear of abandonment and anxiety and expect others to remain stable and secure despite their emotional reactivity and volatility. However, as with most narcissistic abuse stories, they often don't begin toxically. Just like the film illustrates, there's an erosion over time with red flags along the way that are often ignored.

My ex-wife was probably the sexiest woman I ever met. She was beautiful, confident, and super smart. She approached me at a bar, told me a silly joke, and then left her phone number. She didn't even say anything else. I was intrigued, so I called her, and we talked on the phone for three hours that night. On our first date, she wanted to pick me up, pay, and do everything that usually the guy would do. It was a whirlwind, and I was obsessed. But there were signs. She would have these outbursts where she'd get super jealous and paranoid about exes or even waitresses at restaurants. She'd swear I was hitting on them by tipping them. They were intense, and we'd fight for hours. Explosive, crazy glass-breaking fights. She'd apologize, and then we'd have intense sex. It was almost constant drama, and she was always convinced that I was cheating or interested in someone else.

—Lars, 42, professor

They may be alternatingly strict, intimidating, and domineering if they're parents. They then flip to the other extreme and become deeply vulnerable, expect others to fix their emotions, or accuse their kids or other family members of withholding love, attention, or the truth. Usually, this increases when their insecurities and anxieties arise, and they can't self-soothe, expecting others to cater to their fear.

Some people of this subtype will attack others on others' behalf, believing this to be an act of loyalty or bravery. They think they're "sticking up for their people" but will often be overly aggressive, abusive, or violent and then become angry, sulking, or blaming when they're punished, blamed, or face the consequences for their overreactions. Presuming their show of force or "protection" isn't well-received, they turn their anger toward those they were attempting to protect and feel sorry for themselves for being misunderstood or undervalued for their loyalty and bravery.

This subtype may appear put-together, confident, and more like a Three or Eight in professional situations. However, they are likely to exhibit more reactivity. There may be glimpses of their aggression or temper that seep out due to this subtype's higher emotional dysregulation. Some can be professionally vindictive and look for opportunities to crush, humiliate, or undermine anyone who stokes their anxieties or insecurities or makes them look bad. Additionally, they may have trouble with rules as this subtype is more frequently reactive and non-compliant because they hate being told what to do.

This subtype is prone to dramatic displays of anger, violence, or reactivity in the extreme. The Overreactive Rebel's entitlement shows in how they expect others to constantly quell their anxiety and make them feel stable and secure in their intimate relationships. When they don't get their needs met through intimidation, vulnerable emotional manipulation, or coercion, they may resort to stone-walling or vengeful tactics so that they're not one-down. They want to maintain the upper hand to avoid abandonment but have difficulty engaging in meaningful relationships with others due to their narcissism.

**When Dealing with the Overreactive Rebel:**

1. This subtype can be very intense. Find ways to take breaks so that your nervous system doesn't become flooded by their emotional storms.
2. This subtype needs a lot of reassurance that you're invested in the relationship. When they become needy or insecure, do what is in your integrity to alleviate their anxiety without being dishonest.
3. Be aware this subtype is prone to flip-flopping between strength and vulnerability, which can be confusing. Try emotional "gray-rocking" if they become emotionally manipulative because if you respond emotionally, they will utilize that as fuel to intensify the drama.
4. Resist this subtype's provocation; they may become punchy, provocative, or manufacture arguments or problems to see how willing you are to surrender or cater to their discomfort and anxiety as a form of love-testing.

# 15

## Type Seven

### The Excited Enthusiast

Narcissistic Subtypes:
*Self-Preservation Seven: The Selfish Hedonist*
*Social Seven: The Gleeful Charlatan*
*Sexual Seven: The Flippant Rake*

## SELF-PRESERVATION SEVEN

"Enjoy life. There's plenty of time to be dead."

—Hans Christian Anderson

The Self-Preservation Seven is a passionate and vocal proponent of living the good life. They want to chase pleasure, excitement, and new experiences to avoid the anxiety of negative emotions or pain. Sevens focus on ensuring that sensual experiences, adventure, novel ideas, and a joie de vivre keep them out of memories, experiences, or emotions that could threaten a positive future. Self-Preservation Sevens are the gourmets, epicures, and libertines of the Enneagram. For most Sevens, "the more, the merrier" is an applicable euphemism. However, the Self Pres Seven can often feel that other people at times slow them down. They don't want to wait for other people to enroll in their plans and ideas and instead take an "I'm going this way; you're welcome to follow if you want to!" approach to life.

I make it my business to go on some kind of adventure at least once a month. Sometimes it's as little as driving without knowing where I'm going. Other times it's booking a trip to Costa Rica and hiking in the rainforest. I'm lucky to have the means to follow my zany ideas. But I work so I can pay for my playtime. I don't even have a 401k. Which is very ironic considering I'm a financial advisor. But why do I need money for when I slow down? I'm never going to be that girl that just sits at home and watches Lifetime movies.

—Elaina, 51, financial advisor

This subtype possesses the know-how to acquire the things they need to have a good time. They know where the best restaurants, hotels, grocery stores, movies, clubs, and other hidden destinations are to ensure they're never without a steady stream of their essentials. They channel their gluttony into the self-preservation arena, and it becomes vital that they're never without their pleasures. However, unlike some other Self-Preservation types, the Seven tends to shy away from repetitive routines. Indeed, they enjoy their specific comforts, but they fear becoming stale and monotonous, which causes them to seek new experiences. This tendency can lead to frustration for this subtype because without the ideal experience, anger, sadness, or boredom sets in, triggering their existential fear of being trapped in pain.

Seeking the ideal is paramount to this type, and they can be very particular about their homes, clothes, food, and the atmosphere in which they enjoy others' company. Many are attracted to design, innovation, and originality and may seek the newest gadgets or conveniences that can help make their lives easier and, of course, more fun.

The hunger of the Self-Preservation Seven can make them seem almost Eight-like if they encounter obstruction to their plans or dreams. However, unlike Eights, Self-Preservation Sevens will try to charm or convince others of their position. If this doesn't work, they will become rebellious and push forward anyway. They are adept at circumventing rules that they find limiting, and because of their powers of persuasion, they can be very convincing. This subtype constantly sees opportunity everywhere, and every opportunity could potentially lead to more resources to fund their adventures. They make friends wherever they go and generally have an interesting story to share. In fact, like most Sevens, they will pursue most plans (no matter how zany) just to have a story to tell later.

In college, I booked a trip to Cancun, Mexico, for spring break. Of course, we had an amazing time, even though I don't remember most of it. Anyway, we were supposed to leave on Sunday to return to the U.S. because class started on Monday. Somehow my friends thought it'd be funny to go to the airport without me because I was so hungover I could barely move. So, I missed my flight. I also somehow lost my passport and wallet. I was so screwed. So instead of being screwed, I checked out of the hotel and went down to the beach, and asked the guy who worked at a beachside bar if I could work there to earn some money. He was super cool and let me work, and he let me stay in his extra room. I ended up staying in Cancun for two months!

—Chris, 34, attorney

The impulsivity and need for adventure make this subtype fun to be around, but their energy and constant activity can exhaust types who prefer a slower pace. While they often enjoy the good life, they also seek a good deal to save money. They enjoy shopping to find sales and discounts on their favorite things. As one client referred to it, "it's like a scavenger hunt." They are Renaissance people who have often acquired a variety of talents and aptitudes throughout their lives. They can be prone to embellishing or sometimes fabricating details to make a story more exciting or compelling because they secretly fear that other people will find them dull.

*Top Chef* is a popular cooking competition show that has enjoyed an extended run on the Bravo network since 2006. It's enjoyable viewing because of the mouth-watering food the contestants create and the chefs' immense creativity and innovative spirit. I am still amazed at the ratio of Self-Preservation Sevens working as chefs, critics, or restaurateurs in the restaurant industry. As lovers of sensual pleasure, food is often a way to excite their senses and can be an excellent outlet to meet new people and have interesting discussions over a delicious meal. This subtype endeavors to be around like-minded people who appreciate life's pleasures and debate intellectually stimulating topics. They believe that only through sharing ideas and experiences can someone truly consider themselves having lived an exciting and full life. They fear the limitation of no options and thus find themselves in extreme anxiety if someone tries to restrict or place boundaries upon them.

Above all else, the Self-Preservation Seven cannot stand limitations or other people's restrictions. In the face of constraints, they will claw, kick, or scream their way out to regain their freedom. The existential anxiety of being without options or possibilities makes this subtype constantly seek interesting, novel situations. The phenomenon of FOMO (Fear of Missing Out), and its close cousin, FOBO (Fear of a Better Option), was coined by author Patrick McGinnis in 2004. Perhaps no acronyms better describe the constant anxiety of the Seven.[1,2]

## THE SELFISH HEDONIST

Hedonism is a philosophy that positions pleasure as the highest form of good and is the aim of human life. Evidence of hedonism as a philosophy exists as far back as Sumeria. In the *Epic of Gilgamesh*, Siduri stated, "Fill your belly. Day and night make merry. Let days be full of joy. Dance and make music day and night. . . . These things alone are the concern of men."[3] Hedonistic philosophies can similarly be found in ancient Egypt, ancient Greece (most famously espoused by the philosopher Epicurus), Judaism, Christianity, and some branches of Islam. Some of these philosophical approaches are proponents of humankind's right to seek and pursue one's pleasure. However, most are careful to note that the pursuit of pleasure and happiness should not infringe upon or harm another life. The non-narcissistic Self-Preservation Seven naturally ascribes to a hedonistic life philosophy by virtue of their personality structure. But when narcissism is present to any significant degree, the playful and cheerful hedonism of the Seven takes a darker turn into the Selfish Hedonist archetype.

The Selfish Hedonist is relentless about pursuing whatever pleasurable experiences they want at the expense of other people's wishes, happiness, objections,

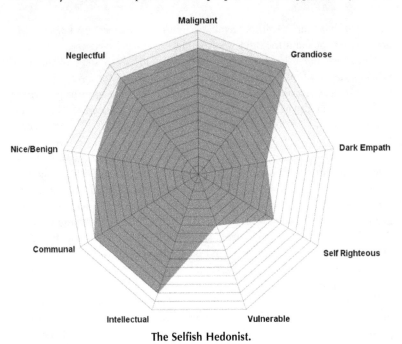

**The Selfish Hedonist.**

or needs. They are aggressive in pursuing whatever is novel and exciting and have a notoriously low threshold for boredom or mundanity. They are prone to mythomania (as are all narcissistic iterations of the Seven personality structure) and see no issue deceiving others if it means getting what they want. They tend to have a noticeably eroded conscience and are adept at rationalizing their actions, typically through the guise of pursuing their bliss or happiness. They do, however, want other people to enjoy themselves too and are champions of the good life for everyone. Nonetheless, if someone else's idea of fun bumps against theirs, they can become vicious and nasty.

> I don't. I don't do anything I don't want to do, and I don't have a problem with it. Usually, I'll just ghost something or someone if it sucks. I do it at work even. Incredibly, I haven't been fired, but I'm so good at sales that they keep me on. Everybody loves me. . . . I've done some wild things in my life, many things I probably shouldn't talk about in an interview. But I kind of think the craziest stuff is the most exciting. I remember when I convinced my drunk friend to drink a capful of bleach just to see what happened. She got a little sick, but it was okay. We chased it with some vodka, and she was a trooper. That kind of shit. Just crazy stuff.
>
> —Meg, 25, sales

Meg's penchant for "craziness" reminded me of a documentary I watched in graduate school about the third Roman emperor, Caligula. He was a notorious hedonist (and narcissist), and many historians argue about some of the more salacious details of his life (such as his apparent penchant for incest). However, most of them agree that he suffered from not only some form of personality dysfunction but also perhaps a neurological condition that increased his impulsivity and lack of executive functioning. He had a predilection for debauchery (extreme sex, brutality, overeating, you name it, he's said to have been into it). He was famously extravagant when it came to his pleasures (food, clothing, palaces, prostitutes) while allowing his people to suffer famine, disease, and war. He was hyper-violent, and rumors abound of his enjoyment of murder and torture. At one point, he claimed himself to be a living god, a testament to his grandiosity and delusional self-aggrandizement. He would walk around Rome dressed as various gods and ordered statues and temples erected in his divine honor. Perhaps one of the more mind-boggling accounts of Caligula's reign is the tale of him making one of his horses, Incitatus, a consul and appointing the animal as a priest.[4]

Whether or not Caligula was legitimately as crazed as accounts suggest, he is undoubtedly an apt example of the Selfish Hedonist. This subtype can derive perverse pleasure from others' pain, humiliation, or discomfort. They often explain away their sadism as humor and encourage people to "lighten up."

Because they are in the mental triad, this subtype is skilled with constructing elaborate intellectual rationalizations for their debauched sensibilities and proclivities.

The Selfish Hedonist can think of nothing more than their immediate gratification, and they will do whatever it takes to make sure they get what they want. They are often quite materialistic and notoriously excessive with money when it comes to their pleasure and desperately frugal with other people. They can be immensely cynical, and as they age, they grow harder and harder to titillate or satiate. They may seek increasingly intense experiences because they lack the subtlety of emotion or depth to savor anything for long. They can become irrationally angry and dangerously aggressive to anyone who steps in the way of something they want, and they can find enjoyment in crushing opponents. They disdain criticism for their selfishness and will lash out against anyone who dares to question the pursuit of their divine right to happiness.

> I believe that I deserve whatever I want whenever I want it. Some people think I'm an asshole for saying that, but I don't begrudge anyone else's right to pursue whatever makes them happy. I'm all about everyone having a good time. I'll probably die early, but I don't care as long as I have fun. My wife s always angry with me because I don't take care of myself much. I make money, so I can spend it and enjoy it. She wants me to be around for our kids when they're old enough to have babies, and I'm like, YOLO.
>
> —T. J., 30, landscape designer

## When Dealing with the Selfish Hedonist:

1. This subtype can be highly acquisitive and opportunistic. Always be aware that they tend to have an ulterior motive that involves gathering more resources, opportunities, or positioning themselves to grab something they want or believe they need.
2. This subtype has "shark-like" energy, and it can often feel like they're hunting for vulnerabilities they can exploit to get something. If you sense them shifting into shark mode, it's best to remove yourself from the situation or, if that's not possible, practice emotional gray-rocking because they will try to charm their way past your boundaries until they get what they want.
3. Their greed can be staggering. They may have plenty of money, food, variety, or resources and still search for more. Their gluttony can be off-putting so try to remember that their obsession with more results from their inner emptiness and try not to personalize it.

4. This subtype can tend to be rough and unwilling to acknowledge people's emotional experiences in any way. Don't expect them to have an emotional conversation or consider your emotional experience because they don't, and likely won't, have the capacity to engage that way.

## SOCIAL SEVEN

Willy Wonka, a man I'm sure needs little to no introduction, conceptualized (and sang about), "a world of pure imagination." Wonka's land of chocolate rivers and lollipop trees is a surrealistic representation of how the Social Seven wants life to be. They are idealistic, upbeat, Utopianists who are willing to sacrifice their temporary pleasure for the future. Social Sevens take the fear of being bored or trapped in pain into the social arena and focus their energy on groups, projects, or causes that they believe will provide a promising and positive future for everyone involved. They are high energy, and excitable but harsh critics of ideas, systems, or structures they believe are outdated or not conducive to a happy life.

The desire to create an ideal world is a hallmark of Social Sevens. While all of them don't build utopian societies, they demonstrate their ideals in smaller-scale projects at work in their personal lives.

> I love my job because I get to create a stimulating curriculum for the elementary school I work for. I started as a teacher, and they loved my style of relating to the children because I often feel like a child myself. I could get into their minds, and I understood what bored them and interested them. The curriculum was stale, so I turned my classroom into a magical playground. . . . My second graders loved it, and it stimulated their imaginations. We'd do all kinds of imagination training exercises because I wanted them to learn how to think outside of the box.
>
> —Laquandra, 32, curriculum development

Quite often, the idealistic views of the Social Seven bump against the frustration this type feels for others not understanding or being able to conceptualize the future they envision. They are frequently many steps ahead of others and enjoy the brainstorming and "riffing" phase of project development. Thinking of all possibilities and potentialities is exhilarating for this subtype. The novelty of ideas, theories, concepts, systems, and design is the lifeblood of the Social Seven. This subtype is forward-thinking, quick-witted, and gregarious. They possess the social skills and charisma to easily enlist people in their visions. However, they may sometimes struggle to execute some of their ideas due to distraction and boredom. This subtype often needs someone to help ground and operationalize their dreams, but they have more than enough energy and enthusiasm to manifest their visions into reality.

Social Sevens are very intellectual and enjoy the energy of theorizing and conceptualizing the future. They have the unique ability to integrate their ideas into funny anecdotes or exciting stories that can often conceal revolutionary and sometimes provocative ideas.

Social Sevens are true generalists in that they make it their business to know a little bit about many things. This is to help them manage the social sphere with ease and avoid awkwardness or appearing inferior. The Seven's fear of inferiority can at times make them overcompensate and elevate themselves to a superior intellectual position. This helps them to feel on equal footing with those around them. The Social Seven strives to be the epitome of the well-traveled, culturally conscious, cool, and intellectually diverse Renaissance person. They are often trendsetters and tend to be on the cutting-edge of music, technology, fashion, film, philosophies, and politics. Being "in the know" helps to stave off fears of being irrelevant or stale.

Social Sevens will sacrifice their immediate gratification or enjoyment for the group. They are willing to endure discomfort, boredom, conflict, or other "negative" states so that others can have a good time and be happy. Therefore, Claudio Naranjo referred to the Social Seven as the martyr. However, their threshold for negativity is relatively low, and they become irritable, bossy, and testy when people in their social spheres won't perk up and get with their positive program. They can become somewhat sarcastic and biting if people don't share their enthusiasm and desire to create "good vibes." Chance the Rapper, likely a Social Seven, is an infectious and gregarious character. His uplifting, witty, and hopeful rhymes indicate this subtype's signature brand of spreading positive vibes. In fact, his philanthropic and political activism have eclipsed his music. In 2017 Chance pledged one million dollars to support Chicago public schools in the hopes of creating a more positive experience for underserved, inner-city children.

This subtype struggles the most with FOMO and can spread themselves too thin. They can be noncommittal and flighty when it comes to commitment because they often hold out for what might be a "bigger, better deal." They can be prone to creating great excitement around a particular idea or plan and then evade the pursuit when something more interesting comes along, leaving other people in the dust. If they learn to create more consistency and systematize and prioritize their ideas, they can ground themselves and bring more fantasies and utopian visions into fruition.

## THE GLEEFUL CHARLATAN

"There's a sucker born every minute." That often-repeated quote is attributed to famous showman, notorious trickster, and politician P. T. Barnum. While the exact origins of the quote are unclear, he was known for popularizing this notion as a frequent purveyor of debunking hoaxes, tricks, and scams, as well as executing his own fraudulent or questionable schemes to ensure a constant flow of funds into his bank account. I classify Barnum as a light narcissist. He was no stranger to the seedy world of fraudsters, schemers, and sociopathic opportunists that populated the entertainment industry in the late 1800s. Barnum, however, also saw the gullibility and fascination of the public with oddities and spectacle. He had an appetite for the avant-garde, taboo and strange, and as such began his obsession with collecting and displaying "freaks." Most of the people Barnum employed in his traveling circus were people with deformations and other conditions that placed them on the outskirts of society. He famously enjoyed the wild excitement that spectators experienced when viewing the spectacle of his circus of oddities. Barnum thought of his traveling circus performers as friends and family, yet he also

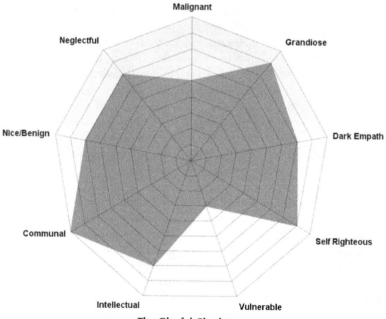

**The Gleeful Charlatan.**

capitalized on their marginalized identities and disabilities. Barnum was a notorious embellisher and was often proud of his ability to convince anyone around him of anything he wanted them to believe.[5] Sascha Baron-Cohen plays an excellent caricature of the showman/conman archetype as Roberto Pirelli in Tim Burton's adaptation of Stephen Sondheim's horror-musical *Sweeney Todd.*

Barnum's ability to spin the truth into whatever "magic" he deemed advantageous to him at any given moment is a hallmark of the Gleeful Charlatan. This subtype is often adept at shifting their presentation, motivations, and delivery to suit their needs. They can be the consummate smooth-talking con-people we see in films about slick gambling sharks or enthusiastic Ponzi-scheme creators. They are grandiose about their ability to convince, persuade, or gaslight people into believing whatever they want. They can be very charismatic and use their charm to manipulate others. They also tend to justify their manipulations as attempts to excite other people into participating in their plans, ideas, or projects. Of course, due to their narcissism, their goals are likely far more beneficial to their agendas, bank accounts, or social standing than they are to those to which they're marketing their wares. The Gleeful Charlatan is a big talker, and they can be prone to making promises they can't or never intend to keep. However, some may have legitimate intentions to execute their fantasies.

The Gleeful Charlatan, once their false stories, fabrications, and exaggerations are exposed, feels little remorse. They may even think of exploiting others' goodwill, investment, or support in them as the other person's problem.

Some people of this subtype are not overtly malignant but may enjoy deceiving or rabble-rousing others. They can have a solid mischievous or antisocial streak and trouble following rules or regulations. They may also be proponents of chaos as a philosophy and may embrace anarchy as a way of life. However, unlike the antisocial narcissistic Type Eight variants, the Gleeful Charlatan is typically upbeat, which helps them get away with far more than they possibly should. They utilize their spritely and gregarious interpersonal skills to circumvent consequences if possible. Leonardo DiCaprio demonstrated this quality quite well in the 2002 film *Catch Me If You Can*, a semi-fictional character study of happy-go-lucky charlatan Frank Abagnale Jr.'s crime spree from 1963–1967. Abagnale was a serial fraudster who impersonated a CIA agent, an airline pilot, a Georgia doctor, a Louisiana prosecutor, and forged his way through millions of dollars. However, his undeniable charm, aptitude for impersonation, and quick wit allowed him to elude to law enforcement. Tom Hanks (a real-life Social Seven) played savvy FBI agent Carl Hanratty.

One last notable example of this subtype is convicted fraudster Martin Shkreli, also known as the "Pharma Bro." Shkreli, a hedge fund manager and

CEO of pharmaceutical companies Retrophin and Turing Pharmaceuticals, is best known for purchasing the manufacturing license to an antiparasitic drug Daraprim and raising its cost from $56 a pill to $750 a pill.[6] The drug reduces the symptoms and morbidity of conditions like AIDS significantly. The price hike was seen as a gross abuse of power and roundly criticized as an evil act that thumbed its nose at human decency. Shkreli was unrepentant and saw himself somewhat like a comic-book supervillain. Before his imprisonment, Shkreli, an avid online gamer, spent long hours live-streaming his views on capitalism, the economy, pop culture, playing his guitar, politics, and boasting about his intellectual superiority. He would spar with fans and seemed to revel in the attention for being a sort of capitalistic boogey-monster. Shkreli was convicted of securities fraud and conspiracy to commit securities fraud. He is a mischievous, sharp-tongued, and enigmatic character but, as Stephanie Starks of *Forbes* magazine notes, Shkreli is a classic narcissistic sociopath who manipulates, gaslights, and then blames others for their eventual misfortune or punishment.[7] When deeply narcissistic, this subtype can be profoundly irreverent, condescending, chaotic, and pathological liars who may wreak havoc on anyone in their path.

### When Dealing with a Gleeful Charlatan:

1. Don't take their flakiness or lack of responsibility personally but prepare for it anyway. Ensure you have a backup plan if something is vital because this subtype will cut corners or avoid the responsibility altogether.
2. Their frequent stories and need to be the center of attention can be exhausting. When they're in performance mode, the best thing is to remove yourself from the situation.
3. Sometimes this subtype can lie, just to lie. They may be attempting to spice up a bland story or trying to get something in a roundabout way that they can't ask for directly. However, shaming them for their lies will only lead to angry reactiveness or evasiveness. For your sanity, it may be best, unless necessary, to take their tall tales or fibs with a grain of salt.
4. While you may have to excuse a lot of their irresponsible and grandiose behavior, do not allow them to transgress your emotional, physical, or financial boundaries without clear consequences or expression of their violation. They will take advantage of others' silence as an excuse to continue their behavior.

## SEXUAL SEVEN

Indian mystic, philosopher, and humanitarian Meher Baba (born Merwan Sheriar Irani) inspired reggae singer Bobby McFerrin with his famous quote, "Don't Worry; Be Happy." Baba died in 1969 but is still revered by his followers and millions worldwide as one of the foremost spiritual leaders of the twentieth century. Some even accept him as the Avatar of the age, a claim he made at nineteen. Baba was profoundly spiritual and claimed God-realization at nineteen when he visited five spiritual personalities known as Perfect Masters in India, whom he says awakened him to his true identity as God in the form of Man. From 1925 until he died in 1969, Meher Baba maintained absolute silence. He spoke enthusiastically and meaningfully using an alphabet board and hand gestures that his Mandali (close disciples) could inexplicably decipher. Virtually all accounts of those who encountered Meher Baba in both the East and the West spoke of the infectious love he inspired.

With many false or questionable spiritual gurus claiming to be divine personalities throughout India, he endured little to no scandal throughout his life. Baba was known for his deep devotion to his disciples, complex and progressive spiritual philosophies, and reputation for wholesome mischief. He loved to play games with his Mandali, and although he could at times be strict and exacting about his spiritual prescriptions, his warmth and respect for all living beings were apparent to those around him. He was known for making plans and changing them abruptly to suit his whims without warning and was notoriously unpredictable and mercurial. Baba loved going to the movies to observe the spiritual concepts woven into the narratives he saw on the silver screen.

Baba had periods where he displayed more elegance and debonair suaveness, mainly during his travels to visit "Baba lovers" in Hollywood and other periods where he slept on a dirt floor in a tiny hut on the grounds of his ashram. Baba was known for washing the feet of lepers and having no fear of the "untouchables" of India, whom he would regularly bless. Meher Baba traveled around India searching for, hugging, washing, and communing with Masts throughout the 1930s and 1940s.

Baba believed Masts were spiritually advanced souls, but they appeared insane to the outside world. There are numerous accounts of him sitting and staring for hours into the eyes of men and women believed by townspeople to be insane. He told his Mandali they were sharing crucial spiritual information and that to assume they were crazy was a gross miscalculation. Baba's ability to exude charisma despite not uttering a word and his unwavering devotion to his spiritual journey and those of his followers is an iteration of the profoundly spiritual Sexual Seven overlooked in extant Enneagram literature.

Baba is an exceptional exemplar of the Sexual Seven due to his intense discipline, ascetic sensibilities, and chosen mutism. He believed his wordless presence was more powerful and not shared among most Sevens. However, the intensity with which he pursued his passion, his devotion, and the value of love for those he cared for, paired with his mischievous, unpredictable, and infectious positivity, are quintessential Sexual Seven.

While not all Sexual Sevens are spiritual masters, they all possess the ability to uplift and inspire others through their joie de vivre. Unlike the other two Seven instinctual subtypes, the Sexual Seven is more apt to explore their emotional world and explore their depths. They may even be more open to emotions like sadness, frustration, or disappointment because they use those emotions to help intensify their almost constant quest for love. Overall, however, they're still Sevens, and they would prefer, whenever possible, not to worry; and be happy. But the Sexual Seven is in love with the idea of love. They are addicted to the euphoria that comes from a new love interest, passion, or exciting idea. They immerse themselves fully into whatever captures their fancy, and they allow themselves to be swept away by the currents of desire. They are very playful and enjoy people who will enable them to express their unbridled enthusiasm and playfulness without censorship. There is an eternally youthful quality to this subtype.

Sexual Sevens are energetic, creative, enthusiastic, fascinated, and fascinating. Many people experience them as uplifting and magical or exhausting and dizzying (or maybe a little of both, depending on the day). Their minds are quickly filled with ideas, possibilities, potentialities, and they're in love with almost all of them. So, picking a course of action or committing to any of their various passions can be challenging.

Peter Pan is a character created by Scottish novelist J. M. Barrie. Peter Pan first appeared in his novel *The Little White Bird* in 1906 and is described as a cross "betwixt and between a boy and a bird." He flew from his nursery, was cared for by fairies and birds, and remained an eternal child. He was a metaphor for the spirit of wonder, escapism, and magic that characterizes childhood. He is also boastful, a trickster, immature, and fickle. The spritely character has taken many iterations on stage and screen. Walt Disney depicted Peter Pan as elf-like, with a fairy companion, Tinkerbell. Peter is a mischievous young playboy archetype, but his ability to create magic and adventure makes him a magnetic and charismatic character. Peter is said to be good at almost everything he tries, from sword fighting to perfect mimicry (which comes in handy when he impersonates his archnemesis, Captain Hook) and heightened vision and hearing. Peter is constantly running away from maturity and getting into various precarious and sometimes dangerous situations so he can stay agile and young. However, Peter is not all frivolity and mischief. In the novel *Peter and Wendy*, the author notes that Peter accompanies young children who have died halfway to the other side, so they are not fearful. He also teaches Wendy, her siblings, and other young children to fly using "lovely, wonderful thoughts" and fairy dust.

"Lovely, wonderful thoughts" and fairy dust are sentiments that most Sexual Sevens would find apt metaphors for their approach to life.

> I love nothing more than to make someone feel amazing. As we age, we become stuck in ourselves, in the heaviness of life and adulthood. We lose that sense of magic and wonder, and sometimes all you have to do is sit down with someone and remind them of their magic. I do this in my yoga and sound healing practice. I love to sit down and talk to my clients before and understand what pain they've been experiencing, whether emotional or physical.
>
> —Silver Moon, 30, holistic healer

Sexual Sevens are excellent when they can offer quick and profound assistance without the expectation that they will stick around once the initial triage is completed. They can be immensely compassionate and administer deep aid to those in need in a crisis.

Commitment issues can be a problem for all Sevens but can be particularly challenging for Sexual Sevens. They simultaneously want deep, meaningful relationships with chosen intimates but fear the limitations those relationships might impose on their freedom. The Sexual Seven is highly suggestible and can easily be swept away by a new idea, philosophy, creative interest, or potential love connection. Most are aware of the free-spirited nature. If they are in a committed or monogamous relationship, they may even uncharacteristically reject potential love interests that threaten to disrespect their primary relationship.

Many Sexual Sevens identify with a hidden sadness or longing akin to Type Four. However, they do not struggle with envy or need to construct a sophisticated image, although they do crave creativity and need passion and excitement to feel fully alive. Sometimes the amount of excitable energy can overwhelm the Sexual Seven. Their desire to stay upbeat, magical, and enthusiastic can become overwhelming and lead them to uncharacteristic crashes that surprise them and their intimates. Comedian and actor Robin Williams was undoubtedly a Sexual Seven and a ball of pure energy. He was immensely talented, warm, ambitious, and seemed to run one thousand miles a minute. But like most clowns, there were tears behind his shiny, happy facade that reveal the longing of the Sexual Seven. The frenetic energy covers this type's inner emptiness and fear of never feeling fully satisfied. They are running from their existential anxiety that they will never sustain the magic and passion they seek.

## THE FLIPPANT RAKE

During one of our regular sessions, a client mentioned the 2003 biopic *Sylvia* about the late poet Sylvia Plath. Casually we began to recount the significant plot points and Enneagram types of the characters. Gwyneth Paltrow played Plath, and the film centered around her tumultuous marriage to poet Ted Hughes. After determining that Hughes fit the bill as the charismatic Sexual Seven, I realized he was an apt exemplar of the Flippant Rake. Hughes, a celebrated poet in his own right, was known for being irresistible and careless with women. He was a large, hulking, and dashing young man. The intensity of his connection with Plath is well documented in both her diary and their respective poetry.

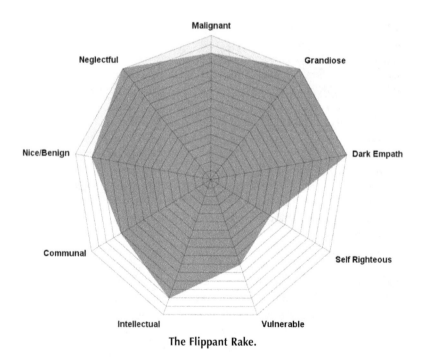

**The Flippant Rake.**

The film, loosely based on biographies and Plath's diary entries, depicts their first meeting as electrifying, ending with the quirky decision of Plath to bite his lip so he'd remember her among his many admirers. We see the progression of their whirlwind relationship shift and cruise through the honeymoon phase. The two marry within a year, and rumors of Hughes' cheating began not long after. Many people attribute Plath's descent into turmoil to Hughes' emotionally callous gaslighting of Sylvia's intuition (and direct knowledge) of his infidelities. Hughes finally admitted to his affair with Assia Wevel, a mutual friend, and the two separated in 1962.[8] He left her to care for their two young children in the coldest winter in 100 years. She moved on her own and struggled to make ends meet as her depression grew more severe until her eventual suicide in 1963. According to biographer Jonathan Bate, Hughes' history with women (many, many women) and his infidelity with most, if not all, women is not the real story. Hughes had a pervasive pattern of seduction, love-bombing, and cruel abandonment once another option revealed itself.[9]

Hughes's poetry is filled with beautiful metaphors and alliterations where he conceptualizes himself as a hawk, fox, crow, jaguar, and other sly yet predatory creatures. He was also known for his sexual brutality, which he dismissed as intense passion and a love of pleasure. However, Bate notes there was always a trail of broken and aggrieved women in his wake. Ostensibly, more than one woman went mad due to Hughes's careless relationship behaviors. Not to mention the opportunistic way he capitalized on his late wife's poetry.

Accounts of those close to Hughes in the aftermath of Plath's suicide say he quickly leveraged her poetry into a publishing contract and that while notably affected and saddened by Plath's death, felt no guilt or bore no sense of responsibility for her degraded emotional health. The poems written by Plath in the months leading up to her death hauntingly alluded to the emotionally devastating effect the dissolution of her marriage had on her. The poems, which ended up being her most celebrated work, speak of the corrosive impact of Ted's infidelity and lying on her mental health. Of course, this doesn't suggest that Hughes was solely responsible for her suicide. A failed affair on her part and a long history of severe clinical depression were more than enough fuel to catapult her into hopelessness. However, Hughes's unapologetic philandering, lying, and abandonment of the mother of his children, so he could be free and pursue his passion are endemic to the careless, romantic hedonism of the Flippant Rake. Despite his reputation, Hughes became the Poet Laureate of England and is still regarded as one of the most prolific writers and poets of his generation.

This subtype struggles to contain their impulses, and they can be incredibly charming, sophisticated, and demonstrative in their enthusiasm for others. Many people are attracted to their charisma and affability. They have an ease with people that allows them to seduce with ease. They are expert love-bombers. It's easy to fall prey to their seduction because they weave attractive fantasies. Whether business, friendship, or love relationships, the Flippant Rake is unparalleled in their ability to weave a beautiful image of the future. However, they often spin the same fantasies to multiple people. The gluttony of the Seven makes it difficult, if not impossible, for this subtype to limit their options. They cast a wide net, suck the juice from a particular situation or relationship, and move on quickly without much thought or concern for those they've left behind. They are unapologetic about their restlessness and take great offense at people criticizing or guilt-tripping them for chasing their bliss. Brendan was a charming, handsome, and enthusiastic young man who reached out to participate in my research study. He exemplifies this subtype's confident charm, infectious mystique, and flippant seduction.

> I met a woman at my hot yoga class a few years ago, and I knew she'd been having trouble in her marriage. After class, we started talking a lot, and I was giving her some perspective on her husband's disengagement from their relationship. I gave her some books on attachment theory and other things that I thought would be meaningful. She was beautiful, and I knew she was interested in me, but I kept my distance for a while. I needed her to come to me. She needed some passion, intrigue, and excitement in her life. I love beautiful women, and I was there to help her get out of her marriage with this boring dude she seemed to hate from her description of him. But they have kids, blah blah blah. It's that old story. One day I walked her out to her car, and I kissed her. She looked stunned but ended up inviting me back to her place, and we made love before her husband and kids got home. She told me she had never felt more alive than when she was with me. I'm not trying to brag, but I've gotten that feedback a lot. Anyway, she wanted more than I told her I was willing to offer. I did love her, but she needed to go back to her normal life because she was always complaining about how bad she felt. I don't have those feelings of guilt about love, sex, and pleasure. We have karma together, and it needed to play out. But I never told her I would be with her forever.
>
> —Brendan, 32, architect

Brendan saw himself as a sort of avenging angel that would deliver her from a mundane, lifeless marriage. He was baffled about the woman's anger and animosity toward him because, like most people of this subtype, he sees himself as a nice, well-intentioned person. He was adamant that his pursuit of her was in no way to break up her marriage or make her upset. He just "wanted to put some magic back in her life." However, when the emotional reality of his behavior bore down on him, he couldn't "handle the negativity." The avoidance of negative emotion, conflict, and the inability to take responsibility for their emotional recklessness is a hallmark of this subtype.

If their empathy is sufficiently eroded, this subtype takes a "devil may care" attitude toward most responsibilities in their life. They can be wildly irresponsible professionally and interpersonally. Their lack of concern or care for the consequences of their behavior on others can be staggering. However, understanding why they evade responsibilities and consequences is crucial. As Sevens, the idea of being criticized or even acknowledging that their lousy behavior impacts other people causes anxiety and feelings of inferiority. Healthy Sevens can adjust and accept that they cannot indulge their libertine fantasies all the time. However, the Flippant Rake has difficulty not indulging their fantasies and whims, no matter how irresponsible, perverse, or damaging to others.

Some people of this subtype can be open advocates for complete chaos, hedonism, and become wildly antisocial and reckless in their behavior. Although fictional, the classic comic book iteration of The Joker exemplifies this archetype.

## When Dealing with the Flippant Rake:

1. It's easy to get swept up in this subtype's fantasies and dreams of the future because of their persuasiveness. Remember to mitigate your expectations to avoid frustration or disappointment when they inevitably switch course because something more compelling comes into their awareness.

2. It's best to approach this subtype as peripherally as possible. Getting too deeply embroiled in a relationship with them is likely to lead to a lot of hurt feelings if you become too deeply invested. They can be demonstrative and intentional, only to abandon their sentiments later.

3. This subtype has a notoriously low threshold for negative emotions. They can become angry, condescending, and even gaslight people away from their authentic feelings. They're particularly prone to this behavior, primarily if your emotions result from something they've said or done.

4. Continue to be a voice of reason, particularly if you are responsible or affected by their physical, emotional, or financial safety in some way as they can sometimes have wholly abandoned their reasonable inner dialogue.

# 16

## Type Eight

### The Powerful Protector

Narcissistic Subtypes:
*Self-Preservation Eight: The Cynical Tyrant*
*Social Eight: The Mafia Don*
*Sexual Eight: The Charismatic Bully*

## SELF-PRESERVATION EIGHT

The Self-Preservation Eight's energy exudes sheer strength and force of will that is hard to ignore. They are earthy, lusty, direct, and formidable opponents. They are certainly someone you'd rather have on your side than against you due to their propensity toward vengeance and impressive tempers. However, despite their bluster and aggression, they are also incredibly protective, loyal, and an inexhaustible source of strength for those they allow into their inner circle of care. Certainly not warm and fuzzy, this subtype can come across to others as brusque and abrupt, particularly in their youth. Many Eights struggle to understand the value of diplomacy until later in life and tend to come on like a Mack truck, particularly about their self-preservation needs.

Self Pres Eights, not unlike Fives, fears being without the resources and comforts they deem vital to their survival. However, unlike Fives, they are not withdrawn and meek but rather command that the world give them their rightful spoils, or else they'll come and take what they want. People often misunderstand Self-Preservation Eights because of their characteristically unrefined,

226

straightforward manner of conducting their life affairs. They don't want to beat around the bush and prefer others approach them with the candor and directness with which they conduct themselves.

This subtype is the powerhouse of the Enneagram, and they endeavor to amass enough resources to ensure they're never without the things they want or need. Not unlike the Self-Preservation Seven, they have big appetites and require a plethora of their favorite things (food, people, sex, money, comforts) at their fingertips. However, unlike the Self Pres Seven, they don't require the same level of variety and novelty. They like what they like and hate any expectations that they'll change their preferences.

Self-Preservation Eights are unpretentious, and while they may enjoy the power communicated by luxury items; big houses, expensive cars, or expensive clothes, they're more impressed by their ability to secure and sustain their independence. They can become easily triggered when threats to their security are sensed and may become intimidating, threatening, or explode in anger if pushed far enough. They channel their fear of being weak, vulnerable, or "pathetic" into acquiring resources that can ensure they maintain their power and control over their life course. They are power brokers no matter their profession, and others often instinctively look to them to help manage or control things, particularly in a crisis. While typically slower-paced than the Social or Sexual Eight, they spring into action if they detect any threat to their resources, family, or power.

Self-Preservation Eights often rule their domains with an iron fist and expect those they protect to respect them and their rules. However, they are also like teddy bears to those who gain access to the inner circle.

People think I'm a hard-ass, and I guess I am with almost everybody. But my kids know I'm a huge pushover. There are few red lines you can't cross with me if you're one of mine. My kids know that they probably get a million chances with me, even when they piss me off. But some Joe Blow off the street. Hell no, I'm not taking crap from some stranger or somebody who isn't my blood or that I care about.

—Ella, 44, entrepreneur

Thirty-sixth President Lyndon B. Johnson was an imposing figure at 6'3" and one of the more forceful and determined presidents of the twentieth century. Johnson was known for giving people "the treatment," which was "was an incredible blend of badgering, cajolery, reminders of past favors, promises of future favors, predictions of gloom if something doesn't happen. When that man started to work on you, all of a sudden, you just felt that you were standing under a waterfall and the stuff was pouring on you."[1] His intimidation tactic was synonymous with his effectiveness in passing legislation. Johnson was notoriously determined, and although those close to him knew him as a kind but brusque man, he learned how to negotiate using whatever means necessary.

The Self-Preservation Eight is concerned, first and foremost, with ensuring that their needs and demands are satiated. In the case of Johnson, he merged his aspirations and needs with those of his legislative agenda. He was said to have taken policy criticisms as personal attacks on his character, which drove him even more, to ensure that his proposals were supported and passed by congress. Biographer Robert Dallek noted that Johnson had an insatiable desire to fill an inner need or emptiness.[2] This sense of lack is common among most human beings. However, for the Self-Preservation Eight, only through satiating one's desire can one amass power, independence, and resources for a sense of safety.

Johnson was notoriously intolerant of being alone and leisure time because of his drive to grab and consolidate power and influence. He saw the country as intrinsically tied to his survival as a leader and a man, thus channeling his self-preservation into his political ambition. Before serving as the president, he was elected as vice president under John F. Kennedy, a job that did not suit him because of his disdain for not being "top dog." He disdained dissent and the Vietnam War protests that characterized much of his presidency and are seen as the most damaging to his presidential legacy. He became angry and dictatorial and struggled to deal with the conflict diplomatically. He preferred brute force and proclamations to peace talks and efforts to quell anxieties and anger from critics. He, like all Eights, expected loyalty and devotion from those he sought to protect, including the American people he claimed benefited the most from the Vietnam War.

I recall sitting in an Enneagram conference breakout session taught by Enneagram teacher and author of the *Enneagram and Movie Guide*, Tom Condon, as he discussed the Self-Preservation Eight. Condon noted that a Self Pres Eight conceptualized themselves like a "junkyard dog" because of their propensity to guard what's theirs (however grand or modest) with great ferocity. So, when my client Valencia shared her experience around her "stuff," I was reminded of Tom's analogy:

> I don't have a lot of things. I never have. I grew up poor, and I still don't have a lot but what I have is mine. I don't like to think of myself as greedy, but I suppose I can be. But when you walk into my house, if you're "good people," then what's mine is yours. I feel terrible when I can't help my kids or another family member get something they want or need. I feel like it's a failure. I suppose I feel like one of those guard dogs that is supposed to protect the junk heap from squatters and pillagers. I will bite your head off if you try to take something from me or mine. It's instinctive, and if I get to that point,

there's no returning for me. I worry about what I might do if someone didn't back off. Everyone gets one warning. Then it's game on.

—Valencia, 35, debt collector

The guilt or shame around being unable to provide her children or family members something they want or need is pervasive among people of this subtype. They believe they must ensure their satisfactory survival and provide for their inner circle. They have difficulty denying their intimates things they want because they know how upsetting it is to have their needs impeded by someone else. Therefore, they are hard workers and have a natural talent for money and resource management. President Johnson knew how to wear different hats and play different roles as a negotiation tactic, a natural propensity for all Self-Preservation Eights. However, unlike Threes, who are fully inhabiting a new image to get ahead, Self Pres Eights can't maintain the adoptive image for long. They conceive it less of an image and more of a strategy.

Despite their gruff and tank-like energy, this subtype is incredibly supportive and protective toward others with normal to high-level empathy. They understand the power of their energy and influence, and they wield it not just to meet their own needs but also to benefit those around them. They can be incredibly generous, loyal, and expect the same in return.

## THE CYNICAL TYRANT

Tudor King Henry VIII is most famous for his penchant for beheading people, particularly his wives, who expressed dissent. Henry was said to have been a robust, athletic, confident, and spoiled child. Early on, he learned how to manipulate his childhood advisor and consort to ensure that whatever desire or whim arose within him was satiated. By some historians' accounts, he was a romantic man who had an intense lust for women paired with a religious propensity toward the values of chastity. He waited some years to consummate his marriage to Anne Boleyn and was usually faithful (for a medieval ruler) and was said to have only taken a few mistresses while married to Katherine of Aragon. Many, however, agree that as he aged, his love for pomp, circumstance, and grandiose, dramatic displays of his power grew more frenetic.[3]

As Henry's ego increased, so did his penchant for brutality and paranoia. The famous beheading of his once beloved wife Anne Boleyn was not merely a result of his anger at Boleyn for failing to deliver a male heir or her notable lack of submission. The ordering of her execution was more likely due to her public dissent and criticism of the king's religious policies. Rumors of witchcraft and

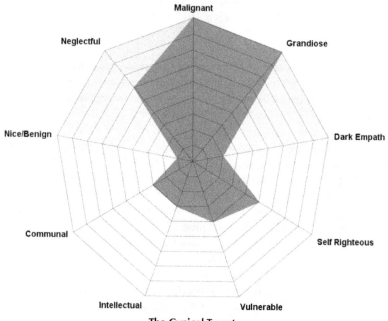

**The Cynical Tyrant.**

adultery and complaints of tyrannical behavior were other possible catalysts. Henry VIII was already tied to numerous extramarital affairs (one of his mistresses was Boleyn's sister). His rage about her final miscarriage seemed to catapult the two's relationship into deadly terrain.

The Cynical Tyrant perceives any threats to their power or dominance as threatening their literal survival. If they sense disloyalty or insubordination from those they consider under their rule, they fill with a cold and calculating rage. They become relentlessly focused on seeking revenge and punishing those who dare to question their power. There is more than a little psychopathy at play in this subtype's psychological profile. They are notoriously brutish and lack subtlety most of the time. However, they can be charming and manipulative for periods to get what they need. An animalistic charisma exudes from this subtype (as with all three narcissistic Eight subtypes). If they choose to cajole others, there is almost always a sentiment of threat or subtle violence behind their charm.

This subtype is the most preoccupied with wealth out of the twenty-seven narcissistic subtypes. They view money (and the power it affords) as the key to unlocking their control over their domain and the people within it. They are feudal by nature and see life as a series of conquests and maneuvers to gain increasing power. Of course, like all Eights, the original goal of their power grabs is to maintain their independence and autonomy. However, they become unable to ascertain how much force is enough. They claim to be brutally honest, but their communication style is cruel and harsh. They demand people talk straight to them; however, they can often be manipulative and both implicitly and explicitly threatening.

Eights, by nature, are confident and have some degree of natural grandiosity. However, self-aware and non-narcissistic Eights are aware of their tendency to make themselves legends in their minds, whereas the Cynical Tyrant is fully convinced of their power and significance in the world and behaves as absolute rulers of their domain. Due to their aggressive and determined disposition, they often accumulate actual power and resources to some degree. They demand control over their selected kingdoms, but as their narcissism increases, they become dissatisfied with what they have and begin seeking more power, resources, money, control, and security.

The HBO series *Succession* stars real-life Self-Preservation Eight Brian Cox as the media mogul Logan Roy. I discussed this series in chapter 14 with my analysis of the Roy family heir-apparent Kendall Roy as the Ambivalent Underminer. However, Logan sucks the proverbial air out of the room as the Goliath-like king of RoyCo media. Logan is blustery, unapologetically offensive, foul-mouthed, cantankerous, ruthless, and unempathetic. Despite his advanced age, Roy is unwilling to legitimately consider handing the mantle of his organization over to his children, simply because he resents the assumption of his ineptitude or ability to manage his empire. He doesn't think twice about dressing down anyone in his organization (including his children) who challenges his decisions. But also, ever the consummate powerbroker, he knows how to charm others for just long enough to put his enemies in a vulnerable position so he can strike. We repeatedly witness his rageful explosions toward his children. Everyone walks on eggshells around Roy, who stomps around like a petulant emperor. Cox's convincing performance, no doubt informed by his psychological reserves, also clearly conjures references to another real-life autocratically inclined, influential Self-Preservation Eight, the forty-fifth president of the United States, Donald J. Trump.

It is evident throughout the series that Logan Roy's primary objective is to maintain control over his empire and its considerable fortune at all costs. As the prospect of losing command over his security and, more importantly, his legacy grows more evident, Roy lashes out viciously. He inspires loyalty and devotion not because he's necessarily a good person, boss, or father but because others fear the repercussions of not submitting. This subtype's focus on not only seeking revenge for those who have wronged them but also crushing and humiliating opponents is vital to understanding this subtype's ruthlessness.

The Cynical Tyrant is not interested in psychological introspection of any kind. Even when introverted, their thoughts center on ways to amass more resources or what vulnerability or weakness to exploit in others to satiate a personal desire.

> I don't have a lot of time to be thinking about my feelings or other people's feelings. I have things to do; if you have a problem with how I do things—tough. I do it the way I do it, and I don't have to cater to anyone else's precious feelings. I'm not a violent person, but there was a time in college when this stupid kid thought it was a good idea to cut in front of me in the line in the cafeteria. I didn't say a word, and I just knocked his ass out. And nobody called the cops or even said anything.
>
> —Kirby, 53, energy company CEO

This subtype can be rather glib and unaware of how they're coming across to others. Their narcissism is typically quite grandiose, malignant with a dash of vulnerable narcissism for good measure. They often believe other people love and adore them but become pouty, reactive, and rageful when they find out about their poorly received behavior. However, instead of correcting course and modifying their approach, this subtype pushes forward with little to no adjustment to their presentation. They typically view empathy as weakness and may bully others into toughening up and insisting others not bother them with excuses, problems, or emotional appeals.

This subtype can be violent and predatory if their empathy is sufficiently eroded. The Cynical Tyrant lacks any actual moral code and instead will justify their abuse of others as a necessary evil to ensure their survival and the maintenance of power.

One of the few documented American female serial killers, Aileen Wuornos, was likely the Cynical Tyrant. Wuornos had a particularly abusive and troubled childhood and entered prostitution at the age of eleven when she would offer sex for food, cigarettes, alcohol, and drugs. Wuornos's intense survival instinct allowed her to circumvent what many people would consider decency to ensure her independence and autonomy. Notoriously Wuornos hated men, mainly since she had been on the receiving end of their brutality throughout her youth and early adulthood. Wuornos had a history of criminal activity before killing at least seven men, at least some of whom were customers of hers. Wuornos justified her murders by often claiming that the men had assaulted her (which was likely true) and felt that men deserved her self-defined and often fatal brand of vigilante justice. She was notoriously protective of her girlfriend Selby. It's worth noting that Wuornos had other severe psychological diagnoses, including Borderline Personality Disorder, Post-Traumatic Stress Disorder, Antisocial Personality Disorder, and a score of 32 on the PCL-R inventory, which measures psychopathy.[4]

### When Dealing with the Cynical Tyrant:

1. You must have tough skin when dealing with this subtype. Don't take their abrasiveness and roughness personally. If they become too blunt or insensitive, it's best to remove yourself from their presence.

2. Showing your emotions around this subtype can be detrimental to their respect for you. They are often contemptuous of vulnerable feelings, both in themselves and others. If you become emotional, prepare yourself for more aggressive attacks as they project their disgust of weakness onto you.

3. Stand up to them if they become bullying or overly controlling. If this subtype is in a power position over you, you mustn't show fear and stand your ground, which will engender more respect from them. If you're a partner, friend, or family member, you must communicate your boundaries and dictate how you are willing to be treated.

4. Don't be offended by this subtype's transactional nature. Remember that their cynical understanding of the world tells them that others are only out to get what they need and want, which significantly informs their decision-making and treatment.

## SOCIAL EIGHT

Power without love is reckless and abusive, and love without power is sentimental and anemic. Power at its best is love implementing the demands of justice, and justice at its best is power correcting everything that stands against love.

—Rev. Martin Luther King Jr.[5]

Martin Luther King Jr. is a name synonymous with the principles of justice and equality. While much of his public image has been sanitized over the past sixty years, the influence of his mission remains intact in America. Dr. King's obsession with equality, justice, and the mitigation of unfair power was not merely a battle he forged due to his identity as a Black man in Jim Crow America, but also a testament to him being a Social Eight. Much of the history of King's personality misses his radicalism and role as a very vocal, strident, and forceful social justice advocate. Indeed, he was raised within the Christian Baptist tradition and was staunchly non-violent. He was nonetheless a formidable and intimidating opponent. He saw it as his job to stand up for justice and protect everyone from the tyranny of racism, segregation, economic inequality, and injustice. As a social subtype, being cast out and excluded by other white children, businesses, and educational opportunities in his formative years greatly impacted him (as it did/does for most Black children in the U.S.). However, as a Social Eight, King channeled his rage at the injustices he endured and witnessed into the social arena and became a protective figure at a very young age.

By the time King was fifteen years old, he had garnered notoriety for his public speaking ability. His exposure to the Baptist church's liturgical call and response style and deep, resonant baritone voice made him an authoritative figure among peers and teachers.[6] He was naturally confident and known for being a proud and slightly vain man (he had a notorious attraction to nice clothes and shoes); he seemed wise beyond his years. King's fearlessness in the face of authorities, racist attacks, and attempts to stymie his crusade left him undeterred for the entirety of his life until his death in 1968.

Naranjo saw the Social Eight as the countertype or exception to the usual pattern of Eight's seeking and consolidating power for themselves to avoid vulnerability.[7] While they are noticeably more affiliative, cooperative, and adept at learning and practicing diplomacy, they still seek power and autonomy. However, they focus their avoidance of weakness or being harmed or manipulated into the social arena and believe that by consolidating power through the protection of others, they can earn people's loyalty, trust, and hopefully protection. Most Social Eights do not think of themselves as seeking the protection of others; however, when introspecting about their behavior with groups, they typically realize their protective measures are partially self-protective.

> People have always naturally looked to me to be a leader. Even in pre-school, I was the one that told everyone what we were playing and how to play it. I would rather oversee than be in the thick of it. I have never felt like I could genuinely let anyone very close, even though I have a lot of acquaintances and people who know who I am. I know I have the strength and fortitude to protect people. Sometimes I feel like if I don't do it, no one will.
>
> —Lisa, 47, nonprofit director

The tendency for this subtype to view themselves as protector to many and friend of no one is pervasive. They fear losing power and influence if people see their vulnerabilities and weaknesses, thus abdicating their contribution to the group. They feel they must remain unflappable, strong, and authoritative. However, because they are often unaware of insecurities or fear, it is easy for them to forge ahead and lead their proverbial troops wherever they need to go. Eights, in general, utilize war and battle metaphors (whereas Threes use sports metaphors more frequently). The Social Eight often sees themselves as a general or commander, and many who reach that level of distinction in the military are, in fact, Social Eights. They are strategic thinkers who can quickly assess potential flaws or weaknesses in a particular plan. Their minds naturally focus on minimizing losses and maximizing power, influence, and gain. They are all focused, in one way or another, on justice. Of course, their conception of justice is highly dependent on their ideologies and largely self-defined.

Social Eights often feel like they must push down their more abrasive qualities. They know they can be a bit "rough around the edges," and because their instinctual fears are most triggered in the social arena, they fear that if they truly express the full force of their aggressive energy, they will be exiled from the group. However, they half expect that they will be pushed out at some point.

Social Eights with normal to high empathy can be magnanimous and amass great pride and pleasure in empowering, supporting, and leading other people or groups. They are relentless justice fighters and are unafraid to stand up for whatever they believe is the valorous or right thing to do. And most importantly, they take care of "their people" and feel immense satisfaction when they see others learn to stand on their own under the direction of their leadership.

## THE MAFIA DON

"You can do anything but never go against the family." The words uttered by Mafia leader Don Vito Corleone in Francis Ford Coppola's masterpiece *The Godfather* remains one of the most enduring quotes from American cinema. Mario Puzo's 1969 novel *The Godfather* inspired Coppola's films and painted a compelling and dramatic picture of the mafia. Puzo's antihero character, named Vito Andolini (played by Robert DeNiro and Marlon Brando), was sent to America from Corleone, Sicily, after being spared by the local mafia Chieftain that murdered his brother and father. Vito Andolini (renamed Corleone upon arriving in New York City to commemorate his heritage) is quickly given a crash course in surviving in the tough mafia-run streets of Little Italy, New York City. After first working an honest job at a grocery store, Vito soon learns that lucrative money, a sense of community, and the opportunity for power and prestige are more readily available if he gets into "the business."

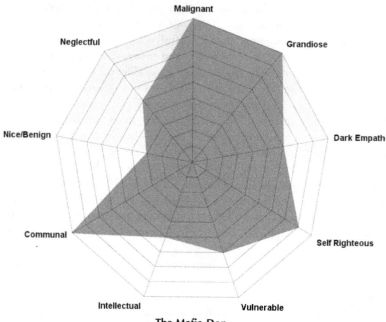

**The Mafia Don.**

Vito develops an aptitude for hustling at first, fencing stolen dresses for favors and loyalty. Eventually, Don Fanucci, the neighborhood Don in charge, learns of his hustle and threatens to turn him and his friends into the police if he doesn't give him a cut. However, the growing psychopath Vito devises a plan to kill Fanucci and take over the neighborhood. And thus begins the story of the most famous fictional Mafia Don in America.

I recognized elements of Don Corleone's leadership style and personality traits in nearly all narcissistic Social Eights I studied. I, therefore, decided the subtype should appropriately be named the Mafia Don. Corleone was not all violence and intimidation. He ran the neighborhood he oversaw with great care. He protected the people. He also squeezed for money, loyalty, and influence. This subtype is highly transactional (as are most narcissists). They utilize their considerable ability to provide people with physical protection, financial support, or some other real or symbolic currency for leverage. They are the "you scratch my back, and I'll scratch yours" subtype. Nothing they do is without a cost. Just like Corleone in the film, they gladly perform favors for people under their care, knowing that they will be able to collect later. They are cunning negotiators and can be suddenly violent or threatening to show others they won't be disrespected. Respect is essential for all Eights, but it is the only thing that truly matters for the Mafia Don. Even more than money or security (as is the aim of the Cynical Tyrant), they demand respect from their flock. However, respect often means unquestioningly loyalty and devotion to whatever they want or need.

This subtype often leads through intimidation, manipulation, blackmail, or other abusive tactics. They are, however, very adept at concealing or hiding their threats through veiled language or insinuation. They know that leaving any trail behind them could result in their ruin, so they prefer to ambush people privately without witnesses. Whether this is a small-scale confrontation with a co-worker, employee, child, friend, or spouse, they are socially conscious enough to avoid showing their hand in such a way that they can't be implicated in the proverbial crime.

The Mafia Don is often gregarious, charismatic, and strives to be well-known and respected in whatever group or community in which they've aligned themselves. They are not satisfied being at the lower rungs of any organization or group and will intimidate their way to the top of the heap. Even for those that work in jobs where bureaucratic structures are well established, this subtype is adept at gathering the necessary ammunition to ensure they can grab the power and influence they need to feel valuable and important. They are often better at coercion and manipulation than the Cynical Tyrant because they make it their business to effectively learn interpersonal skills to navigate the social world. Of course, their decorum, appropriateness, and style will differ depending on the environment and the cultural milieu of the group.

> I see empathy as a deterrent to getting things done. If I were overly empathetic, I wouldn't be able to execute my job. I can listen for a few minutes to someone's issues if they're related to work or a particular problem, but beyond that, it's best to take that to someone else. There's an H.R. department for that. . . . My kids go to their dad if they have an emotional problem. They know my patience runs thin with whining. If they need someone to go to the school and talk to a teacher that's giving them a hard time or I need to deal with someone, I do that. I'm good at that. But I know what I am good at; I have learned how to be more "social facing" at work because they wanted me to be a bit more approachable to hospital donors, politicians, etc. I dealt with a lot of disloyalty and complaints during the pandemic, and it was too much for me. . . . When a nurse or a nurse's aide would threaten to quit, I just let them go . . . I've paid your bills all these years, and you aren't going to stick it out during the worst crisis in my hospital's existence. Bye. No regrets. Never any regrets, that's what I always say.
>
> —Li Sun, 50, hospital administrator

This subtype often expects unquestioned obedience and view questions about their approach or motivations as a direct threat. Meanwhile, they demand complete transparency from others. They quite frequently claim that if they don't know everything, they can't solve a problem if it arises. And, admittedly, this is a common sentiment of the Eight. However, the Mafia Don's obsession with transparency can feel oppressive. As their paranoia grows, they may become convinced that people try to undermine or usurp their power. They can justify privacy violations and boundary-crossing because of their entitlement to control aspects of what they've seized as their domain. They strategize how to make pre-emptive strikes against perceived threats, or if blindsided by an attack, they will undoubtedly seek revenge. They can be cold, calculating, and brutal in defense of their power or influence. But this subtype would often prefer other people do their dirty work so that any repercussions or consequences don't fall on them.

This subtype can be prone to rage and vengeful violence if empathy is sufficiently eroded. They are incredibly unforgiving and can become paranoid and obsessed with identifying and punishing those that dare to cross or question their authority. Predatory by nature, the Mafia Don will utilize whatever charm, favors, resources, social capital, or dirt they can to consolidate their power and bend people to their will.

## When Dealing with the Mafia Don:

1. If this subtype offers to help you or protect you, be aware that there is an expectation that you will give them something in the future. Be sure that you are prepared to pay them back if you accept their assistance or protection. If not, either find another source of aid or be very clear about the terms of your transaction.

2. Keep in mind that their expectations of loyalty are pretty high, and they may perceive seemingly innocuous actions, comments, or decisions on your part as a betrayal. Know that this isn't necessarily due to any actual transgression but their cynicism about others' behavior and intentions (which is more often a projection of their behavior).

3. This subtype can become fixated on self-defined justice and may believe it's their job to right the wrongs of some perceived betrayal. Provide as much realistic feedback as possible but don't be surprised if they become angry or turn their ire toward you if you object to their justice crusades or their methods of retribution.

4. Take note that if you are trying to signal your friendship, they will likely doubt or question your motives, even if they are outwardly friendly, due to their inherent mistrust and cynicism about human relationships.

## SEXUAL EIGHT

*Behind the Music* is a documentary-style series that aired on VH1 regularly. I loved the show because it gave viewers an intimate look inside the lives of some of the most famous artists in the music industry. One episode focused on pop singer Alicia Moore, known by the stage name, P!nk.[8] I was already a fan of the artist's music. Her audacious style, honest lyrics, and in-your-face attitude set her apart from her contemporaries. *Behind the Music* walked viewers through the formative years of P!nk's childhood, adolescence, and career. While finishing my master's degree, I was deep in Enneagram analysis mode, and I remember thinking how Fourish the singer seemed, but something wasn't quite right. I wavered between types Four and Eight for some time, but the documentary revealed a gutsy groundedness typically not present in Fours. She was emotional, moody, creative, and expressive (like a Four), yet nonchalant, mischievous, confident, and unflappable. The documentary revealed the singer's emotionally turbulent teenage years as she dealt with her parents' divorce (an experience that shaped one of her hits, "Family Portrait").

When interviewed for the series, the singer spoke about her revolt against her parents' attempts to control her. She was undeterred by any attempts to rein in her behavior. She had a "nasty attitude," and she knew it. She picked fights with people at school and got herself (and her friends) into trouble. However, underneath her rebellious teenage shenanigans was a rage at feeling betrayed by her parent's decision to end their relationship. She channeled her anger and sadness into music. Record labels shaped P!nk's early career. They wanted her to market herself as a polished R&B singer because of her soulful vocals and lyrical sassiness. Yet the singer fought hard to be represented as a pop-punk, rock, and folk artist, which she felt represented her spirit. After many fights with producer and mentor L. A. Reid, she won the war. Her sophomore album "M!ssundaztood" debuted a more raw, unadulterated series of songs she co-wrote with Four Non-Blondes front-woman-turned-producer Linda Perry. The result was that the world was introduced to the real Alicia Moore. She was in-your-face, reactive, lusty, a consummate romantic, and, at times, difficult to get along with.

*Behind the Music* also gave viewers a peek into P!nk and now-husband Carey Hart's courtship. The on-again, off-again romance was fraught with intense power struggles, electrifying chemistry, and a connection that was irresistible for both as Sexual subtypes. By the end of the series, I knew without a shadow of a doubt that P!nk was the poster child for Sexual Eight. Their unique blend of audaciousness and raw vulnerability is confusing to many people who feel thrown off by the juxtaposition.

Sexual Eights channel the fear of losing a profound connection and being undesirable to chosen intimates into exaggerated strength and a lusty insistence that others notice them. It's hard to miss the Sexual Eight as they naturally project their charisma and authoritative self-confidence into any space. They see themselves as the de facto alpha, so they don't need to perform their desirability (like a Two, Three, or Six). They *know* that they can attract a mate once they set their sights on someone. Like Sexual Eight Chrissie Hynde, lead singer of the Pretenders, once famously sang, "I'm gonna make you, make you, make you notice."

Sexual Eights see relationships of any kind as a power struggle. They want to surrender themselves and put down their proverbial weapons for a partner who can handle them but fear exposing their soft underbellies.

> I am a hardcore romantic. I'm hardcore with anything I do. I was a really intense athlete and got a lot of injuries, but that didn't stop me. I go hard on anything I'm interested in, including my girlfriends. I don't mean in a creepy asshole kind of way, but I want to know that the person has the balls (excuse my language) to handle me. I like to tease, and I f*ck with people a little bit (okay, a lot) to see how the person will deal with me. If they push back, then I can relax. If I can run over them too easily, I lose interest fast. See, once I love somebody, it's forever, even if we break up or the friendship ends if you need me, even if I kinda hate your guts because of something you did, I will be there in a pinch. So I guess that's what I don't want people to exploit. That's why I seem impenetrable. I am unless you're in, then that's when the fun begins.
>
> —Ryan, 27, teacher/wrestling coach

Sexual Eights see abdicating their power in relationships as a conundrum. On the one hand, they want to surrender some of the control to relax. On the other hand, they fear being humiliated or harmed if others wield too much power. So, much like the Four and Six, they engage in a kind of push/pull dynamic with others. Enneagram teacher Tom Condon aptly characterized the Sexual Eight as a "Boxer/Poet" due to their alternating inner and outer struggle between being a fighter and a lover.[9] However, they are indelibly both the boxer and the poet, possessing an enormously sensitive and vulnerable core armored by a formidable and fierce exterior.

This subtype is notoriously opinionated, and some of the diplomatic restraint present in the Social Eight gives way to a bold expressiveness. They are incredibly charming and charismatic, and they often see themselves as predator, hunting prey in their search for intensity and excitement. Easily bored but unwilling to be uncomfortable, this subtype can alternate between a gut-type-like languorous quality and a high-octane drive toward satiating their desires. Like the Sexual

Four, this subtype sees themselves as transformative truth-tellers. However, the Four calls out emotional truths or what's missing, while the Eight calls out motivations and the power dynamics in each situation.

Devotion is essential for this subtype. They require loyalty from others and, in turn, like a medieval knight, will pledge theirs to their inner circle. However, they are sometimes rough around the edges, temperamental, and can be challenging to please. They are surprisingly easily hurt and underestimate their intimidating qualities. Many are horrified to learn that others interpret their behavior as malicious or angry.

This subtype can be possessive of anything they deem to be theirs. However, it is most evident in their relationships. They claim "their people" and resent intrusions on their relationship territory. While this can sound like a "toxic" trait, healthy Eights use the term "mine" as a term of endearment and want people to have the latitude to do as they please in relationships. If others consider and respect their needs and wishes, they're generally okay. Also, it's worth noting that this subtype does not like to show jealousy, and many claim not to get jealous or compete for others' attention. This is because jealousy can be exploited as a weakness, so instead, they display a nonchalance that communicates a "take it or leave it attitude" to relationships that they may hold quite dear.

> I had to learn how to tell people how I felt about them. I thought it was evident through my teasing, protection, and how much I wanted to be around them. But I'm not good at telling people, I think, because once that's out there, it's like an open wound, and they can pour salt on it or stitch it up. I'm afraid of the salt. Always been afraid of the salt. So, I can be like a steel trap. But almost like one that someone has heated in an oven because I know people feel my fire and passion. It's pretty palpable.
>
> —Akente, 43, fire chief

## THE CHARISMATIC BULLY

I remembered as a child hearing the expression, so-and-so "drank the Kool-Aid." I thought it was just a funny adult saying that meant someone was trying to fit in by acting cool, hence the term "Kool-Aid." It seemed like a cute turn of phrase. However, once I learned of the Jonestown Massacre of 1978 and its charismatic and psychopathic leader, Jim Jones, the phrase "drank the Kool-Aid" took on a much darker and more sinister meaning. The devastation of the massacre was more horrifying because the sheer number of people (909 deaths) that died either by suicide or murder is incomprehensible. What is even more unbelievable is that many of them died at the instruction of one man by the sheer force of his charisma, charm, and psychological and emotional violence.

One of the world's most infamous and dangerous cult leaders, Jim Jones, began his religious career as a "Christian Socialist" minister. He was by all accounts an engaging, charismatic, energetic, and at times volatile young man. He grew up in a poverty-stricken and tumultuous home and found a sense of purpose and family in the church. He was genuinely devout and longed to spread his passion for the redemptive power of Christianity. However, there were signs of something more sinister brewing in Jones.

At one point, his mother caught him impersonating a pastor at a church and giving a charismatic and entertaining sermon. Neighbors remembered Jones being obsessed with death and religion, and he believed that he had special spiritual powers to heal. He believed he could fly and once jumped off the roof to demonstrate his abilities to friends and broke his arm. He became enamored with Adolph Hitler and Joseph Stalin and reportedly role-played as Hitler and made his friends goosestep. Jones hit the children who refused to follow his orders. Jones was obsessed with his spiritual power and loved evangelizing and proselytizing to people in his neighborhood. He frequently stole

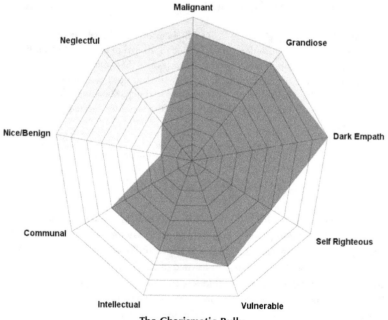

**The Charismatic Bully.**

from local candy stores and used profanity despite his religious devotion. At other times, he put other kids in danger with his antics and ridiculed or punished kids who didn't obey his sadistic suggestions. Jones said of his childhood, "I was ready to kill by the end of the third grade. I mean, I was so aggressive and hostile, I was ready to kill. Nobody gave me love, any understanding. In those days, a parent was supposed to go with a child to school functions. There was some kind of school performance, and everybody's parent was there but mine. I'm standing there, alone. Always was alone."[10]

Jones knew how to pinpoint people's deepest vulnerabilities and prey on them. He could be empathetic and kind and then become callous. He was notoriously possessive of his intimates (which he collected like trophies despite his marriage). He always made others initiate conversations with him first, as a power play. This way, he knew that the person was interested in him and could leverage their interest to his advantage.

Jones controlled his congregations through carefully meticulous cultivation of the suggestion that he was a divine prophet sent to deliver them from the ills of socialism, racism, and inequality.[11] The Charismatic Bully loves the power of controlling and grooming elite, handpicked people through years of careful manipulation, brainwashing, and gaslighting. Jones groomed his congregation to trust implicitly in him. He governed with intimidation and paranoia. Until finally, in 1978, when investigators attempted to uncover what was happening at the People's Temple, he instructed the congregation to drink their cyanide-laced Kool-Aid to avoid the government's attacks and the apocalyptic events to come. He told them they would reach the "promised land" through their deaths, and he would see them on the other side.

I write at length about Jones because, with all his charisma, intelligence, and cunning, he was able to orchestrate the largest mass murder–suicide in the world. The grandiosity of not only Jones's belief in his divinity but his sway over 909 people is truly remarkable. The Charismatic Bully is specifically equipped to engender intense loyalty and devotion. They are more emotionally aware than the Cynical Tyrant and the Mafia Don, yet utilize similar strategies to consolidate power. Of course, not all Charismatic Bullies end up being cult leaders and killing hundreds of people. However, all of them possess the kind of magnetism that can be intoxicating and frightening. This subtype is often the Dark Empathic narcissist, with a fair amount of malignant grandiosity and vulnerable narcissism. They possess a mystical sway over their intimates or any group, organization, or space they occupy. They often come across as mysterious, compelling, and a little dangerous. They, like all Eights, crave power, but they prefer to have control over people's emotional, spiritual, or psychological states.

This subtype is more aware of how they're coming across to others and use their propensity toward ascertaining motives to help them craft their language to deliver the most significant impact, depending on their needs. They can be genuinely transformative to people; however, they derive great pleasure and a considerable ego boost from seeing how their influence on others takes shape. However, unlike the Tempestuous Diva, whose need to be emotionally validated to maintain their identity, or the Untouchable Star, who molds their intimates to be the image they most desire, the Charismatic Bully enjoys knowing that they possess the other entirely. Their satisfaction stems from seeing their control, influence, and power in all aspects of someone's life.

Finding research participants of this subtype to contribute to the data was difficult because they are resistant to revealing weaknesses or any information that could disempower them with others. However, I did manage to interview a Charismatic Bully, Kurt, which was illustrative of the way this subtype manipulates others to gain power. I must settle for characterizing the interview as he requested that he didn't want his responses appearing in any kind of book, even with a pseudonym. He is a clinical psychologist, who also identifies as a sociopath. He assured me that he was more effective because of his "specialness." Kurt was by turns charismatic and menacing. His eyes would frequently go cold, particularly when I would probe further about his process. There were periods where he would launch into long self-important stories about how people loved him and how good he was at his job, and then he'd just stop talking and stare at me or turn the questions back on me as though he were the clinician, and I was the client. He seemed to enjoy the back and forth. It was exciting to him on some level, but he was determined to maintain the upper hand, and finally, when he received a phone call and abruptly left, I got the sense that he felt like he won.

Compared to the other two Type Eight narcissistic subtypes, the Charismatic Bully is less interested in power over a group, money, or fame (although these are certainly perks). They want complete domination over someone's mind, body, and soul. They want to see the effects of their influence on those around them, particularly their intimates. This subtype is attracted to psychology and other one-on-one, spiritual, or personal growth disciplines because of the intimacy these endeavors can afford. Their desire to possess the other is an adrenaline rush that reaffirms their power and strength.

Not uncommonly, this subtype claims to be vehemently against physical violence or may appear quite self-righteous, spiritual, or conscientious. However, they will be openly hypocritical, like Jim Jones's religious evangelism juxtaposed with his penchant for theft, drugs, and sex. The lust of the Eight mingles with the sexual instinct and narcissism and creates a person who desires close, intimate bonds with many people for control and manipulation. They have difficulty getting close to others and very rarely if ever, reveal their vulnerabilities. However, they can strategically elicit others' sympathy through complaining about their unappreciated contributions to their career, relationships, or families. They see themselves as a sort of divine protector of their flock, whoever that is, but are often aggrieved and victimized by their perception of others' selfishness and lack of respect or loyalty.

This subtype often struggles with various addictions (extreme sex, eating, drinking, drugs, etc.). Once they notice they've lost control of their desires, many become restrictive to regain control over their lusty impulses. They hate being out of control and are selective about who sees their anger and how it's displayed so as not to lose credibility or power. As parents, they can be protective and intimidating. They may engender great loyalty and devotion from their kids, spouses, and families and be powerful advocates and protectors against other bullies. They are intolerant of anyone else controlling or having influence over their people. The Charismatic Bully is masterful at gaslighting and can frequently lie to ensure that they always seem to come from the best intentions. They demand loyalty and devotion and become testy and badgering if they feel people are not executing their orders or prescriptions in the way they'd prefer.

This subtype is immensely cynical about others' motives and intentions. They can become paranoid and erratic if they think someone is trying to take advantage of them. Because of their megalomania, many see threats, betrayal, insults, and slights where none exist. This allows them to justify seeking revenge on those with whom they may have been "deeply connected." If their empathy is sufficiently eroded, they can be uncaring, emotionally, or physically violent, and recklessly self and other-destructive.

### When Dealing with the Charismatic Bully:

1. Being around this subtype can, at times, feel exhilarating and intense. However, notice how often they feed you thoughts, feelings, beliefs or end their sentences with "don't you agree" or some other phrase that is subtly pushing you into submission to their way of thinking.

2. Notice how frequently they share stories, accounts, or anecdotes where they've done something wrong or were unkind or insensitive. This subtype can masterfully hide their vulnerabilities or weaknesses by stoking or soliciting yours without revealing any of their proverbial cards.

3. This subtype can be meticulous and perfectionistic at work or in any working relationship. They can seem impossible to please and may demand and push for things to be done "their way" and may make un-

reasonable demands on your time and energy. While the Charismatic Bully hates boundaries, stating and enforcing them is essential.

4. If this subtype demonstrates Dark Empath traits, be aware of subtle emotional manipulation over time. Notice the red flag if they claim empathy, compassion, and understanding yet frequently backbite, undermine, or are upset with others over usual mistakes. It's best to gray rock or distance yourself (although this will elicit their rage); in the long run, it may save your sanity.

# 17

# Type Nine

## The Peaceful Mediator

Narcissistic Subtypes:
*Self-Preservation Nine: The Neglectful Slacker*
*Social Nine: The Ambivalent Avoider*
*Sexual Nine: The Unassuming Manipulator*

### SELF-PRESERVATION NINE

The Self-Preservation Nine exemplifies the energy of comfort and ease. While the most relaxed of all twenty-seven instinctual subtypes, this subtype experiences tension around the presence of stress in their lives. They strive to maintain an even-keeled, simple, and comfortable existence through mitigating potential conflicts and anxiety.

Self-Preservation Nines are the most grounded and solid of the Nine subtypes. They can appear like less reactive Eights as other people sense the underlying rage and aggression of the Nine. However, because one of the core Nine fears is conflict with those they're close to in their lives, they repress and deny their anger and transfer their aggression into maintaining their physical comfort. Self-Preservation Nines are typically more explicit about their boundaries, needs, and expectations regarding their physical requirements. They may be particular about food, the chair they sit in, the comfort of their bed, or ensuring they have their favorite shows and movies available to them. The anxiety of disconnection and disharmony drops away if they feel cozy, relaxed, and centered. However, any discordant energy or disruption in their comfortable routines can destabilize this subtype, and they can become anxious and grumpy.

All Self-Preservation Nines are somewhat traditionalists when approaching their lives. What each Nine considers "traditional" will vary depending on culture and upbringing, but they need to feel anchored in the sense of familiarity. So, if their family always watches *It's a Wonderful Life* on Christmas Eve, they must maintain that tradition to feel grounded and safe. Routines are critical for Self-Preservation Nines. Knowing what to expect in their lives and having access to the things that make them feel safe and contented help them avoid things that could be potentially upsetting.

Self-Preservation Nines often collect, catalog, and adopt varying hobbies as part of their self-soothing behaviors. They are often quite interested in preserving things and feel connected to the past.

> I prefer simple things. The simpler, the better. I try to keep my life free of unnecessary stuff. Whether it's drama, material items, activities, I just want things calm and simple. My favorite thing to do is collect photos and familial genealogical information. I am the family historian because I have such an appreciation for the past. I think it's important to any family (or society for that matter) to preserve their history. But it's more than preserving the information. It helps me to feel connected to my roots. I have a room with a bookshelf filled with photo albums. Some are mine; some are my grandparents', others are news-clippings and other mementos that I think someday someone will want.
>
> —Leona, 44, bookstore manager

The Self-Preservation Nine can struggle with knowing what is essentially important. They can at times channel their anxiety (which is often unconscious) into things others might find frivolous or unimportant. They also feel that feeling satisfied and satiated is best achieved through accumulating resources or essentials that can help allay fears of being cut off from their proverbial security blankets. Quite often, their reliance on food, substances, movies/television, collecting, exercise, and other busy work increases when more essential needs or responsibilities arise. Like all Nines, they become clueless, forgetful, or diffuse when stressed. They often repress or sublimate their discomfort, sadness, and anger into one of their comforts. Once they allow their awareness to entertain the thought, emotion, or distressing experience, they feel like they are jolted from a deep sleep and feel an urgency to act to change or eliminate the discomfort.

> I was in a lousy marriage for fifteen years. It wasn't abusive or anything like that; it was just unfulfilling. It was easy for me to get caught in the day-to-day of just

going to work, coming home, eating dinner, taking care of the kids, etc. I know everybody says that about their lives, and yes, I think that's just life, to some extent. However, I was lulled into this muted world of routines and familiarity that I didn't even realize I was depressed for ten years. I had checked out so much because I had become just like this robot on repeat. I did or said whatever I needed to survive and prevent any conflicts. So, my wife and I didn't fight. But if I couldn't watch at least two hours of ESPN every night or certain sporting events, I would get furious and stomp around like a teenager. It was like the only thing I wanted and needed.

—Clay, 48, mattress sales

The tendency for this subtype to go to sleep utilizing their routines and comforts is quite prevalent. However, once jolted awake Self-Preservation Nines can make rapid, meaningful changes to their behavior. The tendency to fall back into the lull of indulging in their comforts is always possible, but it is mitigated by their awareness that other people want them to show up and be fully present and engaged with life. This subtype can be very calming and a source of profound balance and practicality in the lives of the people they care about. They are often quite strong, albeit reservedly, and if self-aware, they can be confident, steady, and reliable in the face of chaos.

## THE NEGLECTFUL SLACKER

Kevin Spacey plays Lester Burnham, a forty-two-year-old magazine executive, in the film 1998 film *American Beauty* directed by Sam Mendes. Lester is deeply dissatisfied in his life and married to a high-strung real estate agent and narcissistic Social Three, Carolyn (played by Annette Benning). Burnham is undersexed, disgruntled about his job, and thoroughly checked out from his life and the people in it. He is hopelessly on autopilot, living the "perfect" suburban life. Lester, who attends a high school basketball game where his teenage daughter is cheering, becomes infatuated with her best friend, Angela, and fantasizes about her. Lester starts resisting his suburban life, quits his job (after blackmailing his supervisor), starts working out, becomes verbally abusive to his wife and daughter, starts smoking marijuana, works at a fast-food restaurant, and eventually molests his daughter's friend. Lester believes that he is more "alive" than he's been in years; however, what has activated is the full extent of his latent vulnerable and neglectful narcissism.

As Lester's narcissism grows, his cantankerous and nasty attitude also changes. He loses his filter when speaking to almost everyone he interacts with and is no longer interested in fathering his daughter. His obsession with

The Neglectful Slacker.

winning the attention of Angela and chasing his sexual fantasies becomes all-consuming.

Lester's descent into the furthest reaches of his narcissism, pedophilia, and complete abdication of being a responsible father and husband is a sharp departure from his boring life. However, in the end, it proves to be too much for him to bear when his daughter's friend Angela reveals (before they're about to have sex) that she's a virgin. Lester's reality check comes witnessing Angela's innocence. Nonetheless, his appetites before the encounter with Angela became all-consuming, forcing him to neglect the other people in his life. He seeks what he believes will be the most satisfying route to his happiness: satiating all his desires. The film is beautifully made and meditates on many aspects of human life, including social norms, suburbia, meaning, and happiness. And although not intentionally about narcissistic personality disorder, Lester represents how narcissism expresses itself in the Self-Preservation Nine.

Often narcissism in Nines is somewhat hidden and more challenging to detect due to their propensity to undervalue themselves and their importance as a feature of their overall personality structures. As I mentioned in chapter 6, Nines often have an ego about not having an ego. However, when lacking empathy and other conditions are present for narcissistic personality traits, the

Nine's narcissism can "activate." As was the case with Lester, they may believe that the only way to be noticed and exist is to permit their narcissistic traits to run the show. Their self-neglect extends to carelessness, dismissal, and active erasure of other people's needs, wants, emotions, and overall existence. They turn the rage that they've been suppressing for years outward and begin to justify their poor treatment of others because they've been overlooked for so long.

The Neglectful Slacker is inattentive, insensitive, dismissive, and unconcerned with other people's needs. They believe that their immediate needs and resources are more critical. They do not want to be bothered with other people's emotional problems and often justify avoiding responsibilities (particularly if they interfere with their comfort or peace).

> My ex-wife has been trying to get me to pay this stupid amount of money in child support for my two kids. She claims that they need $2000 a month, apiece. I don't know what she spent when we were together, but I know I didn't spend $2000 a month on them, especially since they've been over the age of six or so. Well, I'm not paying for it. I make good money, but I know she's just going to use it to buy herself stuff. . . . She always said I was cheap, but I'm not. She told the mediator I bought myself a new $4000 TV and sound system. I don't know how she found that out, but it's none of her business what I do with my money. I'll quit my job before I pay her. Anyway, I probably sound like a colossal asshole to you. I'm a nice guy. Which is why I don't understand why she's doing me like this.
>
> —Roy, 34, master electrician

Roy justified his decision to withhold child support for as long as possible because he genuinely felt that, since his wife decided to divorce him (he revealed he had been unfaithful, and she found out), she should have to suffer the consequences of her decision. Unable to take responsibility for his actions, his anger manifested as a stubborn refusal to acknowledge his ex-wife's feelings or his young children's needs. He claims that they are trying to manipulate him to feel bad and that they're just spoiled because of their mother's influence. The Neglectful Slacker thinks of themselves as friendly and kind and often has difficulty acknowledging their role in any conflict or disagreement. They see themselves as constantly reasonable and calm. However, quite often, people of this subtype are prone to fits of rage that can be devastating and terrifying for those on the receiving end of their fury.

Identifying the Neglectful Slacker can be challenging because they don't necessarily peacock like the grandiose narcissist or attack others like the malignant variant. They keep their self-importance and selfishness hidden. However, if someone transgresses their needs, comfort, resources, or pursuit of peace, they can become snide, blustery, and potentially violent. More typically, they are incredibly dismissive of others' concerns and think most everything is unimportant. They take the phrase, "don't sweat the small stuff, and it's all small stuff" to a whole new level. There is a stubborn refusal to be bothered by anyone or anything.

The more this subtype tries to repress their emotions or anything in their lives that they find uncomfortable, too complex, conflictual, or inconvenient, the more their rage grows. Eventually, they become wholly intolerant of everyday human problems or feelings in themselves and others. They have to work even harder to shove down their rage and misery and resent and neglectfully punish anyone who reminds them of the uncomfortable things they have chosen to ignore.

**When Dealing with the Neglectful Slacker:**
1. Avoid disrupting their routines too much, as this is when you'll get the most pushback from this subtype. Instead, suggest variations or deviations from their norm and let them decide whether or not to adopt it. Still, don't avoid things you want to do because you don't want to upset them.
2. When this subtype is at its worst, they can be exceptionally neglectful and callous. Remember, this stems from their own self-neglect, and you must prioritize your needs because they likely won't or are unable to do so.
3. At times the Neglectful Slacker will cut corners, be miserly, or reticent about putting forth more energy or effort than they need to. Getting into a conflict will only make them dig in their heels more. It's best to carry on and find ways to give yourself what you need.
4. If they become angry or hateful, it's best to leave them alone rather than try to fight with them. The depth of their rage can be explosive and destructive.

## SOCIAL NINE

Social Nines want to be associated with a particular group and enjoy helping the group be more cohesive and harmonious. They don't need to be the center of attention and often prefer being peripherally involved in helping to meet a common goal or simply absorbing the energy of a group while socializing. Many are optimistic, idealistic, and congenial. Some Social Nines report an aptitude for mixing or identifying with a wide array of people, making it easy for them to make friends or acquaintances.

I'm introverted, so I don't like making the first move when it comes to socializing. But I have always been good at just fitting in. I don't share my opinions too much unless someone asks me or something I feel passionate about. Most of the time, I don't have much of a preference, and I'm fine, just kind of doing whatever everyone else is doing. It's not because I don't have a personality or anything. I'm just not picky. I like most people; as long as they're nice.

—TJ, 30, history teacher

The Social Nine is often reticent about expressing their opinions; however, they usually have established convictions about a few topics and will suddenly make powerful proclamations or stand against things they think are wrong. Claudio Naranjo identified their propensity toward "soap-boxing," a phenomenon where the Social Nine grabs a proverbial apple cart, stands upon it, and proclaims their opinion about a particular issue, quite forcefully and passionately. They can enjoy intellectual debates and, if inclined, can be surprisingly adept, like TJ, at debating. Most of the time, however, Social Nines just want to be around people they feel like match their "vibe" and want to feel connected and merged with a group or cause.

Queen Elizabeth II is perhaps one of the most reticent and private monarchs in recent history. She is notoriously reluctant to give interviews, and she has cultivated a public image that reveals little of her personal opinions, feelings, or thoughts. Many have written about her conscious choice to surrender individuality in favor of adopting the role of the Queen. However, it seems she was naturally well suited to this role. Her sister, the charismatic, often audacious, and troubled Princess Margaret (a Social Seven), famously wanted a more public-facing role. Both Elizabeth and Margaret agreed she was better suited for the politicking and social gregariousness often required of royalty. Nonetheless, "heavy is the head that wears the Crown," and her naturally enduring and neutralizing temperament was an asset for her reign.

Elizabeth could easily relinquish her preferences and passions more completely to perform the role. As with most Nines, they prefer to erase their identities somewhat to blend in with the groups' expectations. Groomed from an early age to accede to the throne yet reluctant to lead a country due to the complications and complexities of royal life, she nevertheless accepted her fate.[1] She is the longest-reigning monarch in British history. Notoriously conventional and stoic, her ability to mediate the personalities of various colorful and ambitious Prime Ministers is well documented. Her staunch orthodoxy and respect for the Crown have contributed to a successful royal career.

Like any Nine, she is a master of steadiness and has weathered the shifting winds of favor toward the Crown with steadfast resolve and a grounded love for the symbolism of the Crown's unifying potential. Elizabeth is notoriously sensible and straightforward and avoids, whenever possible, overt displays of pomp and circumstance. She even resisted the decadent displays of wealth and status customary of a royal coronation.[2] Over the years, she has reportedly learned to live with the expectations of grandeur and ceremony that are part of her job. Queen Elizabeth is notoriously conflict-avoidant but can be stern, dismissive, and emotionally cold, a reported source of tension between her and some of her more expressive children, namely, Prince Charles and Princess Anne.

Like all Nines, this subtype is terrified of their anger. Many aren't aware of the extent of their aggression until it bubbles to the surface when a conviction is challenged or boundary transgressed. However, some Social Nines have become adept at repressing their anger that they claim they haven't been angry in years. A Social Nine student, "Anne," once told me, with a straight face, she couldn't remember the last time she had been angry. She claimed she wasn't sure if she'd ever been very angry in her life at all. So, I gave Anne an assignment. I asked her to go home and make a list of things that annoyed or irritated her. She said she didn't know if she'd be able to come up with anything substantial but humored me. The next day she came back with a two-page list (front and back) full of grievances, annoyances, and irritations. I asked her to share some items on the list, and she vehemently expressed her anger at many things, most of which related to things her friends do that "pissed her off."

At the end of the semester, Anne thanked me for helping her get in touch with her anger. However, she told me she had burned the sheet by the end of the class because she was so ashamed that she had written it. I asked her what distressed her most about the exercise. She shared that it wasn't that she was angry, but rather that she had been so "hard" on her friends, even though they knew nothing of the exercise. Social Nines feel a sense of danger if they express dissent within their chosen groups because it means they are, to eloquently quote my student, "out of harmony with the flow of [their] lives."

## THE AMBIVALENT AVOIDER

The 1999 film *Fight Club,* based on the Chuck Palahniuk novel of the same name, explores the inner world of a dissatisfied "everyman" that's called "The Narrator" (named Jack in Palahniuk's book). The Narrator (a Social Nine played by Edward Norton) is an average white-collar worker who falls into a rut. He feels disconnected from his life and, to manage his depression, attends various support groups under different aliases, primarily for the free coffee and sense of connection with other people. At the apex of the Narrator's anger and disconnection, he meets the ruggedly handsome Tyler Durden, a narcissistic Social Seven soap salesman played by Brad Pitt, on a business trip.

Tyler is everything the Narrator isn't—sexy, violent, emotionally reckless, and deeply unempathetic. Durden tells the Narrator that all his belongings were destroyed in an explosion. In a moment of desperation, the Narrator asks Durden to hit him in a parking lot. He finds the violence exhilarating and cathartic, and they agree they should do it again. The Narrator moves into Tyler's home, and they frequent a local bar, often fist fighting in the parking lot. Eventually, Durden and the Narrator start a "Fight Club" in the bar's basement. The fight club grows and becomes an anti-capitalist, anti-establishment haven for men to express their rage and discontent violently. The Narrator blackmails his former boss for funds to help finance Fight Club, and we witness the Narrator's descent into malignant narcissism.

As Durden's brutality, insensitivity, hatred, and thirst for more intense fights grow, the Narrator becomes increasingly bruised and battered. In the film's third act, we learn that Durden was a projection of the Narrator's repressed rage, hostility, and feelings of being overlooked and discarded. Tyler Durden

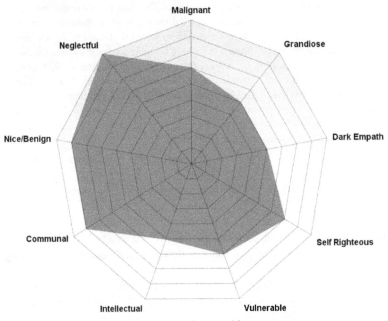

**The Ambivalent Avoider.**

is a mechanism to explore the Narrator's narcissistic and violent fantasies in real life. The Narrator's split into Durden is representative of the inability of the Ambivalent Avoider to acknowledge their rage. Quite often, this subtype sees themselves as a nice person. Norton's character floats from support group to group, not contributing, at times even lying about addictions or other problems.

His latent narcissistic traits are finally activated, and rather than face his inherent unkindness, he creates a character to deal with his distress. While not all Ambivalent Avoiders create alter-egos, they all disown their aggression. Very often, this subtype seems relatively "normal" to others. They may be more than able to adopt a pleasant, unassuming, and easygoing image that masks their rage. This subtype most aligns with the Nice or Benign Narcissistic variants. However, they're unwilling to concern themselves with other people's problems or emotions underneath the pleasant exterior. They may even be the comic relief or simply the "tag-along" in group relationship dynamics. Their narcissism can go undetected except when serious or essential matters arise and they're unable to deal with them in an empathetic or thoughtful manner.

> My friends are so annoying because they always tell me that I'm not empathetic. I guess because I just don't care about their drama. They had a literal empathy intervention with me where they told me they felt dismissed by me all the time. I just sat there and listened but honestly, it was ridiculous and hurtful. . . . I'm the one that always makes everyone laugh and tries to be upbeat, but I guess it translates as dismissive. I need new friends, not a new attitude. I will keep hanging out with them because I know they love me or whatever. I'll just keep my mouth shut. . . . The main problem I've had in the past is when people get super emotional, or things get deep. I'm not very interested. I just want to hang out. I keep my problems to myself, and I guess I want other people to do the same. So yes, that's gotten me into trouble in my life before, to answer your question.
>
> —Carolyn, 25, student

Typically, this subtype's narcissistic orientation goes undetected unless they encounter a challenge to their empathy deficits. However, if they can't circumvent criticism through their agreeable and affable demeanor, they become rageful and undermining. This is particularly true if they feel like they've been forced to stuff down their true feelings, thoughts, and opinions to get along with others.

The Ambivalent Avoider knows how to circumvent attention so they can work quietly behind the scenes to get their immediate needs met. However, they struggle to assert themselves the most out of the twenty-seven narcissistic subtypes. If they find themselves in a situation they cannot easily evade, they grow desperate, and their repressed rage can have dangerous consequences.

Chris Watts made headlines in 2018 for the horrific murder of his pregnant wife, Shanann Watts, and their two daughters. The family was the picture of suburban perfectionism. Chris was described by nearly all that knew him as a "nice guy." Everyone was shocked to find out that Watts had committed the crimes. Watts was reportedly engaged in an extramarital affair before the murder. By some accounts, his behavior before the murders was suspect only because, previously overweight, he began working out heavily and was even more detached than usual.

Some described Chris as agreeable and quiet. He acknowledged some difficulties in his marriage with Shannan, who was known to be slightly demanding and at times overbearing. Chris confessed he wanted a divorce and had grown disdainful of Shannan and didn't know how to cut ties with her because of the children.[3] However, he didn't want to be "the bad guy" for ending a marriage and having an affair. Some might say that Watts's behavior was so uncharacteristic that it was a crime of passion precipitated by a psychotic break of some sort. However, Chris lied to authorities for weeks before finally confessing, changing his story several times, and even appearing on television to plead for his murdered wife to come home.[4]

Forensic psychologists noted that Chris's initial inability to clearly state why he dumped his daughters in an oil storage facility tank is evidence that he can't conceptualize himself as the perpetrator.[5] He preferred saying, "they died" during his "confession" rather than, "I killed them." During the investigation, Watts claimed his wife grew angry and strangled their daughters in response to his request for separation, so he strangled her and dumped all the bodies. However, he later recanted and told the whole story. In 2021 Watt's revealed to a prison pen pal that he tried poisoning Shannan with Oxycontin for several weeks to terminate her pregnancy. He also shared that he planned the murders of his family for weeks before executing. He even tried smothering his daughters in bed before resorting to strangulation. It's worth noting that most perpetrators of familicide commit suicide after murdering their families. Watts claims he contemplated it, but ultimately the whole act was intended to clear his slate so he could be with his girlfriend without an ex-wife or any other parental obligations.

No one would have suspected nice guy-next-door Chris Watts to commit such a heinous act, which underscores the Ambivalent Avoider's propensity toward concealing their rage and lack of empathy. They are adept at going through the motions to avoid conflict or complication. They are often better able to get their needs met without obstruction if they don't draw attention to themselves. However, in moments of desperation, they can easily snap, perhaps not as dramatically as Watts, but fits of rage, extreme passive aggression, or displays of emotional callousness.

**When Dealing with the Ambivalent Avoider:**
  1. Be aware that this subtype at times creates traps whereby they allow themselves to be overlooked or neglected and then punish others for it. Try to elicit their input to avoid the manipulation that results in their increased anger and resentment.
  2. When backed into a corner, the Ambivalent Avoider may lie or, more typically, omit the truth to avoid a problem, emotion, or reaction. Remember, this stems from their insecurity around owning their motivations and actions.
  3. This subtype can be surprisingly negative and erosive to a group process. While they may not strongly oppose anyone, their ambivalence and silent judgment can be a challenge. They do this because they want others to seek their insight or opinion, and if they don't get it, they obstruct the process through stubbornness or resistance.
  4. Because this subtype is frequently the Nice/Benign or Communal Narcissist, they often see themselves as nice, good, and kind people. And they may have moments of showing their benevolence. However, pointing out when they haven't met their persona will only result in mounting resentment and a tendency to seek revenge for the criticism of their character.

## SEXUAL NINE

In 2022 pop megastar and Jackson family royalty Janet Jackson released a documentary chronicling the highs and lows of her long career.[6] Jackson is soft-spoken, gentle, and reflective, and much of her commentary centered around her search for love, connection, and independence in her relationships. Jackson discusses her marriages to James DeBarge and René Elizondo in detail in the documentary. She reveals a pattern whereby she unconsciously recreated a relationship with her father, Joe Jackson, who famously tried to control her career, image, and love life until she fired him as her manager. After ending her professional relationship with her father, Jackson claimed her independence and released her hit album "Control."

Freedom, discipline, and a search for ideal love have characterized Jackson's personal life and fueled her musical career. Notoriously private, Jackson follows a predictable pattern of Sexual Nines who seek total and complete merging with a chosen partner or loved one. However, their tendency to merge entirely creates a dynamic where they lose their identity and feel anxious about losing autonomy and independence. Janet's focus throughout her life on control is a common refrain for this subtype who recognizes their tendency to lose themselves in romantic relationships. Throughout the documentary, friends and family members noted Janet's propensity toward disappearing into relationships that were typically unhealthy or oppressive in some way.

Janet Jackson's soft-spoken, coquettish, "airy," and gentle demeanor is quite common for Sexual Nines of any gender expression. They want to merge with those around them and do so unconsciously and almost immediately. Connecting with others is their primary way of understanding and relating to the world. For this reason, many Sexual Nines can seem unintentionally flirtatious or seductive.

> Men always think they're in love with me. Come to think of it, so have a few women! It's been a problem my whole life, even when I was a teenager. I don't mean this in an egotistical way. I think it's because whoever I'm with, I want to be with them at that moment. I am very receptive, and I absorb people's energy and words. I think that's what makes me a good massage therapist, but it's also what helps me get close to people. I don't know how quite to describe it, but I can feel it when the other person's energy and mine are in flow, and we synchronize.
>
> —Tara, 43, massage therapist

Tara's experience when connecting with others is ubiquitous with Sexual Nines, making them excellent therapists and healers. Many are attracted to fields where they can utilize their natural ability to create a deep connection. However, just as important, were Tara's comments about not necessarily being interested in the people with whom she's connecting. The unconscious merging of Sexual Nine does not presuppose that they have feelings for the other person. It's a defense mechanism that allows them to feel connected to other people and dispel the Sexual instinctual fear of being undesirable. They learn early that letting the other person project themselves onto you creates fleeting feelings of intimacy and connection, which is often pleasurable for both people at any given moment. However, like any other Sexual type, the Sexual Nine is looking for perfect attunement with someone they've chosen. If they can't have the ideal partner at any moment, many will choose someone just to feel connected. Without the feeling of merging, they report being unable to feel themselves.

Sexual Nines report that their identity conception alternates between feeling very diffuse and boundless and very solid with definite boundaries. They alternate between wanting to feel totally and completely merged with the object(s) of their affection and then feeling fearful that they've lost their individuality. Janet Jackson's career search for control, independence, and autonomy juxtaposed with her search for the perfect love is a testament to the Sexual Nine's constant inner conflict. Sometimes this internal struggle is externalized, and the Sexual Nine may split themselves to deal with the dichotomy.

At a workshop on the instinctual subtypes, Claudio Naranjo stated that the Sexual Nine is "nobody special."[7] Not because he believed that the Sexual Nine has no unique qualities or is inherently unremarkable, but merging with others and adopting other people's preferences is a strategy that makes them nobody special so that the other person can be the focus. They are like empty vessels that they hope to fill with a desirable other's preferences, opinions, thoughts, and emotions. This is, however, partially unconscious, as Tara mentioned earlier, and there is also a process called "counter-merging" that occurs when they realize that they've lost themselves in the other.

Once this subtype has entered the counter-merge state, they typically disconnect emotionally from the other person. However, they may stay in failed or inappropriate relationships longer than they should because, like all Nines, they fear the disconnection of the breakup. The fear and pain of ending a relationship are worse than living in a state of denial or disconnection in a relationship that isn't ideal.

This subtype can seem like a Four because they demonstrate a dreamy intensity that the other Nine subtypes do not. They also experience significant melancholy and crave intensity and depth. The difference is that the Sexual Nine doesn't have a cultivated image. They become the other person while the Four is staunchly independent and protective of their image. They rely on their ability to fuse with the other to quell their instinctual fears of being alone or undesirable.

The pensiveness and moodiness of the Sexual Nine is usually not even completely understood by the Nine themselves because they aren't identified with being emotional. However, they feel increasingly alienated when not in a relationship with someone else because it's challenging to know who they are.

It's important to remember that the Sexual Nine can merge with a best friend, parent, spiritual ideology, creative pursuit, or lover with equal intensity. However, they all crave the romantic merging they experience in a relationship with a desired other.

## THE UNASSUMING MANIPULATOR

The 1992 psychological thriller *Single White Female* stars Jennifer Jason Leigh and Bridget Fonda and is a dramatized and admittedly over-the-top portrayal of the Unassuming Manipulator. Allie Jones (Fonda) is a successful fashion software developer who kicks Sam, her fiancé, out of her apartment after revealing his infidelity. She subsequently decides to solicit a roommate to move in and help share living expenses and provide companionship. After numerous unsuitable candidates, the final applicant, Hedra "Hedy" Carlson (Leigh), mysteriously arrives. Hedy is homely, quiet, awkward, and unassuming. The two hit it off, and their cohabitation begins innocently enough. However, Hedy has some striking boundary issues. She is immediately comfortable being naked around Allie and walks into her room unannounced like they've known each other for years. Hedy provides Allie with emotional support amid her breakup and begins to feel possessive and protective over Allie.

Hedy begins screening calls from Allie's ex, Sam, and even hides a letter he sent apologizing for cheating on her with his ex-wife. The film builds tension as the two grow closer together, and Hedy becomes more and more obsessed with Allie. Hedy begins to dress like Allie and even gets her hair cut and colored in the same style, all the while claiming she doesn't understand why Allie would be upset by her mimicry.

When Allie decides to reconcile with Sam, Hedy becomes angry and derisive. She reminds Allie of all the support she's given and assures her that he will cheat on her again. Hedy feels betrayed because the couple wants to live in the apartment alone, forcing Hedy to move out. Hedy grows more desperate, afraid of losing the connection, and her more sinister sociopathic tendencies are revealed. Allison learns that Hedy's deceased twin (who supposedly died at birth) died by drowning at nine years old with her sister Hedy present. Allie begins to put two and two together and realizes that she is wholly unsure of whom she's living with. Hedy embarks on a series of unhinged violent attacks, one on Allie's upstairs neighbor Graham with whom she hears Allie discussing her fear of Hedy. She sneaks into Graham's apartment and attacks him with a crowbar. She also murders Sam after impersonating Allie and raping him by performing unwanted fellatio and then gouging his eye out with a stiletto shoe. By the film's third act, Hedy has descended into total violent psychopathy and killed two people, bound and abused Allie, and grown more and more unhinged as Allison discovers the full extent of Hedy's destruction.

The film is an over-the-top Hollywood interpretation of psychopathy, malignant narcissism, and delusional disorder, so there's a lot to parse through from a psychological perspective when analyzing Hedy. Nonetheless, she

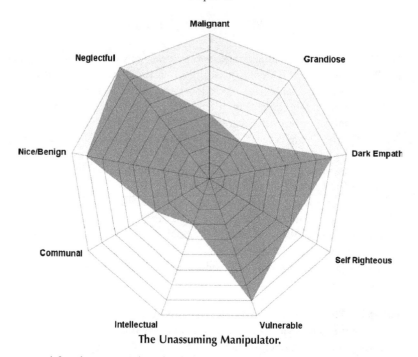

**The Unassuming Manipulator.**

exemplifies the extreme lengths the Unassuming Manipulator is willing to go to avoid disconnection from a perceived love object. The propensity toward merging and seeking fusion with a desired other that we see in non-narcissistic Sexual Nines takes a decisively darker turn when narcissism enters the picture. The tendency for extreme boundary-crossing, stalking, angry outbursts, and even erotomania.[8]

This subtype feels entitled to invade the other person's privacy and even adopts aspects of the other's identity to feel close to them. They can at times be utterly clueless of their boundary-crossing behaviors and become irate when people suggest that their attempts to merge with the other are invasive. In cases where erotomania is present, their obsessiveness and delusions of romantic grandeur lead them to transgress others by incessant stalking, interference in other people's relationships or families, or even violence.

For the Unassuming Manipulator, the lines between fantasy and reality often blur. That is not to say they are all schizophrenic or erotomaniacs, but the tendency toward delusional thoughts increases due to their romantic grandiosity. Unable to imagine why anyone wouldn't be in love with them, particularly people they've chosen to attach to, this subtype has difficulty taking no for an answer. This is not unlike the Sexual Two, but this subtype is more patient than the impatient and willful Two. The normally conflict-avoidant and anger-averse Sexual Nine can turn into a rageful, possessive abuser. Their contempt for others manifests in their belief that they are better than other options for their love interests, even if they are married or otherwise spoken for.

The following excerpt is from an interview with a benign narcissistic Sexual Nine, Jaxon. Jaxon was attractive but relatively ordinary. His affect was sedate, but there was a glint of anger in his eyes which would flare every so often when I would say something that didn't match his picture of reality.

> Jaxon: I know she loves me because I've seen the way she looks at me. I've been waiting ten years for her to realize she wants to be with me.
>
> Me: Does she know you love her? Have you told her?
>
> Jaxon: [Angrily] No! It hasn't been the right time. I just watch and make sure she's okay. She's been with that douche bag for two years now, and I just want to make sure they don't have a baby together. I'm way hotter and nicer than him. I've seen how he talks to her and how she looks at him. She doesn't even like him!
>
> Me: So you two are friends, and you talk about your relationship?
>
> Jaxon: I wouldn't say, friends. We work together. I've had a crush on her since the moment I laid eyes on her. You know how Jim is in love with Pam from *The Office*. Well, I'm Jim, and I'm just going to wait it out while she realizes that Roy isn't the one for her.
>
> Me: Oh, I see, so this is an unrequited love situation?
>
> Jaxon: Well, that reduces it to something weird. Like I'm some kind of loser. I'm not a loser, Dude. She's flirted with me before. I think she's in love with me too. There's no way she likes him. I'm smarter, in better shape, and I make more money than him. She'll realize.
>
> Me: So have you not told her because you don't want to risk the rejection.
>
> Jaxon: She wouldn't reject me! I've never been rejected before in my life. I'm just a gentleman, and I want it to be perfect. I like all the same movies, music, and food she likes. I like everything she likes. I'm just waiting for her to notice.
>
> —Jaxon, 29, account manager

Jaxon was unable to entertain that his crush wasn't romantically interested in him, and for all I know, she could very well be. However, what was striking (besides his significantly low empathy scores) was his self-assured, almost cocky belief in her love for him. Jaxon's disdain for her husband and his efforts to manipulate her by adopting her favorite preferences as his own were narcissistic red flags. Often, this subtype only adopts the other's preferences to mold the other person to their needs and desires. At one point, I considered that he could be the Manipulative Pleaser, but he isn't aggressive enough in real life. Much of his aggression and overtures are understated and bubble underneath the surface. He admittedly didn't even speak to her that much at work and tried to avoid being "annoying," so he avoided too much interaction. I didn't press too much to discover how he knew intimate details about his crush's relationship with her husband. I suspect there has been at least some stalking and boundary-crossing behavior on Jaxon's part.

At work, this subtype is relatively unassuming, and one might only encounter their grandiosity or entitlement when they need to demonstrate their superior value over others in a particular environment. For example, they may boast about their ability to charm or persuade others to get them to do what they want. Still, even these behaviors will be relatively sedate compared to other narcissistic subtypes.

If the Unassuming Manipulator is in a relationship, they can be controlling and smothering and insist on being emotionally, materially, and sexually satisfied. They can have dependent or neglectful features where they may expect partners, intimates, or family members to take care of basic needs or do more than their fair share of domestic or financial work. They can be lazy and seek stimulation through risky or intense behaviors like frequent affairs or adrenaline-seeking behaviors. As Nines, this subtype often has an increased deadness of feeling. They have difficulty feeling their own individuated sense of self and, as such, must connect to themselves through the other. If the other person disconnects, they can become frantic, demanding, possessive, or rageful. Their lack of a defined sense of self can be problematic for intimates to manage as this subtype may eventually float from relationship to relationship seeking a connection that they cannot provide others. They feel aggrieved, overlooked, and discarded when people inevitably try to pull away due to their neediness and self-absorption.

### When Dealing with the Unassuming Manipulator:

1. Be aware that this subtype develops bonds quickly. However, with narcissism present, they have difficulty going deep with others and choose breadth over depth instead. Try to remember not to take this personally, but be clear about your boundaries and expectations if they violate your trust or confidence.

2. This subtype tends to lie or placate to get out of uncomfortable emotions or situations with no intentions of following through. Hold them accountable for their commitments, and don't be fooled by their soft, kind manipulation tactics. This will reinforce their belief they can manipulate to get what they want.

3. Encourage the Unassuming Manipulator to develop and express their interests, preferences, and tastes outside of yours. Also, remember that

they are only temporarily adopting your likes and interests to sway you to embrace theirs eventually.

4. Suppose they become invasive, boundary-crossing, or engage in threatening or intimidating behaviors. In that case, they likely feel disconnection is on the horizon and then resort to more aggressive tactics to prevent this. Seek help if they become emotionally, physically, or financially abusive.

# Conclusion

We have explored a wide range of human motivations and behaviors from twenty-seven distinct but intrinsically linked personality types throughout these chapters. We've also journeyed through twenty-seven equally specific narcissistic variations on the overall theme of narcissism. There is much to be written about narcissism. While these pages are a snapshot of the subtleties of narcissism, we haven't scratched the surface of healing the behaviors these subtypes can inflict. Nor have we explored the deep work necessary to help repair some of the narcissistic distortions in one's psyche.

There is a much-needed movement toward inclusion and destigmatization of various neurodivergent conditions that affect human beings. Autism spectrum disorders, processing disorders, people-first mental and physical health diagnoses help humanize and normalize variations in human psychological, physical, and emotional processing. However, I want to address a troubling trend where attempts to normalize narcissism have created pushback against calling out narcissistic behaviors and abuse patterns. I am hesitant to move toward depathologizing pathological narcissism because of its frequently damaging effects on those around them. Narcissistic abuse thrives in secret, and many narcissists prefer that their behaviors remain hidden or protected from others' scrutiny.

There are some claims that narcissism doesn't hurt the narcissist. Narcissism is erosive to the psyche because, as research has suggested, narcissists are no happier or more contented than those without narcissism. Pervasive feelings of loneliness and disconnection can exacerbate comorbidities such as depression and anxiety. Narcissism implies disrupted or fragmented object relations, where other people are viewed as objects designed to meet a particular goal or satisfy a need, want, or desire. However, how we view others is rooted in how we view ourselves. Many narcissists view themselves as objects, thus stripping themselves of their humanity.

To me, normalizing narcissism is akin to normalizing war. While war happens and perhaps is sometimes (arguably) necessary, we should strive toward more effective and less destructive means of resolving differences. Narcissism is like war. While it is a fact of human life and a part of human psychology, this does not presuppose that narcissism is beneficial for humanity in the long run. I submit that varying degrees of narcissism (psychological or cultural) underlie humanity's most exploitative, dehumanizing, or violent acts. Narcissism exacerbates selfishness, callousness, indifference, impatience, arrogance, greed, deception, and emotional and physical violence. If we recognize and minimize the effects of narcissism in ourselves, we have taken the first steps to mitigate it in the world.

There are instances in life where narcissistic traits can benefit a particular goal. Who among us hasn't had to channel our inner Narcissus to negotiate to buy a vehicle or when we've refused to take no for an answer or budge on an issue when something is important to us. Also, narcissism in its varying degrees has had the positive effect of highlighting the necessity for empathy and compassion. I've heard the predator/prey analogy about the need for narcissism in the human condition. Yes, in nature, there are predators, and there is prey. However, we are (or presume to be) striving for deeper and more refined states of consciousness as human beings. Reducing the complexity of the human experience to our animalistic instincts may help to explain why narcissism exists but does nothing to justify allowing it to thrive unmitigated in ourselves or humanity overall. This is analogous to saying human beings will die, so medical science is pointless. However, anyone who's taken an antibiotic for an infection or an inhaler for an asthma attack recognizes that, while those medications weren't technically "necessary," they invariably improved their quality of life or saved their lives. Perhaps my romanticism has overtaken my reason, and indeed we may just be meat sacks fumbling to survive. However, I'd prefer to live in a world where we can transcend or at least mitigate our baser, destructive instincts. On the other hand, I am also a realist, and I understand that at times our more basic instincts will (and perhaps should) prevail whether due to necessity, trauma, pleasure, or at times a mixture of all three.

There is enough elevation and adoration of narcissism and its subtle and overt forms of violence in modern media. It can be entertaining to watch some forms of narcissism on the world stage. I have watched my fair share of documentaries and films about narcissists, fraudsters, sociopaths, psychopaths that were damn entertaining. I even secretly rooted for some of them despite their various literal or proverbial crimes. I remember being horrified at my disappointment to learn that one young fraudster who finagled his classmates out of thousands of dollars to raise money for a charity was eventually caught. Even narcissists can have good intentions, and many do various good things for their friends, loved ones, family, and the world. But do the ends justify the means? It's easy to forget that "the road to hell is paved with good intentions" and that their behavior, however well-meaning, has real emotional, physical, financial, and mental consequences for themselves and others.

Efforts to help raise awareness of narcissism are unlikely to eradicate narcissism from the narcissist's psyche. I'm not even sure this is a reasonable or necessary goal of narcissism awareness. Most narcissists believe that their diminished or lack of empathy has been an asset in their lives that has kept them safe from various forms of physical or emotional harm or pain, and they could very well be correct. However, with some elucidation, narcissists can develop increasing awareness to guide realistic behavioral modification and experience less interpersonal struggle. Some are aware of their narcissism and actively work to ensure that their behavior, although habitually turned toward their own needs and desires, doesn't infringe upon the rights, emotions, or boundaries of others. This is the ideal outcome for narcissists. Indeed, they may slip up from time to time. Who among us doesn't have personality traits that can be problematic or even a little toxic at times? Yet overall, awareness of our patterns is a gift I've seen yield satisfying results repeatedly in my coaching practice and among my students. I always recommend the Enneagram as one tool to help us understand why we do what we do and deepen our conscious awareness.

I encourage you to return to this book, not so you can tell everyone in your life that they're narcissistic or use it to pathologize or dehumanize others; the point of this book is not to make anyone wrong or bad, as I mentioned in the introduction. The purpose of this book is to raise awareness and foster continued conversation about narcissism and reduce the severity and pervasiveness of its toxicity in the lives of others. That day may be far away. I believe that narcissistic spectrum disorders will continue to rise before reaching saturation. And, not to sound like the die-hard humanist I am, I think empathy and compassion should be taught in schools, along with math and reading. Does that mean everyone will feel empathetic and compassionate? No.

So long as the human ego exists, narcissism, selfishness, and defensiveness will thrive. This is what makes us unique as a species. However, teaching children the value of empathy or respect for others' feelings and boundaries makes it safer for all of us. Loosening the ego's grip creates space between our automatic desires, impulses, and destructive inclinations. With increased space, our inherent spiritual programming to treat each other with kindness and compassion has more room to blossom. I hope that narcissism can become a transient state rather than a habitual way of functioning with awareness. The cultivation of more profound forms of empathy, even if it is merely cognitive empathy or an understanding of emotional cause and effect, makes us more conscious and, subsequently, more human.

Sterlin Mosley
March 15, 2022

# Notes

## INTRODUCTION

1. Freud, Sigmund. *On Narcissism: An Introduction.* Victoria, BC: Must Have Books, 2021.

2. Freud, Sigmund. *On Narcissism: An Introduction.* Victoria, BC: Must Have Books, 2021.

3. A. Significant impairments in personality functioning manifest by 1. Impairments in self-functioning (a or b): a. Identity: Excessive reference to others for self-definition and self-esteem regulation; exaggerated self-appraisal may be inflated or deflated, or vacillate between extremes; emotional regulation mirrors fluctuations in self-esteem. b. Self-direction: Goal-setting is based on gaining approval from others; personal standards are unreasonably high to see oneself as exceptional or too low based on a sense of entitlement; often unaware of own motivations. a. Empathy: Impaired ability to recognize or identify with the feelings and needs of others; b. Intimacy: Relationships are largely superficial and exist to serve self-esteem regulation; mutuality constrained by little genuine interest in others' experiences and predominance of a need for personal gain

B. Pathological personality traits in the following domain: 1. Antagonism, characterized by: a. Grandiosity: Feelings of entitlement, either overt or covert; self-centeredness; firmly holding to the belief that one is better than others; condescending toward others. b. Attention seeking: Excessive attempts to attract and be the focus of the attention of others; admiration seeking.

4. There are various ways to apply the Enneagram model beyond its use as a personality typology, including the Enneagram of Process. The Enneagram of Personality is a psychological system that identifies nine primary personality types.

# CHAPTER 1

1. Warrier, Varun, Roberto Toro, Bhismadev Chakrabarti, Anders D Børglum, Jakob Grove, David A. Hinds, Thomas Bourgeron, and Simon Baron-Cohen. "Genome-Wide Analyses of Self-Reported Empathy: Correlations with Autism, Schizophrenia, and Anorexia Nervosa," 2016. https://doi.org/10.1101/050682.

2. Perkins, Tom, Mark Stokes, Jane McGillivray, and Richard Bittar. "Mirror Neuron Dysfunction in Autism Spectrum Disorders." *Journal of Clinical Neuroscience* 17, no. 10 (2010): 1239–43. https://doi.org/10.1016/j.jocn.2010.01.026.

3. Ginsburg, Herbert, and Sylvia Opper Brandt. *Piaget's Theory of Intellectual Development.* Englewood Cliffs, NJ: Prentice-Hall, 1988.

4. Kohlberg, Lawrence. *The Psychology of Moral Development Nature and Validity of Moral Stages.* San Francisco: Harper & Row, 1984.

5. Gilligan, Carol. *In a Different Voice: Psychological Theory and Women's Development.* Cambridge, MA: Harvard University Press, 2016.

6. Hoffman, Martin L. *Empathy and Moral Development: Implications for Caring and Justice.* Cambridge, UK: Cambridge University Press, 2010.

7. Baron-Cohen, Simon. *Science of Evil: On Empathy and the Origins of Cruelty.* Philadelphia: Basic Books, 2011.

# CHAPTER 2

1. Baron-Cohen, Simon. "Empathy Quotient for Adults." *PsycTESTS Dataset,* 2004. https://doi.org/10.1037/t00384-000.

2. Baron-Cohen, Simon. *Science of Evil: On Empathy and the Origins of Cruelty.* Philadelphia: Basic Books, 2011.

# CHAPTER 3

1. Twenge, Jean M., and W. Keith Campbell. *The Narcissism Epidemic: Living in the Age of Entitlement.* New York: Atria Paperback, 2013.

2. Dargis, Monika, Joseph Newman, and Michael Koenigs. "Clarifying the Link between Childhood Abuse History and Psychopathic Traits in Adult Criminal Offenders." *Personality Disorders: Theory, Research, and Treatment* 7, no. 3 (2016): 221–28. https://doi.org/10.1037/per0000147.

3. Lowen, Alexander. *Narcissism: Denial of the True Self.* London: Simon & Schuster, 2004.

4. Alexander Lowen was a student of bioenergetic psychiatrist Wilhelm Reich who believed understanding the way that the people held emotional energy in the body revealed psychological defense strategies that could be unlocked through somatic and psychoanalytic therapeutic interventions.

5. Skeem, Jennifer L., Polaschek, Devon L. L., Patrick, Christopher J., Lilienfeld, Scott O. (December 15, 2011). "Psychopathic Personality: Bridging the Gap Between Scientific Evidence and Public Policy." *Psychological Science in the Public Interest* 12(3).

## CHAPTER 4

1. The International Advanced Training in Todtmoos 2010. Auditorium Netzwerk, 2010. https://shop.auditoriumnetzwerk.de/advanced_search_result.php?keywords=Naranjo&x=0&y=0.

2. The International Advanced Training in Todtmoos 2010. Auditorium Netzwerk, 2010. https://shop.auditoriumnetzwerk.de/advanced_search_result.php?keywords=Naranjo&x=0&y=0.

3. Fauvre, Katherine Chernick. *Enneastyle: The 9 Languages of Enneagram Type*. Menlo Park, CA: SelfPub, 1996.

4. Fauvre, Katherine Chernick. *The 27 Tritypes Revealed: Discover Your Life Purpose and Blind Spot*. Menlo Park, CA: SelfPub, 2018.

## CHAPTER 5

1. Naranjo, Claudio. *Enneatypes and Psychotherapy*. Prescott, AZ: Hohm Press, 1995.

2. Fauvre, Katherine. *Enneagram Instinctual Types and Subtypes: The Three Drives That Fuel the Passions of the Nine Types*, eighth ed. Menlo Park, CA: Self Pub, 2018.

3. For more explanation of Freud's concept of the Id, refer to his paper on *The Ego and the Id*, published initially in 1923.

4. On the theme of repulsion: while we endeavor to attract those we find desirable and attractive, the Sexual instinct fuels the desire to repel or thwart the advances of those we find undesirable.

5. Naranjo, Claudio. *Enneatypes and Psychotherapy*. Prescott, AZ: Hohm Press, 1995.

6. For the most thorough research on the Instinctual types, refer to Enneagram researcher Katherine Chernick Fauvre and her bookbook *Enneagram Instinctual Types and Subtypes: The Three Drives That Fuel the Passions of the Nine Types*.

## CHAPTER 6

1. An exploration of Trifix deserves a lengthier discussion; suffice to say that despite Trifix (which creates a whole new type), we use one primary type with greater frequency, ease, and efficiency, and this core type will be our primary concern for the remainder of this book.

2. Fauvre, Katherine Chernick. *Enneastyle: The 9 Languages of Enneagram Type.* Menlo Park, CA: SelfPub, 1996.

3. Mosley, Sterlin. Rep. *Enneagram Lexical Analysis Research Report.* Norman, OK: Empathy Architects, 2021.

## CHAPTER 7

1. For an excellent examination of adolescence's neurological, chemical, and developmental anomalies, I recommend neuroendocrinologist and primatologist Robert Sapolsky's book, *Behave: The Biology of Humans at Their Best and Worst.*

2. In 2001, Torgeson et al. estimated that 0.5 percent of the American population could be diagnosed with NPD. However, recently, researchers in personality disorders estimated the percentage of NPD in the U.S. to be around 7 percent, with anywhere from 10–15 percent of the population exhibiting narcissistic traits. Only 0.2–0.5 percent of NPD sufferers seek treatment, with an equally low recovery percentage.

3. I highly recommend Dr. Durvasula's book, *Should I Stay or Should I Go,* to better understand NPD and narcissistic abuse.

## CHAPTER 8

1. The term *covert* in this instance refers to the emotions that underlie the narcissist's behaviors. Some theorists assert that covert emotions must be inferred because narcissists are not typically communicative about their internal processes, particularly the less-than-ideal emotional states of shame, sadness, or inferiority (Jauk et al. 2017). So, while we may see the grandiose behaviors more frequently, it is reasonable to assume that the vulnerable feelings of worthlessness, emptiness, and shame fuel the amplification of grandiose behaviors.

2. Ramani, Durvasula. *Benign Narcissism: Everything You Need to Know,* 2020. https://www.youtube.com/results?search_query=ramani+benign+narcissism.

3. Heym, Nadja, Fraenze Kibowski, Claire A. J. Bloxsom, Alyson Blanchard, Alexandra Harper, Louise Wallace, Jennifer Firth, and Alexander Sumich. "The Dark Empath: Characterising Dark Traits in the Presence of Empathy." *Personality and Individual Differences* 169 (February 1, 2021): 110172. https://doi.org/10.1016/j.paid.2020.110172.

4. Trauma bonding occurs when an abused person forms an unhealthy, intense connection with their abuser(s). Stockholm syndrome is one example of trauma bonding, as is the common experience of abused cult members believing their leaders (who may be profoundly violent or emotionally abusive) deeply love and care for them. Often the abused person develops sympathy for the abuser.

5. This variant shouldn't be confused for individuals on the autism spectrum. People on the autism spectrum experience forms of empathy divergent from neurotypical

people, and some can learn how to recognize human emotions similarly to neurotypical individuals.

## CHAPTER 9

1. "Love bombing" is a manipulation tactic often used by narcissists where grand love gestures (e.g., immediate promises of marriage on the first date, talk of soul mates, expensive or lavish trips or meals, or fabricating feelings of closeness) are used to seduce and secure potential love interests.

2. Department of Justice, U.S., ed. "Report to the Deputy Attorney General on the Events at Waco, Texas: Child Abuse." The United States Department of Justice, February 14, 2018. https://www.justice.gov/archives/publications/waco/report-deputy-attorney-general-events-waco-texas-child-abuse.

3. Rimer, Sara. "Growing up under Koresh: Cult Children Tell of Abuses." *The New York Times*, May 4, 1993. https://www.nytimes.com/1993/05/04/us/growing-up-under-koresh-cult-children-tell-of-abuses.html.

## CHAPTER 10

1. *The International Advanced Training in Todtmoos 2010. Auditorium Netzwerk*, 2010. https://shop.auditorium-netzwerk.de/advanced_search_result.php?keywords=Naranjo&x=0&y=0.

2. Homer, E. V. Rieu, and Rieu D. C. H. *The Odyssey*. London: Penguin Classics, 2009.

## CHAPTER 11

1. Woods, Tiger. "Tiger Woods Archives." allsportsquotes.com, September 25, 2021. https://allsportsquotes.com/author/tag/tiger-woods/.

2. Michaud, Stephen G., and Hugh Aynesworth. *The Only Living Witness: The True Story of Serial Sex Killer Ted Bundy*. Irving, TX: Autholink Press, 2012.

## CHAPTER 12

1. Plath, Sylvia, and Ted Hughes. *The Unabridged Journals of Sylvia Plath*. New York: Anchor Books, 2000.

2. Factitious disorder is a mental disorder where individuals fabricate or dramatize illness for attention, money, or other forms of support.

3. Wilde, Oscar. *De Profundis*. Portland, OR: Mint Editions, 2021.

4. I highly recommend Middlebrook's book *Anne Sexton: A Biography* for a thorough and compelling character study on Anne Sexton and her art.

5. Naranjo, Claudio. *Enneatypes and Psychotherapy*. Prescott, AZ: Hohm Press, 1995.

## CHAPTER 13

1. Dickens, Charles. *A Christmas Carol*, 2007. http://www.open-bks.com/library/classics/dickens_charles_carol/carol-cover.html.

## CHAPTER 14

1. Guinn, Jeff. *Manson: The Life and Times of Charles Manson*. Farmington Hills, MI: Large Print Press, 2014.

## CHAPTER 15

1. Kozodoy, Peter. "The Inventor of Fomo Is Warning Leaders about a New, More Dangerous Threat." Inc.com, October 9, 2017. https://www.inc.com/peter-kozodoy/inventor-of-fomo-is-warning-leaders-about-a-new-more-dangerous-threat.html.

2. The Harbus. "Social Theory at HBS: McGinnis' Two FOs." The Harbus, August 10, 2015. https://harbus.org/2004/social-theory-at-hbs-2749/.

3. Sandars, N. K. *The Epic of Gilgamesh*. London: Penguin, 2003.

4. Woods, David. "Caligula, Incitatus, and the Consulship." *The Classical Quarterly* 64, no. 2 (2014): 772–77. https://doi.org/10.1017/s0009838814000470.

5. Mansky, Jackie. "P.T. Barnum Isn't the Hero the 'Greatest Showman' Wants You to Think." Smithsonian.com. Smithsonian Institution, December 22, 2017. https://www.smithsonianmag.com/history/true-story-pt-barnum-greatest-humbug-them-all-180967634/.

6. Goldman, David. "Who Is Martin Shkreli? A Timeline." CNNMoney. Cable News Network, December 18, 2015. https://money.cnn.com/2015/12/18/news/companies/martin-shkreli/.

7. Sarkis, Stephanie. "Martin Shkreli and How Narcissists and Sociopaths Lure You In." *Forbes* Magazine, December 21, 2020. https://www.forbes.com/sites/stephaniesarkis/2020/12/21/martin-shkreli-and-how-narcissists-and-sociopaths-lure-you-in/.

8. Dirda, Michael. "'Ted Hughes': A Controversial Biography Shows the Poet's Darker Side." The *Washington Post*. WP Company, October 6, 2015. https://www.washingtonpost.com/entertainment/books/ted-hughes-a-controversial

-biography-shows-the-poets-darker-side/2015/10/06/e67f6a90-6930-11e5-8325
-a42b5a459b1e_story.html.

9. Dirda, Michael. "'Ted Hughes': A Controversial Biography Shows the Poet's Darker Side." The *Washington Post*. WP Company, October 6, 2015. https://www.washingtonpost.com/entertainment/books/ted-hughes-a-controversial -biography-shows-the-poets-darker-side/2015/10/06/e67f6a90-6930-11e5-8325 -a42b5a459b1e_story.html.

## CHAPTER 16

1. Jardine, Lisa. "Lyndon B Johnson: The Uncivil Rights Reformer." The *Independent*. Independent Digital News and Media, January 21, 2009. https://www.independent. co.uk/news/presidents/lyndon-b-johnson-the-uncivil-rights-reformer-1451816.html.

2. Dallek, Robert. "Character above All: Lyndon B. Johnson Essay," PBS (Public Broadcasting Service), accessed March 3, 2022, https://www.pbs.org/newshour/spc /character/essays/johnson.html.

3. Hanson, Marilee. "King Henry VIII Timeline, Personality & Historical Importance." English History, February 16, 2022. https://englishhistory.net/tudor/monarchs /king-henry-viii-timeline/.

4. The cutoff score on the PCL-R is 30 to be granted the diagnosis of a psychopath.

5. King, Martin L. "The Great March to Freedom–Detroit–June 23, 1963–Youtube." The Great March to Freedom–Detroit–June 23, 1963, February 11, 2015. https://www .youtube.com/watch?v=cZbvdMQGitE.

6. Staff, Time. "10 Experts on What We Get Wrong about Martin Luther King Jr." *Time*, April 29, 2021. https://time.com/5197679/10-historians-martin-luther-king-jr/.

7. Naranjo, Claudio. Lecture. *The International Advanced Training in Todtmoos 2010*. Presented at the The International Advanced Training in Todtmoos 2010, May 20, 2020.

8. Gottlieb, Sean, and Gay Rosenthall. "Pink." Episode. *Behind the Music* 11, no. 2. VH1, September 17, 2009.

9. Condon, Tom. *The Enneagram Movie & Video Guide: How to See Personality Styles in the Movies*. Bend, OR: The Changeworks, 1999.

10. Reiterman, Tim, and John Jacobs. *Raven: The Untold Story of the Reverend Jim Jones and His People*. New York: Tarcher/Penguin, 2008.

11. Reiterman, Tim, and John Jacobs. *Raven: The Untold Story of the Reverend Jim Jones and His People*. New York: Tarcher/Penguin, 2008.

## CHAPTER 17

1. Smith, Sally Bedell. *Elizabeth the Queen: The Life of a Modern Monarch*. New York: Random House, 2012.

2. Smith, Sally Bedell. *Elizabeth the Queen: The Life of a Modern Monarch*. New York: Random House, 2012.

3. Dickson, E. J. "What Drives a Man to Kill His Own Family? Inside the Psychology of Family Annihilators." *Rolling Stone*, March 6, 2019. https://www.rollingstone.com/culture/culture-news/chris-watts-family-murder-colorado-why-803957/.

4. Chang, Rachel. "Chris Watts: A Complete Timeline of the Murder of His Wife and Daughters." Biography.com. A&E Networks Television, July 19, 2021. https://www.biography.com/news/chris-watts-wife-daughters-murder-mistress-confession-timeline.

5. Kovaleski, Tony. "Inside the Mind of a Killer: Psychology Experts Discuss Chris Watts' Behavior Following Family's Murder." KMGH, February 22, 2019. https://www.thedenverchannel.com/news/investigations/inside-the-mind-of-a-killer-psychology-experts-discuss-chris-watts-behavior-following-familys-murder.

6. "Janet Jackson." Broadcast. *Janet Jackson*. 1, no. 1–2. Lifetime/A&E, 2022.

7. Naranjo, Claudio. Lecture. *The International Advanced Training in Todtmoos 2010*. Presented at the The International Advanced Training in Todtmoos 2010, May 20, 2020.

8. Erotomania is a delusional psychological disorder where the sufferer believes that someone they barely know or don't know is in love with them.

# Bibliography

Baron-Cohen, Simon. "Empathy Quotient for Adults." *PsycTESTS Dataset*, 2004. https://doi.org/10.1037/t00384-000.

Baron-Cohen, Simon. *Science of Evil: On Empathy and the Origins of Cruelty*. Philadelphia, PA: Basic Books, 2011.

Chang, Rachel. "Chris Watts: A Complete Timeline of the Murder of His Wife and Daughters." Biography.com. A&E Networks Television, July 19, 2021. https://www.biography.com/news/chris-watts-wife-daughters-murder-mistress-confession-timeline.

Condon, Tom. *The Enneagram Movie & Video Guide: How to See Personality Styles in the Movies*. Bend, OR: The Changeworks, 1999.

Dallek, Robert. "Character above All: Lyndon B. Johnson Essay." PBS. Public Broadcasting Service. Accessed March 13, 2022. https://www.pbs.org/newshour/spc/character/essays/johnson.html.

Dargis, Monika, Joseph Newman, and Michael Koenigs. "Clarifying the Link between Childhood Abuse History and Psychopathic Traits in Adult Criminal Offenders." *Personality Disorders: Theory, Research, and Treatment* 7, no. 3 (2016): 221–28. https://doi.org/10.1037/per0000147.

Department of Justice, U.S., ed. "Report to the Deputy Attorney General on the Events at Waco, Texas: Child Abuse." The United States Department of Justice, February 14, 2018. https://www.justice.gov/archives/publications/waco/report-deputy-attorney-general-events-waco-texas-child-abuse.

*Diagnostic and Statistical Manual of Mental Disorders: DSM-5*. Arlington, VA: American Psychiatric Association, 2017.

Dickens, Charles. *A Christmas Carol*. 2007. http://www.open-bks.com/library/classics/dickens_charles_carol/carol-cover.html.

Dickson, E. J. "What Drives a Man to Kill His Own Family? Inside the Psychology of Family Annihilators." *Rolling Stone*, March 6, 2019. https://www.rollingstone.com/culture/culture-news/chris-watts-family-murder-colorado-why-803957/.

Dirda, Michael. "'Ted Hughes': A Controversial Biography Shows the Poet's Darker Side." The *Washington Post*. October 6, 2015. https://www.washingtonpost.com/entertainment/books/ted-hughes-a-controversial-biography-shows-the-poets-darker-side/2015/10/06/e67f6a90-6930-11e5-8325-a42b5a459b1e_story.html.

Durvasula, Ramani. *Benign Narcissism: Everything You Need to Know.* 2020. https://www.youtube.com/results?search_query=ramani+benign+narcissism.

Durvasula, Ramani. *Should I Stay or Should I Go?: Surviving a Relationship with a Narcissist.* New York: Post Hill Press, 2017.

Fauvre, Katherine Chernick. *Enneastyle: The 9 Languages of Enneagram Type.* Menlo Park, CA: SelfPub, 1996.

Fauvre, Katherine Chernick. *The 27 Tritypes Revealed: Discover Your Life Purpose and Blind Spot.* Menlo Park, CA: SelfPub, 2018.

Fauvre, Katherine. *Enneagram Instinctual Types and Subtypes: The Three Drives That Fuel the Passions of the Nine Types,* eighth ed. Menlo Park, CA: Self Pub, 2018.

Freud, Sigmund. *On Narcissism: An Introduction.* Victoria, BC: Must Have Books, 2021.

Freud, Sigmund. *The Ego and the Id.* New York: W.W. Norton, 1962.

Gardener, Howard. *Multiple Intelligences: The Theory in Practice.* New York: Basic Books, 1993.

Gilligan, Carol. *In a Different Voice: Psychological Theory and Women's Development.* Cambridge, MA: Harvard University Press, 2016.

Ginsburg, Herbert, and Sylvia Opper Brandt. *Piaget's Theory of Intellectual Development.* Englewood Cliffs, NJ: Prentice-Hall, 1988.

Goldman, David. "Who Is Martin Shkreli? A Timeline." CNNMoney, December 18, 2015. https://money.cnn.com/2015/12/18/news/companies/martin-shkreli/.

Gottlieb, Sean, and Gay Rosenthall. "Pink." Episode. *Behind the Music* 11, no. 2. VH1, September 17, 2009.

Guinn, Jeff. *Manson: The Life and Times of Charles Manson.* Farmington Hills, MI: Large Print Press, 2014.

Hanson, Marilee. "King Henry VIII Timeline, Personality & Historical Importance." English History, February 16, 2022. https://englishhistory.net/tudor/monarchs/king-henry-viii-timeline/.

The Harbus. "Social Theory at HBS: Mcginnis' Two FOs." The Harbus, August 10, 2015. https://harbus.org/2004/social-theory-at-hbs-2749/.

Heym, Nadja, Fraenze Kibowski, Claire A.J. Bloxsom, Alyson Blanchard, Alexandra Harper, Louise Wallace, Jennifer Firth, and Alexander Sumich. "The Dark Empath: Characterising Dark Traits in the Presence of Empathy." *Personality and Individual Differences* 169 (February 1, 2021): 110172. https://doi.org/10.1016/j.paid.2020.110172.

Hoffman, Martin L. *Empathy and Moral Development: Implications for Caring and Justice.* Cambridge, UK: Cambridge University Press, 2010.

Homer, E. V. Rieu, and Rieu D. C. H. *The Odyssey*. London, UK: Penguin Classics, 2009.

*The International Advanced Training in Todtmoos 2010. Auditorium Netzwerk*, 2010. https://shop.auditorium-netzwerk.de/advanced_search_result .php?keywords=Naranjo&x=0&y=0.

"Janet Jackson." Broadcast. *Janet Jackson* 1, no. 1. Lifetime/A&E, 2022.

Jardine, Lisa. "Lyndon B Johnson: The Uncivil Rights Reformer." The *Independent*, January 21, 2009. https://www.independent.co.uk/news/presidents/lyndon -b-johnson-the-uncivil-rights-reformer-1451816.html.

Jauk, Emanuel, Elena Weigle, Konrad Lehmann, Mathias Benedek, and Aljoscha C. Neubauer. "The Relationship between Grandiose and Vulnerable (Hypersensitive) Narcissism." *Frontiers in Psychology* 8 (2017). https://doi.org/10.3389 /fpsyg.2017.01600.

King, Martin L. "The Great March to Freedom–Detroit–June 23, 1963–Youtube." The Great March to Freedom–Detroit–June 23, 1963, February 11, 2015. https://www.youtube.com/watch?v=cZbvdMQGitE.

Kohlberg, Lawrence. *The Psychology of Moral Development Nature and Validity of Moral Stages*. San Francisco: Harper & Row, 1984.

Kovaleski, Tony. "Inside the Mind of a Killer: Psychology Experts Discuss Chris Watts' Behavior Following Family's Murder." KMGH, February 22, 2019. https://www .thedenverchannel.com/news/investigations/inside-the-mind-of-a-killer-psychology -experts-discuss-chris-watts-behavior-following-familys-murder.

Kozodoy, Peter. "The Inventor of Fomo Is Warning Leaders about a New, More Dangerous Threat." Inc.com., October 9, 2017. https://www.inc.com/peter-kozodoy /inventor-of-fomo-is-warning-leaders-about-a-new-more-dangerous-threat.html.

Lowen, Alexander. *Narcissim: Denial of the True Self*. London: Simon and Schuster, 2004.

Mansky, Jackie. "P.T. Barnum Isn't the Hero the 'Greatest Showman' Wants You to Think." Smithsonian.com, December 22, 2017. https://www.smithsonianmag.com /history/true-story-pt-barnum-greatest-humbug-them-all-180967634/.

Michaud, Stephen G., and Hugh Aynesworth. *The Only Living Witness: The True Story of Serial Sex Killer Ted Bundy*. Irving, TX: Autholink Press, 2012.

Mosley, Sterlin. Rep. *Enneagram Lexical Analysis Research Report*. Norman, OK: Empathy Architects, 2021.

Naranjo, Claudio. *Enneatypes and Psychotherapy*: Prescott, AZ: Hohm Press, 1995.

Naranjo, Claudio. Lecture. *The International Advanced Training in Todtmoos 2010*. Presented at The International Advanced Training in Todtmoos 2010, May 20, 2020.

Nelson, Mark. "Biosphere 2: What Really Happened?" *Dartmouth Alumni Magazine*, 2018. https://dartmouthalumnimagazine.com/articles/biosphere-2-what-really -happened.

Perkins, Tom, Mark Stokes, Jane McGillivray, and Richard Bittar. "Mirror Neuron Dysfunction in Autism Spectrum Disorders." *Journal of Clinical Neuroscience* 17, no. 10 (2010): 1239–43. https://doi.org/10.1016/j.jocn.2010.01.026.

Plath, Sylvia, and Ted Hughes. *The Unabridged Journals of Sylvia Plath.* New York: Anchor Books, 2000.

Reiterman, Tim, and John Jacobs. *Raven: the Untold Story of the Reverend Jim Jones and His People.* New York: Tarcher/Penguin, 2008.

Rimer, Sara. "Growing up under Koresh: Cult Children Tell of Abuses." The *New York Times,* May 4, 1993. https://www.nytimes.com/1993/05/04/us/growing-up-under -koresh-cult-children-tell-of-abuses.html.

Sandars, N. K. *The Epic of Gilgamesh.* London: Penguin, 2003.

Sapolsky, Robert. *Behave: The Biology of Humans at Our Best and Worst.* London: Vintage, 2018.

Sarkis, Stephanie. "Martin Shkreli and How Narcissists and Sociopaths Lure You In." *Forbes,* December 21, 2020. https://www.forbes.com/sites/stephaniesarkis/2020/12/21 /martin-shkreli-and-how-narcissists-and-sociopaths-lure-you-in/.

Smith, Sally Bedell. *Elizabeth the Queen: The Life of a Modern Monarch.* New York: Random House, 2012.

Staff, Time. "10 Experts on What We Get Wrong about Martin Luther King Jr." *Time,* April 29, 2021. https://time.com/5197679/10-historians-martin-luther-king-jr/.

Torgersen, Svenn, Einar Kringlen, and Victoria Cramer. "The Prevalence of Personality Disorders in a Community Sample." *Archives of General Psychiatry* 58, no. 6 (2001): 590. https://doi.org/10.1001/archpsyc.58.6.590.

Twenge, Jean M., and W. Keith Campbell. *The Narcissism Epidemic: Living in the Age of Entitlement.* New York: Atria Paperback, 2013.

Warrier, Varun, Roberto Toro, Bhismadev Chakrabarti, Anders D Børglum, Jakob Grove, David A. Hinds, Thomas Bourgeron, and Simon Baron-Cohen. "Genome-Wide Analyses of Self-Reported Empathy: Correlations with Autism, Schizophrenia, and Anorexia Nervosa," 2016. https://doi.org/10.1101/050682.

Wilde, Oscar. *De Profundis.* Portland, OR: Mint Editions, 2021.

Woods, David. "Caligula, Incitatus, and the Consulship." *The Classical Quarterly* 64, no. 2 (2014): 772–77. https://doi.org/10.1017/s0009838814000470.

Woods, Tiger. "Tiger Woods Archives." allsportsquotes.com, September 25, 2021. https://allsportsquotes.com/author/tag/tiger-woods/.

Zimmerman, Amy. "Inside Fyre Festival Fraudster Billy McFarland's First Big Scam." The *Daily Beast.* The Daily Beast Company, February 2, 2019. https://www .thedailybeast.com/inside-fyre-festival-founder-billy-mcfarlands-first-big -millennial-scam.

# Index

# About the Author

**Sterlin Mosley**, PhD, is assistant professor of human relations at the University of Oklahoma. He teaches classes on personality psychology, social change, cultural awareness, and women's and gender studies. He holds a master's degree in human relations counseling, where he specialized in personality typologies and personality pathology, and a PhD in intercultural communication. Dr. Mosley has conducted research on the Enneagram personality typology for over ten years and is a certified Enneagram coach and teacher.

Dr. Mosley has developed and facilitated numerous undergraduate and graduate courses, professional workshops, trainings, and lectures on personality, empathy, culture, gender, sexuality, spirituality, and communication. Dr. Mosley is the co-founder and CEO of Empathy Architects. He provides personal and professional coaching and develops and facilitates workshops on the Enneagram personality system, empathy, narcissism, and other systems to help foster greater awareness and positive change. Dr. Mosley is also a ballet dancer and founded a dance company where he is a resident choreographer and executive artistic director. He currently resides in Norman, Oklahoma.

CPSIA information can be obtained
at www.ICGtesting.com
Printed in the USA
LVHW041439261122
733997LV00001B/30

9 781538 161746